Blank Canvas

My So-Called Artist's Journey

5

STORY &
ART

**Akiko
Higashimura**

Blank Canvas

My So-Called Artist's Journey

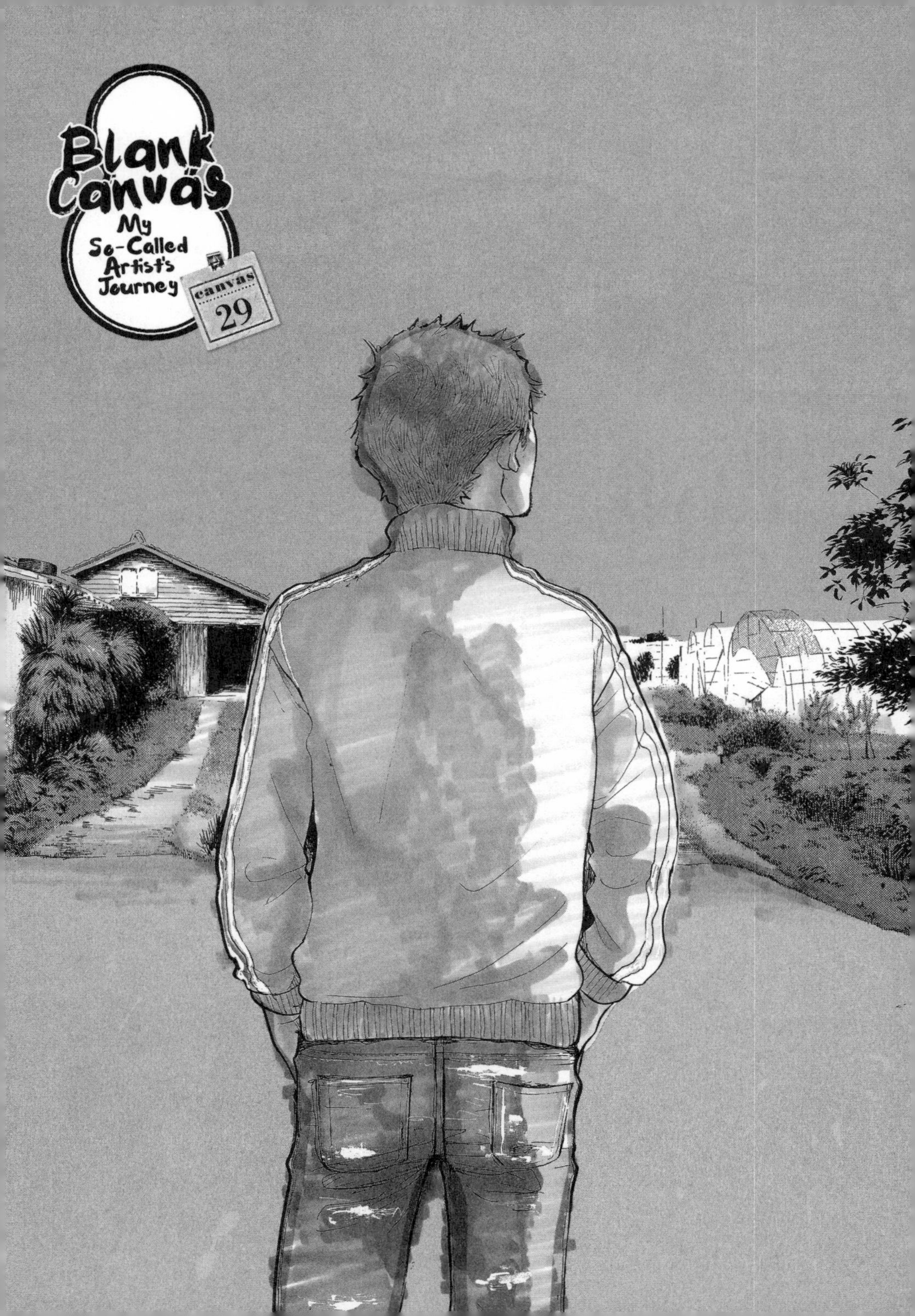
Blank Canvas
My So-Called Artist's Journey
canvas
29

Blank Canvas

My So-Called Artist's Journey

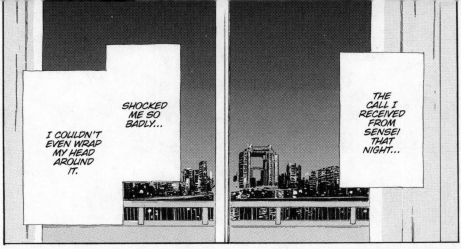

THE CALL I RECEIVED FROM SENSEI THAT NIGHT...

SHOCKED ME SO BADLY...

I COULDN'T EVEN WRAP MY HEAD AROUND IT.

Yer the only one I can ask, Hayashi.

Come back and teach these kids until their exams.

Right now, they all suck too bad to get in **anywhere** without a heap of help.

WHA ...?!

W-WAIT A SECOND!

WHAT ARE YOU TALKING ABOUT, SENSEI?!

THIS ISN'T THE TIME TO WORRY ABOUT YOUR STUDENTS!

THINK ABOUT **YOURSELF!** YOU'VE GOTTA START TREATMENT RIGHT AWAY, DON'T YOU?!

JUST CLOSE THE SCHOOL FOR NOW! IF YOU'RE SICK, YOU SHOULDN'T BE TRYING TO--!

No, the school stays open.

At least 'til the next exams are over.

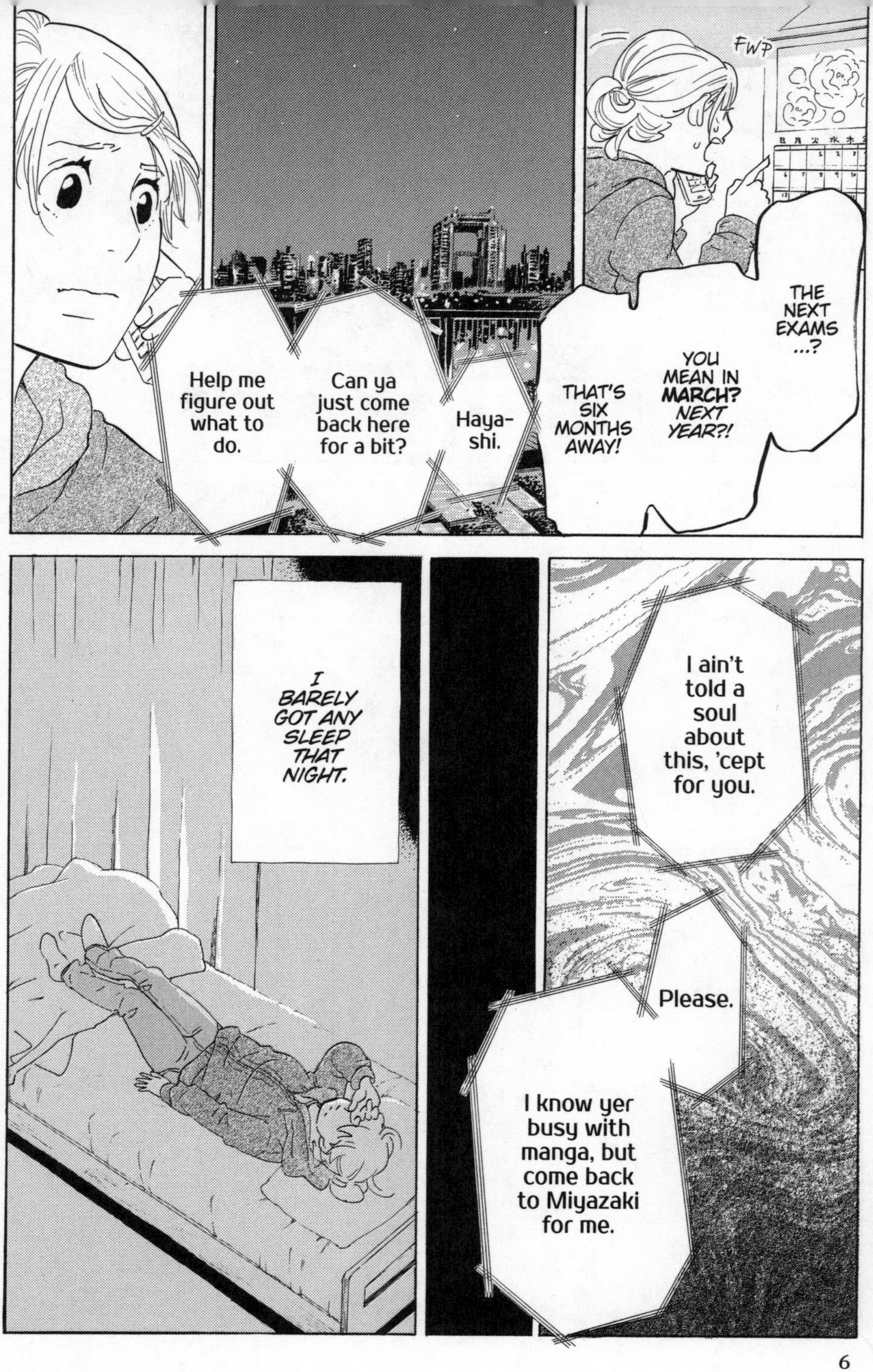
FWP
THE NEXT EXAMS ...?
YOU MEAN IN MARCH? NEXT YEAR?!
THAT'S SIX MONTHS AWAY!
Haya-shi.
Can ya just come back here for a bit?
Help me figure out what to do.
I ain't told a soul about this, 'cept for you.
Please.
I know yer busy with manga, but come back to Miyazaki for me.
I BARELY GOT ANY SLEEP THAT NIGHT.

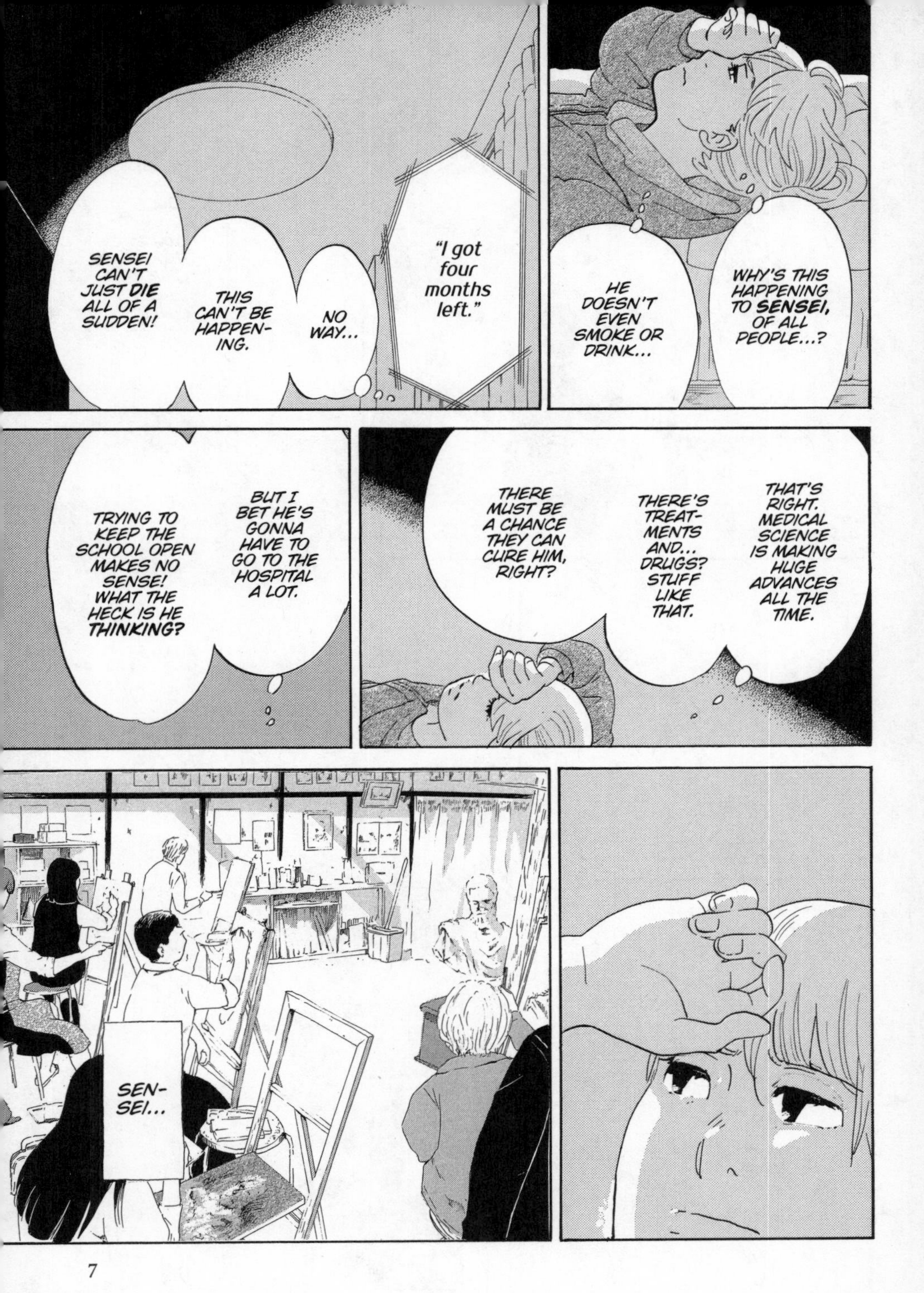
WHY'S THIS HAPPENING TO SENSEI, OF ALL PEOPLE...?
HE DOESN'T EVEN SMOKE OR DRINK...
"I got four months left."
NO WAY...
THIS CAN'T BE HAPPEN-ING.
SENSEI CAN'T JUST DIE ALL OF A SUDDEN!
THAT'S RIGHT. MEDICAL SCIENCE IS MAKING HUGE ADVANCES ALL THE TIME.
THERE'S TREAT-MENTS AND... DRUGS? STUFF LIKE THAT.
THERE MUST BE A CHANCE THEY CAN CURE HIM, RIGHT?
BUT I BET HE'S GONNA HAVE TO GO TO THE HOSPITAL A LOT.
TRYING TO KEEP THE SCHOOL OPEN MAKES NO SENSE! WHAT THE HECK IS HE THINKING?
SEN-SEI...

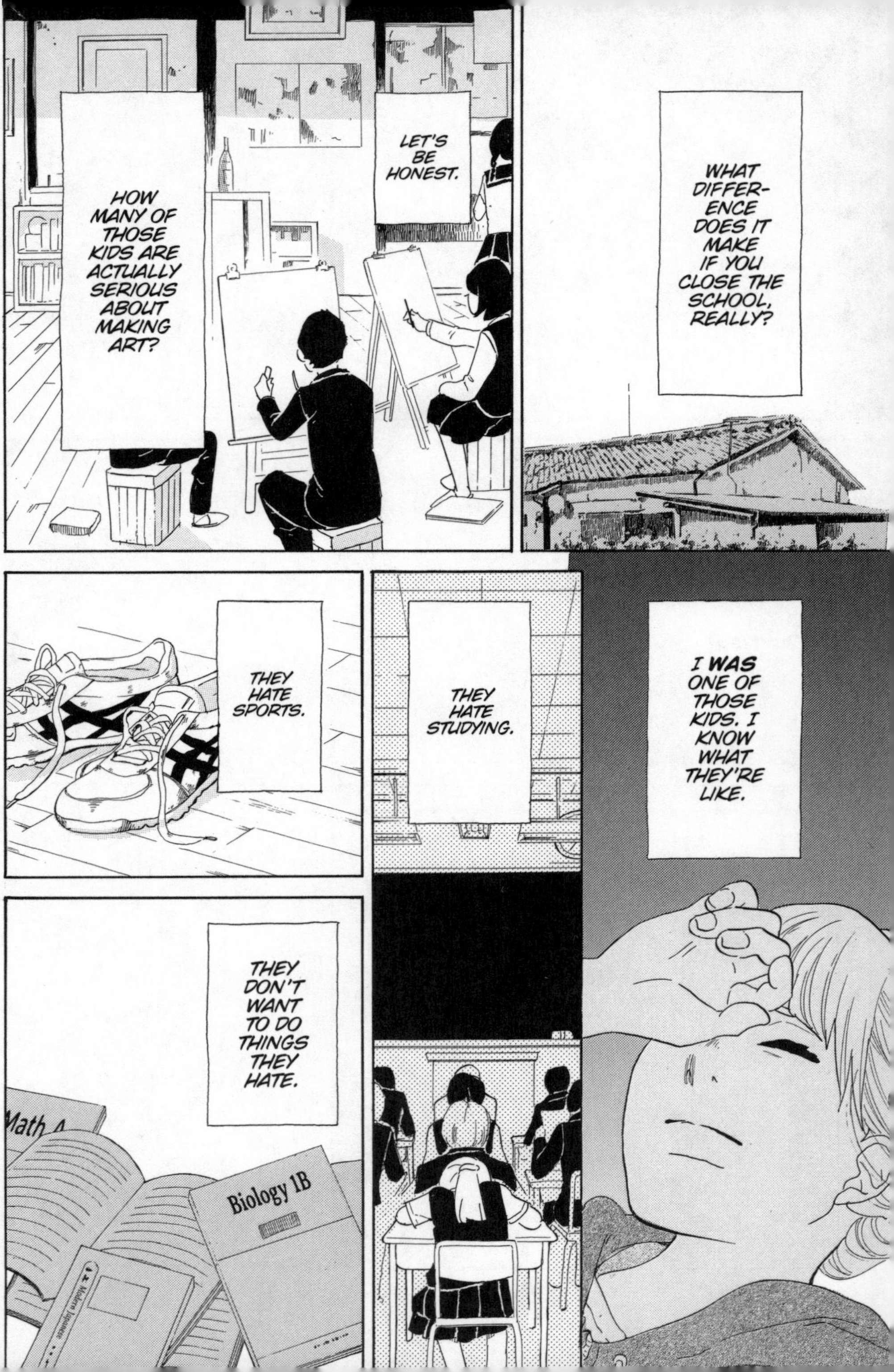
WHAT DIFFERENCE DOES IT MAKE IF YOU CLOSE THE SCHOOL, REALLY?
LET'S BE HONEST.
HOW MANY OF THOSE KIDS ARE ACTUALLY SERIOUS ABOUT MAKING ART?
I WAS ONE OF THOSE KIDS. I KNOW WHAT THEY'RE LIKE.
THEY HATE STUDYING.
THEY HATE SPORTS.
THEY DON'T WANT TO DO THINGS THEY HATE.
Biology IB
Math A

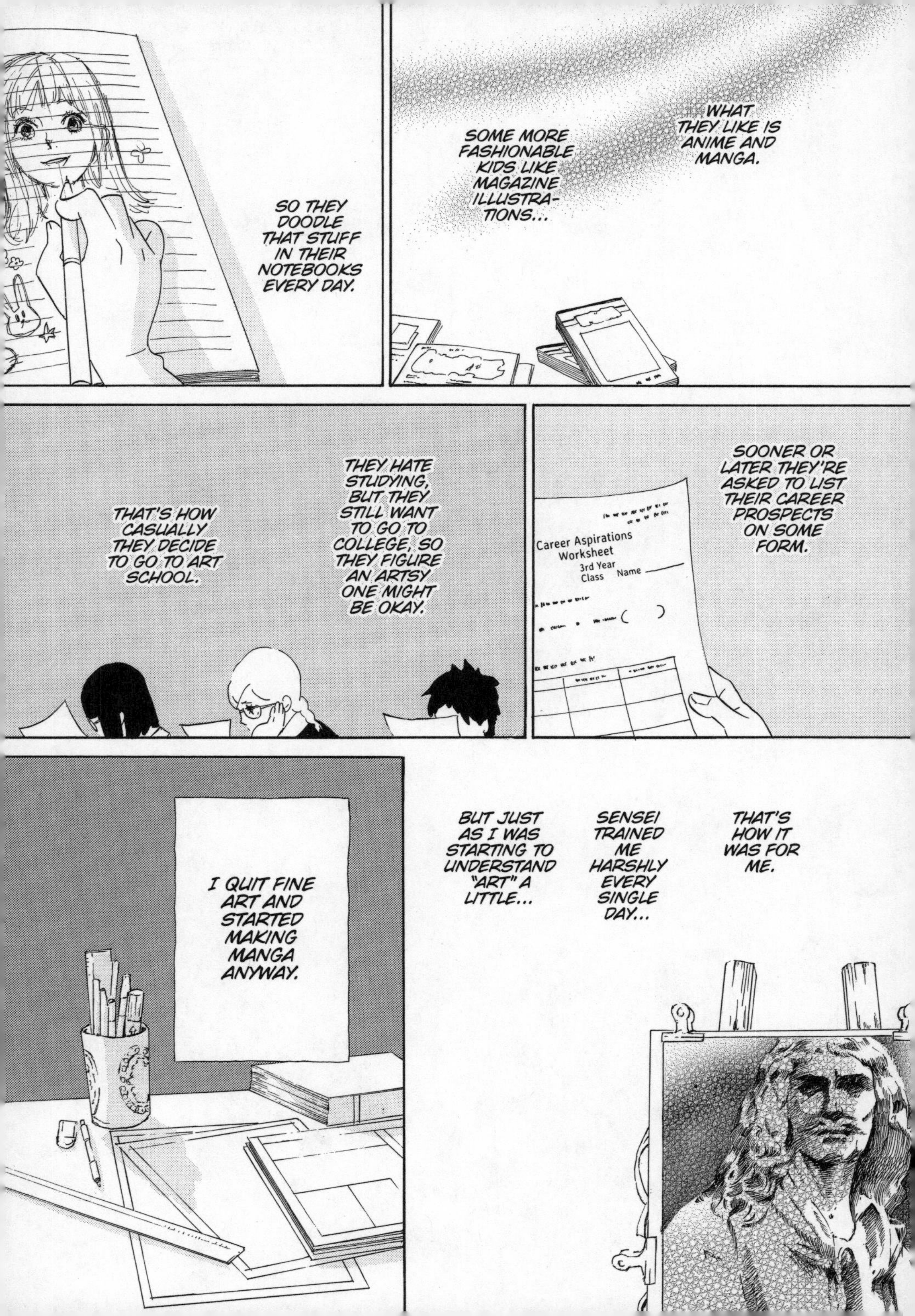
WHAT THEY LIKE IS ANIME AND MANGA.
SOME MORE FASHIONABLE KIDS LIKE MAGAZINE ILLUSTRATIONS...
SO THEY DOODLE THAT STUFF IN THEIR NOTEBOOKS EVERY DAY.
SOONER OR LATER THEY'RE ASKED TO LIST THEIR CAREER PROSPECTS ON SOME FORM.
Career Aspirations Worksheet
3rd Year
Class Name
THEY HATE STUDYING, BUT THEY STILL WANT TO GO TO COLLEGE, SO THEY FIGURE AN ARTSY ONE MIGHT BE OKAY.
THAT'S HOW CASUALLY THEY DECIDE TO GO TO ART SCHOOL.
THAT'S HOW IT WAS FOR ME.
SENSEI TRAINED ME HARSHLY EVERY SINGLE DAY...
BUT JUST AS I WAS STARTING TO UNDERSTAND "ART" A LITTLE...
I QUIT FINE ART AND STARTED MAKING MANGA ANYWAY.

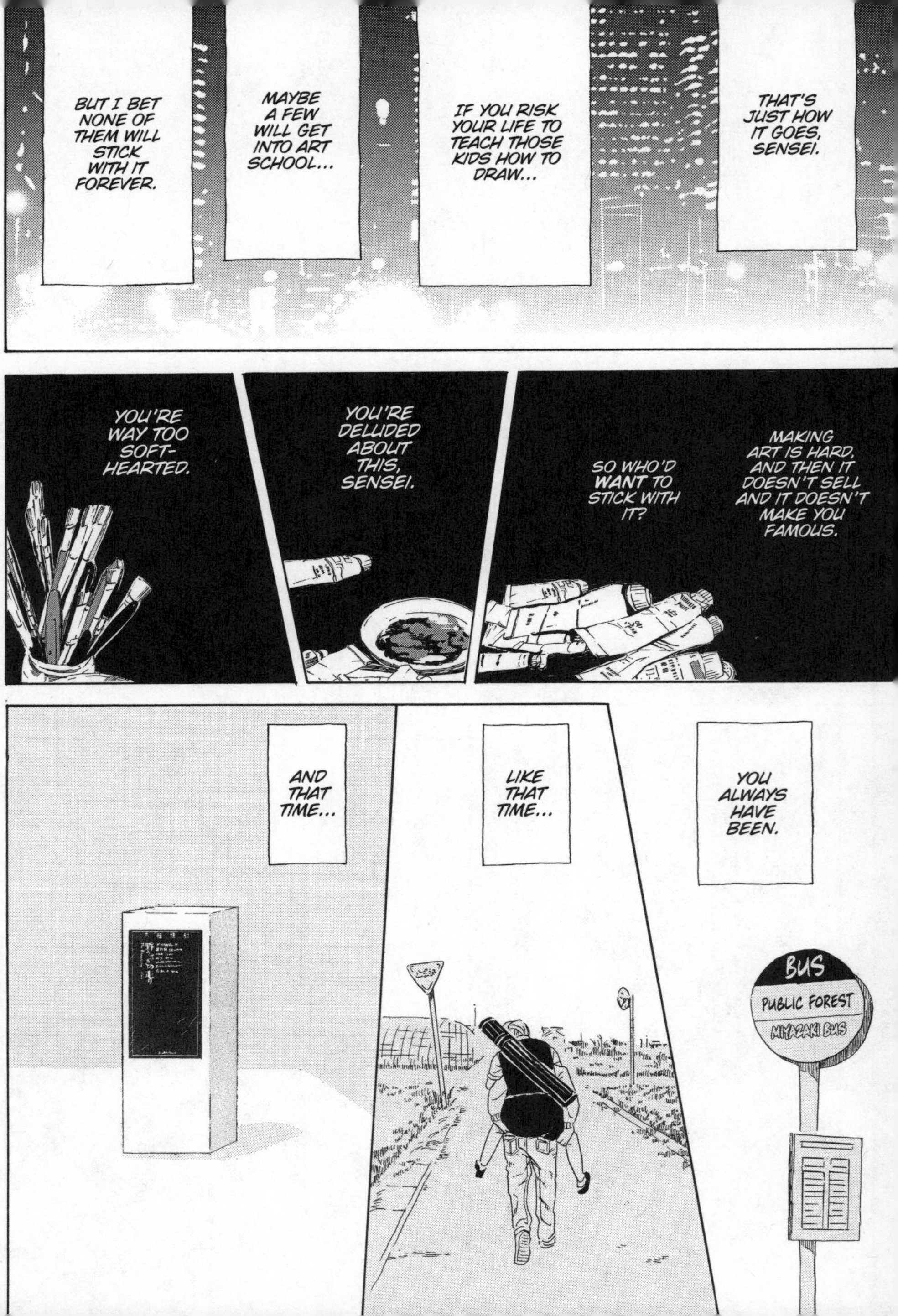
THAT'S JUST HOW IT GOES, SENSEI.
IF YOU RISK YOUR LIFE TO TEACH THOSE KIDS HOW TO DRAW...
MAYBE A FEW WILL GET INTO ART SCHOOL...
BUT I BET NONE OF THEM WILL STICK WITH IT FOREVER.
MAKING ART IS HARD, AND THEN IT DOESN'T SELL AND IT DOESN'T MAKE YOU FAMOUS.
SO WHO'D **WANT** TO STICK WITH IT?
YOU'RE DELUDED ABOUT THIS, SENSEI.
YOU'RE WAY TOO SOFT-HEARTED.
YOU ALWAYS HAVE BEEN.
LIKE THAT TIME...
AND THAT TIME...
BUS
PUBLIC FOREST
MIYAZAKI BUS

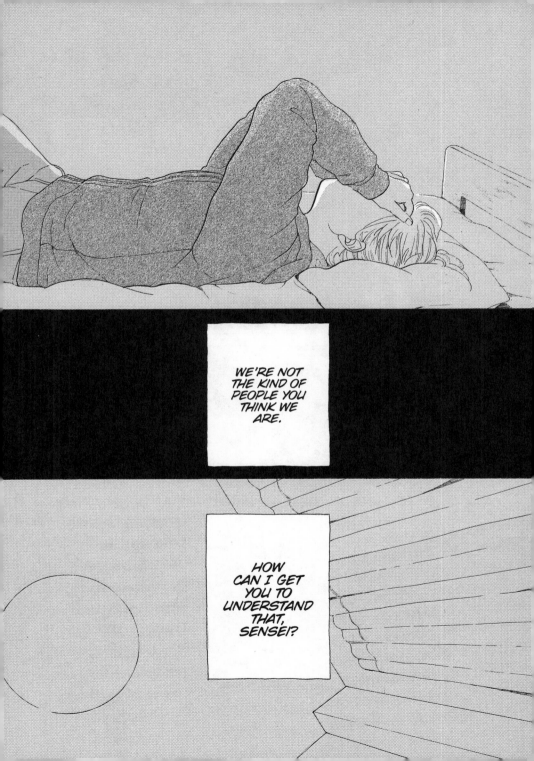

WE'RE NOT THE KIND OF PEOPLE YOU THINK WE ARE.

HOW CAN I GET YOU TO UNDERSTAND THAT, SENSEI?

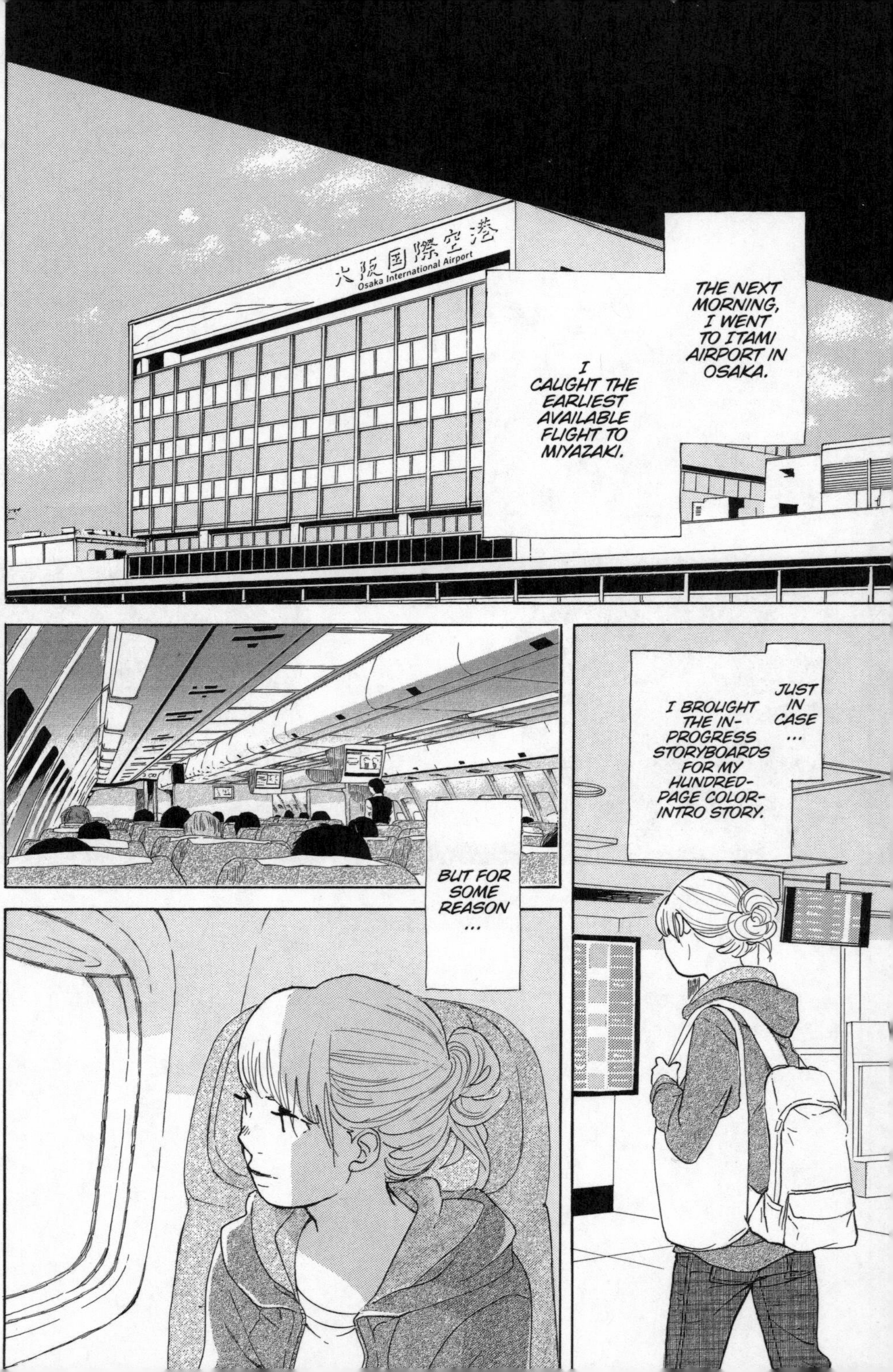
THE NEXT MORNING, I WENT TO ITAMI AIRPORT IN OSAKA.
I CAUGHT THE EARLIEST AVAILABLE FLIGHT TO MIYAZAKI.
大阪国際空港
Osaka International Airport
JUST IN CASE...
I BROUGHT THE IN-PROGRESS STORYBOARDS FOR MY HUNDRED-PAGE COLOR-INTRO STORY.
BUT FOR SOME REASON...

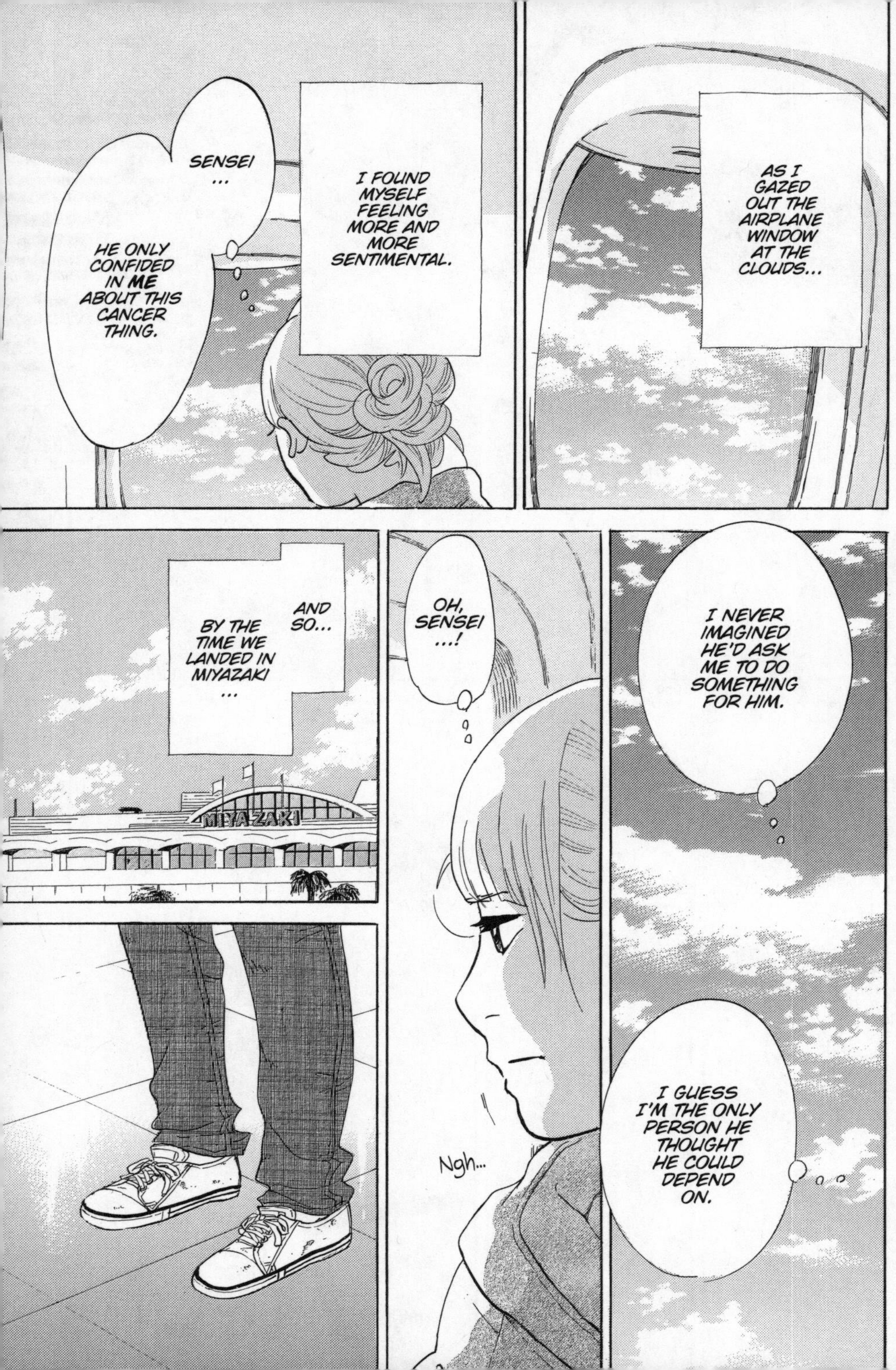
AS I GAZED OUT THE AIRPLANE WINDOW AT THE CLOUDS...
I FOUND MYSELF FEELING MORE AND MORE SENTIMENTAL.
SENSEI ...
HE ONLY CONFIDED IN ME ABOUT THIS CANCER THING.
I NEVER IMAGINED HE'D ASK ME TO DO SOMETHING FOR HIM.
I GUESS I'M THE ONLY PERSON HE THOUGHT HE COULD DEPEND ON.
OH, SENSEI ...!
Ngh...
AND SO... BY THE TIME WE LANDED IN MIYAZAKI ...
MIYAZAKI

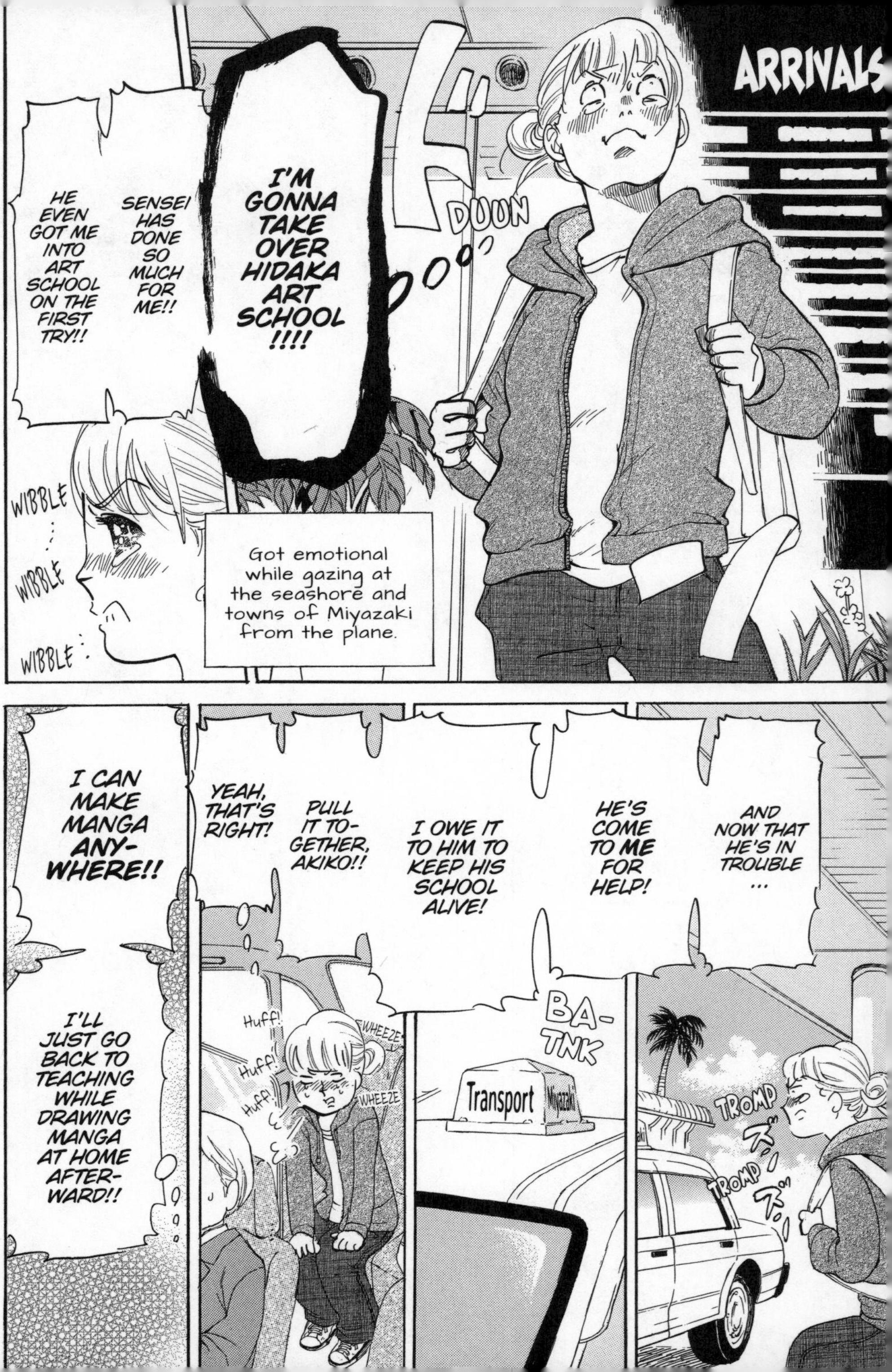
ARRIVALS
DUUN
I'M GONNA TAKE OVER HIDAKA ART SCHOOL !!!!
SENSEI HAS DONE SO MUCH FOR ME!!
HE EVEN GOT ME INTO ART SCHOOL ON THE FIRST TRY!!
Got emotional while gazing at the seashore and towns of Miyazaki from the plane.
WIBBLE
WIBBLE
WIBBLE
AND NOW THAT HE'S IN TROUBLE ...
HE'S COME TO ME FOR HELP!
I OWE IT TO HIM TO KEEP HIS SCHOOL ALIVE!
PULL IT TO-GETHER, AKIKO!!
YEAH, THAT'S RIGHT!
TROMP
TROMP
BA-TNK
Transport
Miyazaki
Huff!
Huff!
Huff!
WHEEZE
WHEEZE
I CAN MAKE MANGA ANY-WHERE!!
I'LL JUST GO BACK TO TEACHING WHILE DRAWING MANGA AT HOME AFTER-WARD!!

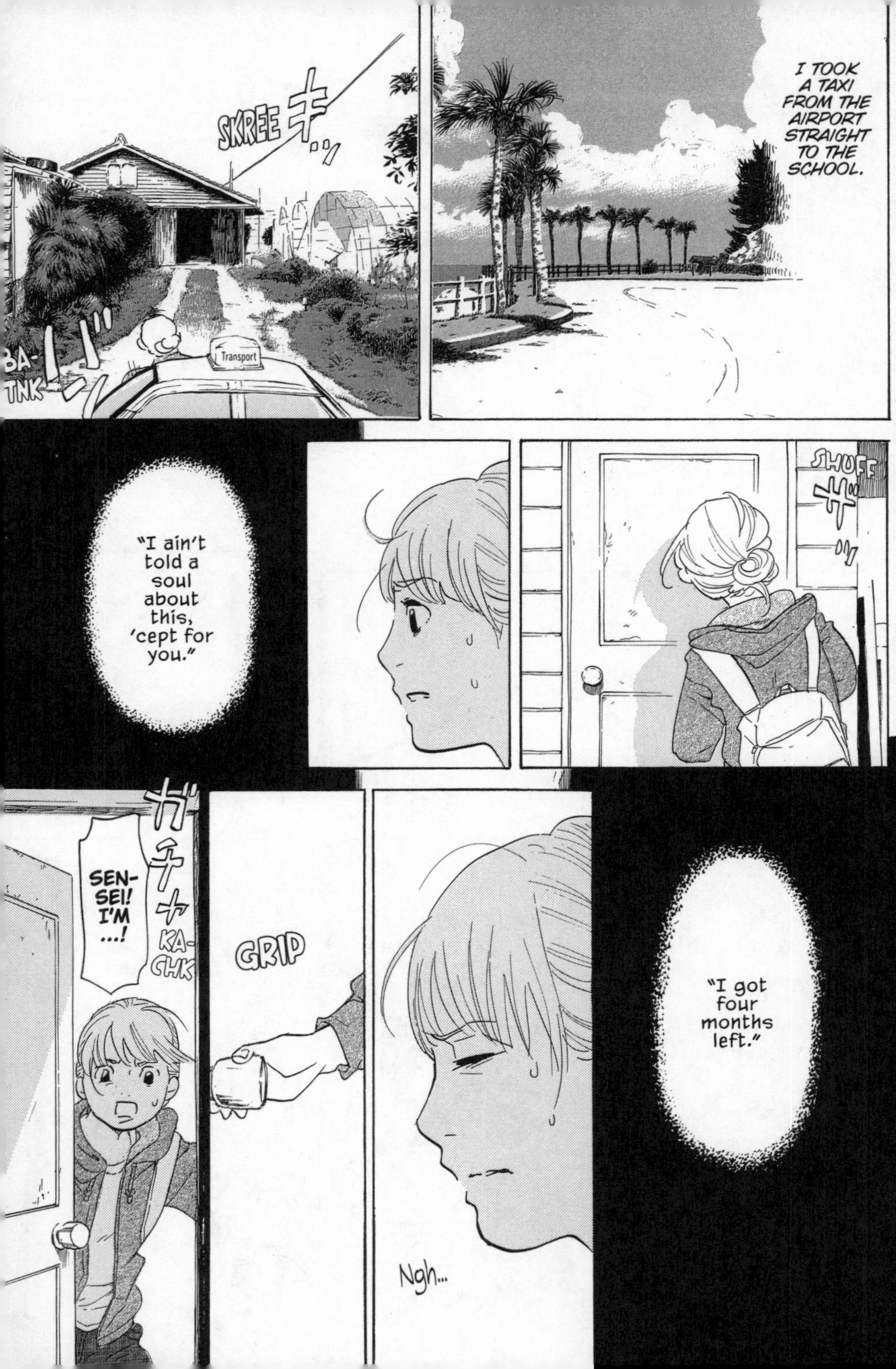
I TOOK A TAXI FROM THE AIRPORT STRAIGHT TO THE SCHOOL.
SKREE
Transport
BA-TNK
SHUFF
"I ain't told a soul about this, 'cept for you."
"I got four months left."
Ngh...
GRIP
KA-CHK
SEN-SEI! I'M ...!

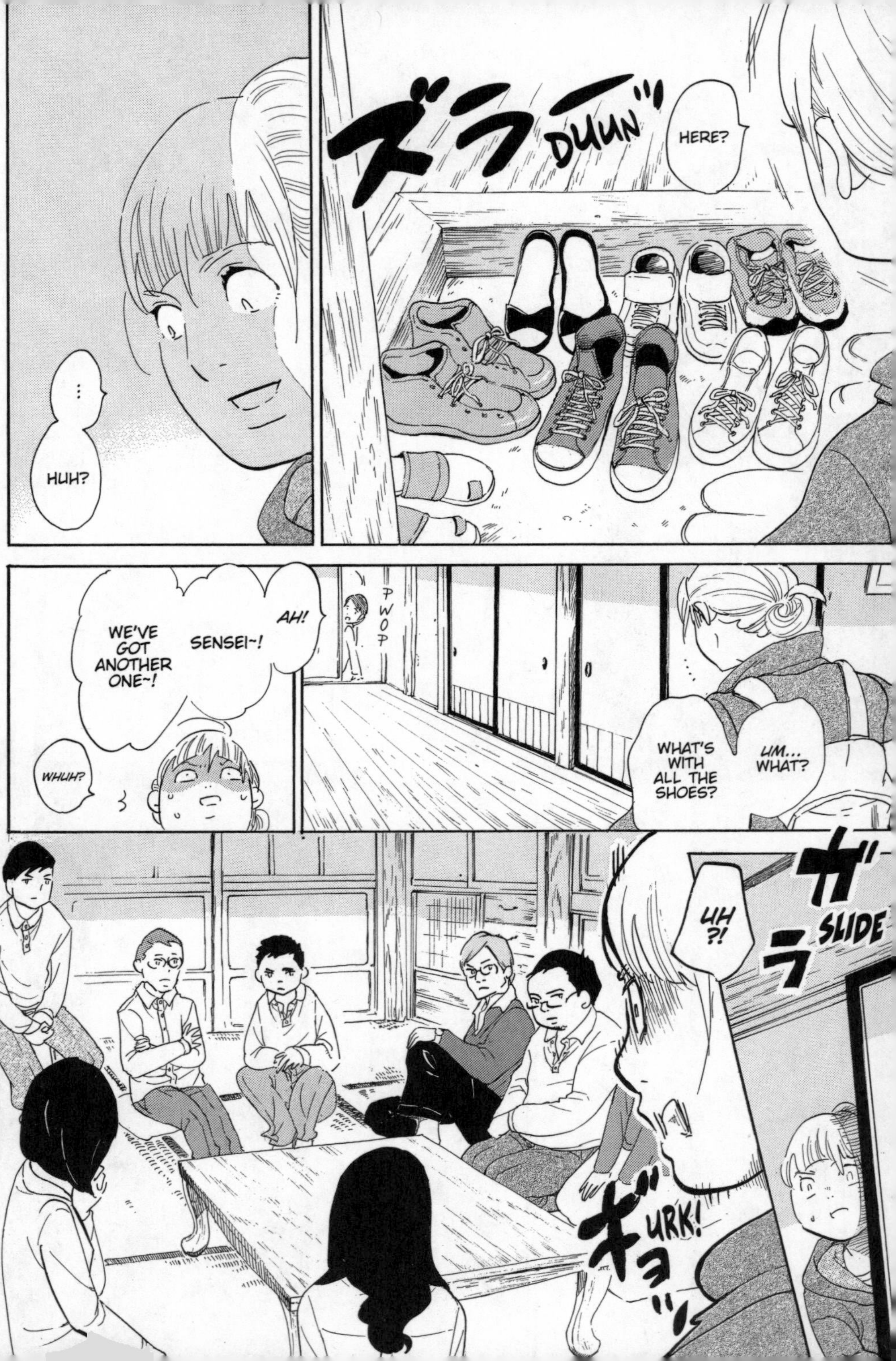

ズラー
DUUN
HERE?
...
HUH?
...
UM... WHAT?
WHAT'S WITH ALL THE SHOES?
PWOP
AH!
SENSEI~!
WE'VE GOT ANOTHER ONE~!
WHUH?
ガラ
SLIDE
UH?!
ギョッ
URK!

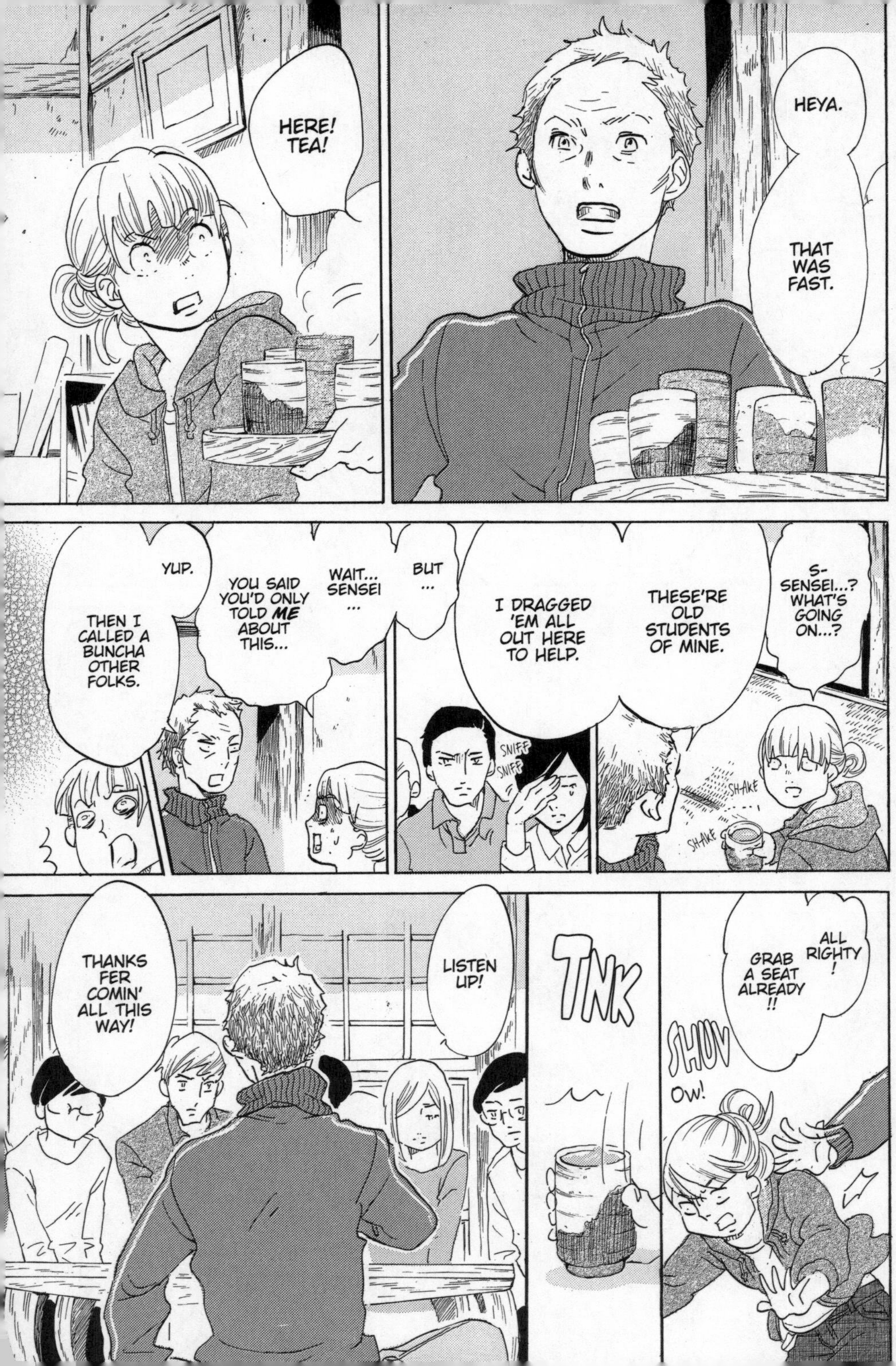
HEYA.
THAT WAS FAST.
HERE! TEA!
S-SENSEI...? WHAT'S GOING ON...?
SHAKE
SHAKE
THESE'RE OLD STUDENTS OF MINE.
I DRAGGED 'EM ALL OUT HERE TO HELP.
SNIFF
SNIFF
BUT ...
WAIT... SENSEI ...
YOU SAID YOU'D ONLY TOLD *ME* ABOUT THIS...
YUP.
THEN I CALLED A BUNCHA OTHER FOLKS.
ALL RIGHTY!
GRAB A SEAT ALREADY!!
SHUV
OW!
TNK
LISTEN UP!
THANKS FER COMIN' ALL THIS WAY!

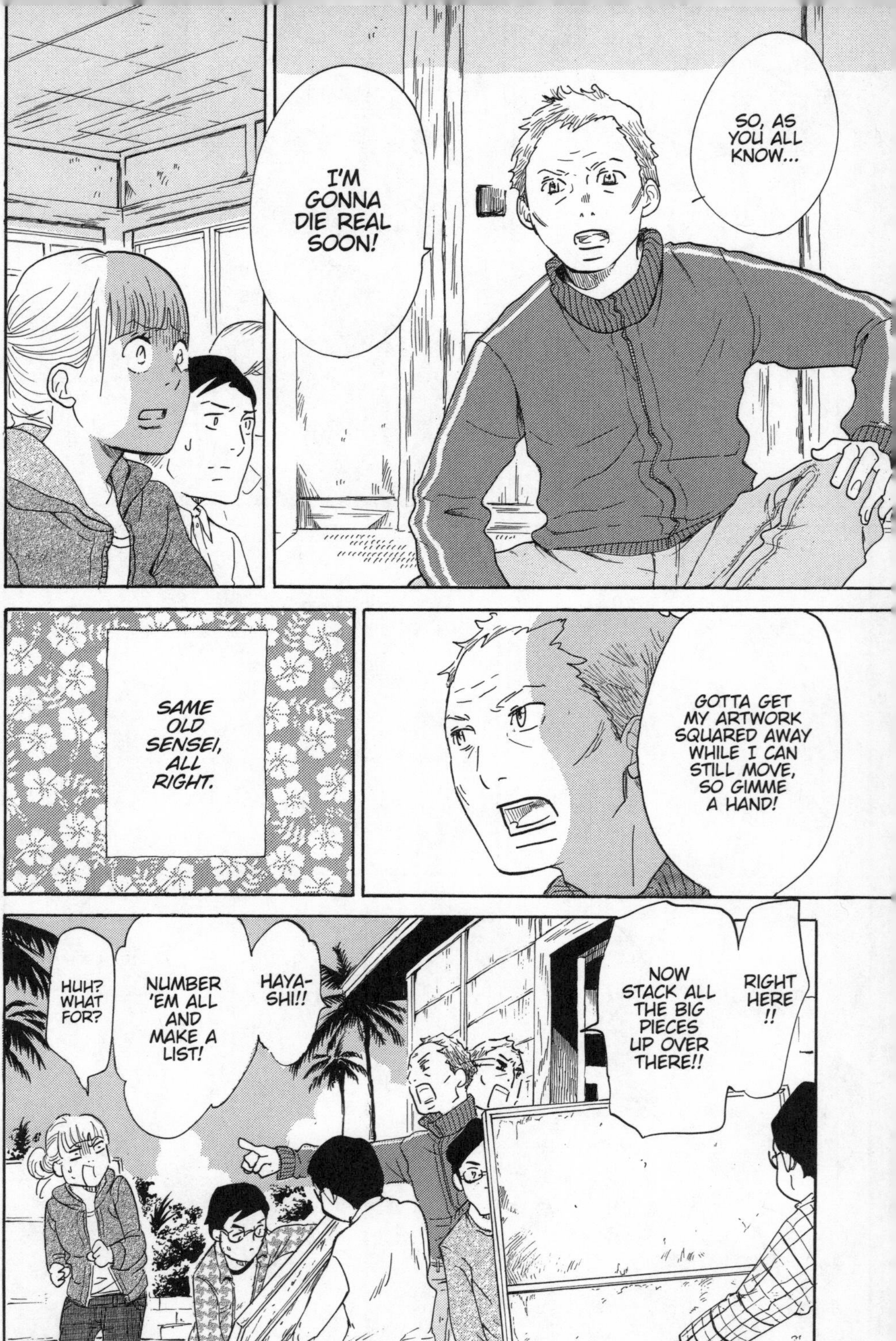
SO, AS YOU ALL KNOW...
I'M GONNA DIE REAL SOON!
GOTTA GET MY ARTWORK SQUARED AWAY WHILE I CAN STILL MOVE, SO GIMME A HAND!
SAME OLD SENSEI, ALL RIGHT.
RIGHT HERE!!
NOW STACK ALL THE BIG PIECES UP OVER THERE!!
HAYA-SHI!!
NUMBER 'EM ALL AND MAKE A LIST!
HUH? WHAT FOR?

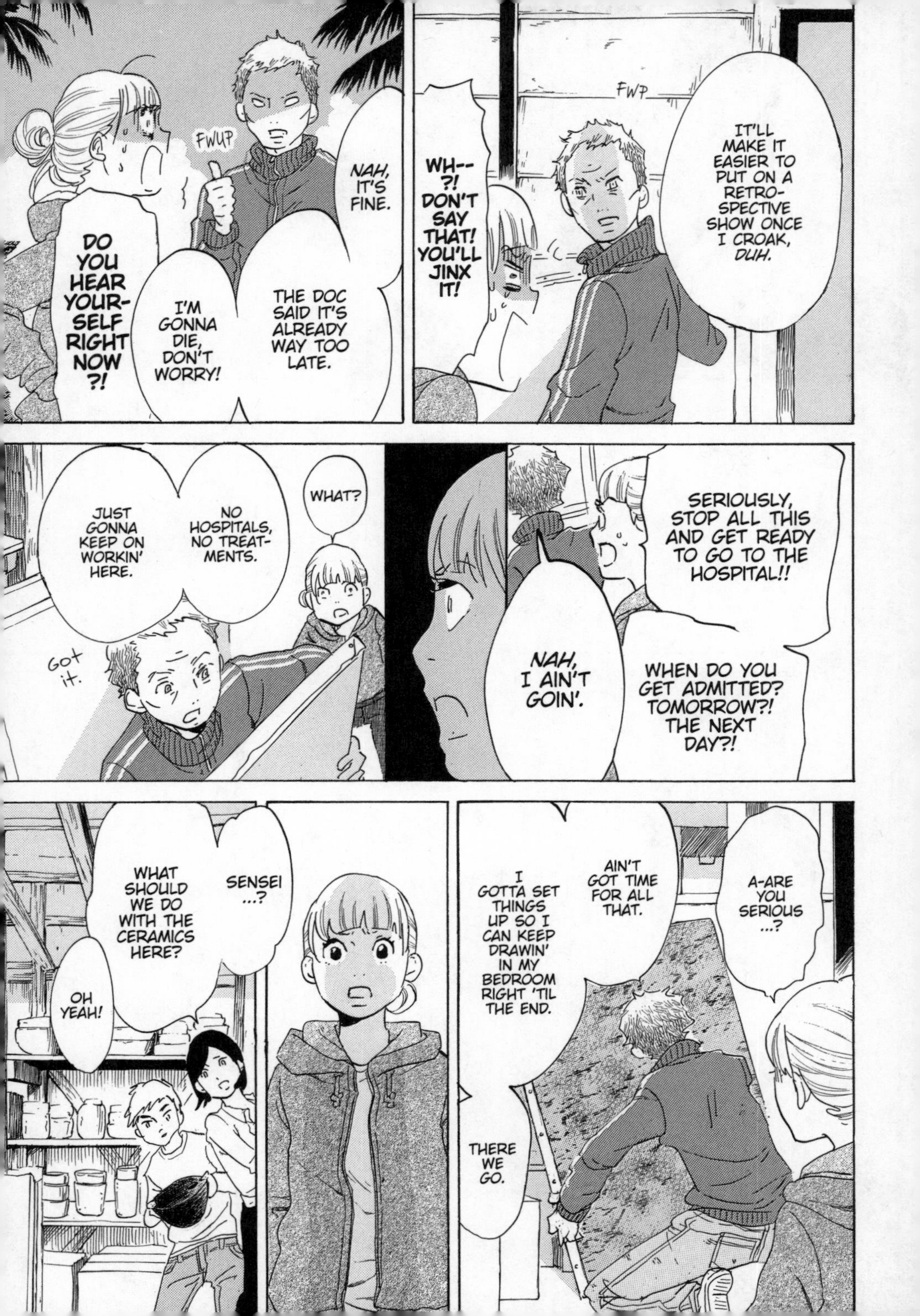
FWP
IT'LL MAKE IT EASIER TO PUT ON A RETRO-SPECTIVE SHOW ONCE I CROAK, *DUH.*
WH--?! DON'T SAY THAT! YOU'LL JINX IT!
NAH, IT'S FINE.
FWUP
THE DOC SAID IT'S ALREADY WAY TOO LATE.
I'M GONNA DIE, DON'T WORRY!
DO YOU HEAR YOUR-SELF RIGHT NOW?!
SERIOUSLY, STOP ALL THIS AND GET READY TO GO TO THE HOSPITAL!!
WHEN DO YOU GET ADMITTED? TOMORROW?! THE NEXT DAY?!
NAH, I AIN'T GOIN'.
WHAT?
NO HOSPITALS, NO TREAT-MENTS.
JUST GONNA KEEP ON WORKIN' HERE.
Got it.
A-ARE YOU SERIOUS ...?
AIN'T GOT TIME FOR ALL THAT.
I GOTTA SET THINGS UP SO I CAN KEEP DRAWIN' IN MY BEDROOM RIGHT 'TIL THE END.
THERE WE GO.
SENSEI ...?
WHAT SHOULD WE DO WITH THE CERAMICS HERE?
OH YEAH!

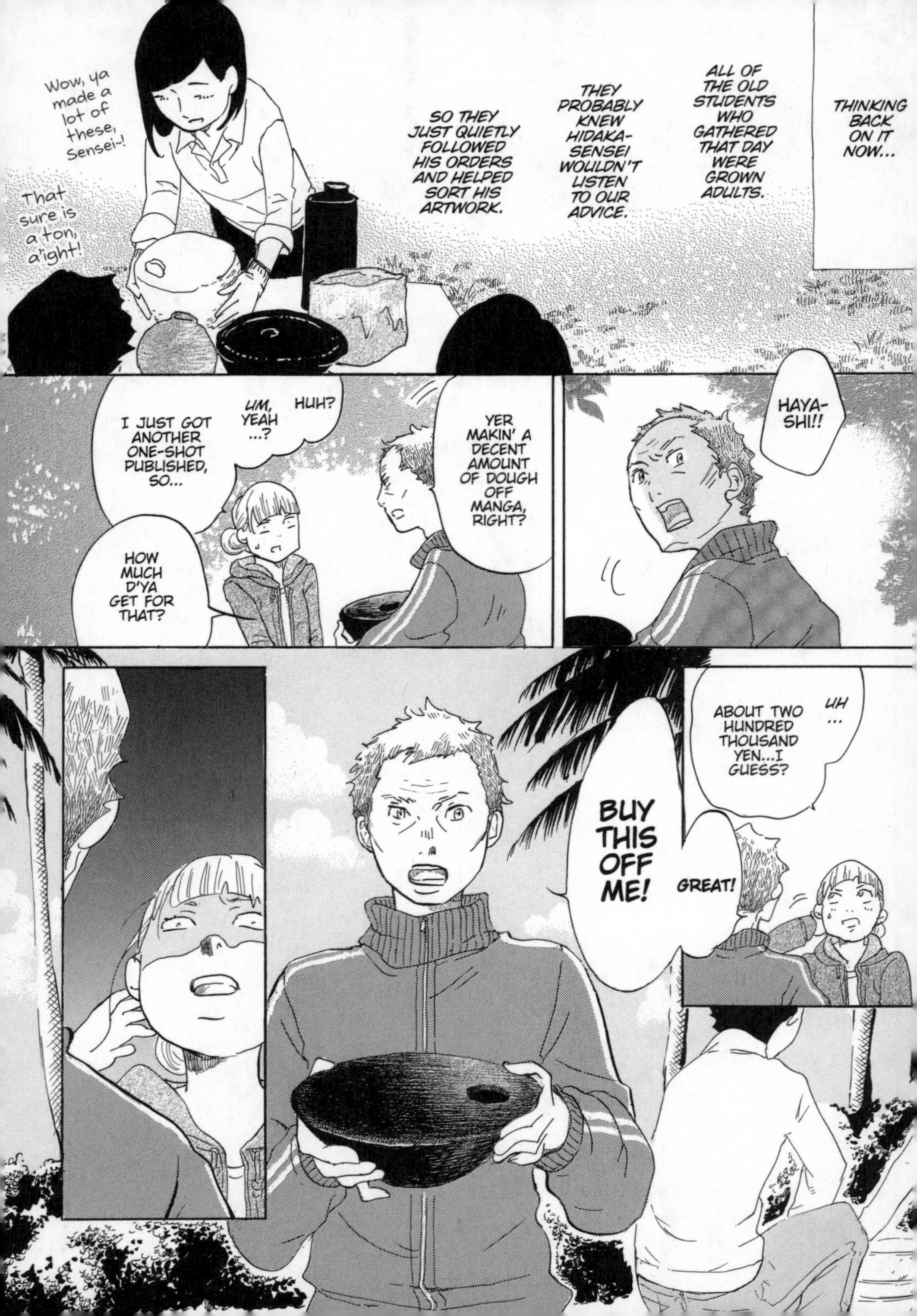
THINKING BACK ON IT NOW...
ALL OF THE OLD STUDENTS WHO GATHERED THAT DAY WERE GROWN ADULTS.
THEY PROBABLY KNEW HIDAKA-SENSEI WOULDN'T LISTEN TO OUR ADVICE.
SO THEY JUST QUIETLY FOLLOWED HIS ORDERS AND HELPED SORT HIS ARTWORK.
Wow, ya made a lot of these, Sensei~!
That sure is a ton, a'ight!
HAYA-SHI!!
YER MAKIN' A DECENT AMOUNT OF DOUGH OFF MANGA, RIGHT?
HUH?
UM, YEAH ...?
I JUST GOT ANOTHER ONE-SHOT PUBLISHED, SO...
HOW MUCH D'YA GET FOR THAT?
UH ...
ABOUT TWO HUNDRED THOUSAND YEN...I GUESS?
GREAT!
BUY THIS OFF ME!

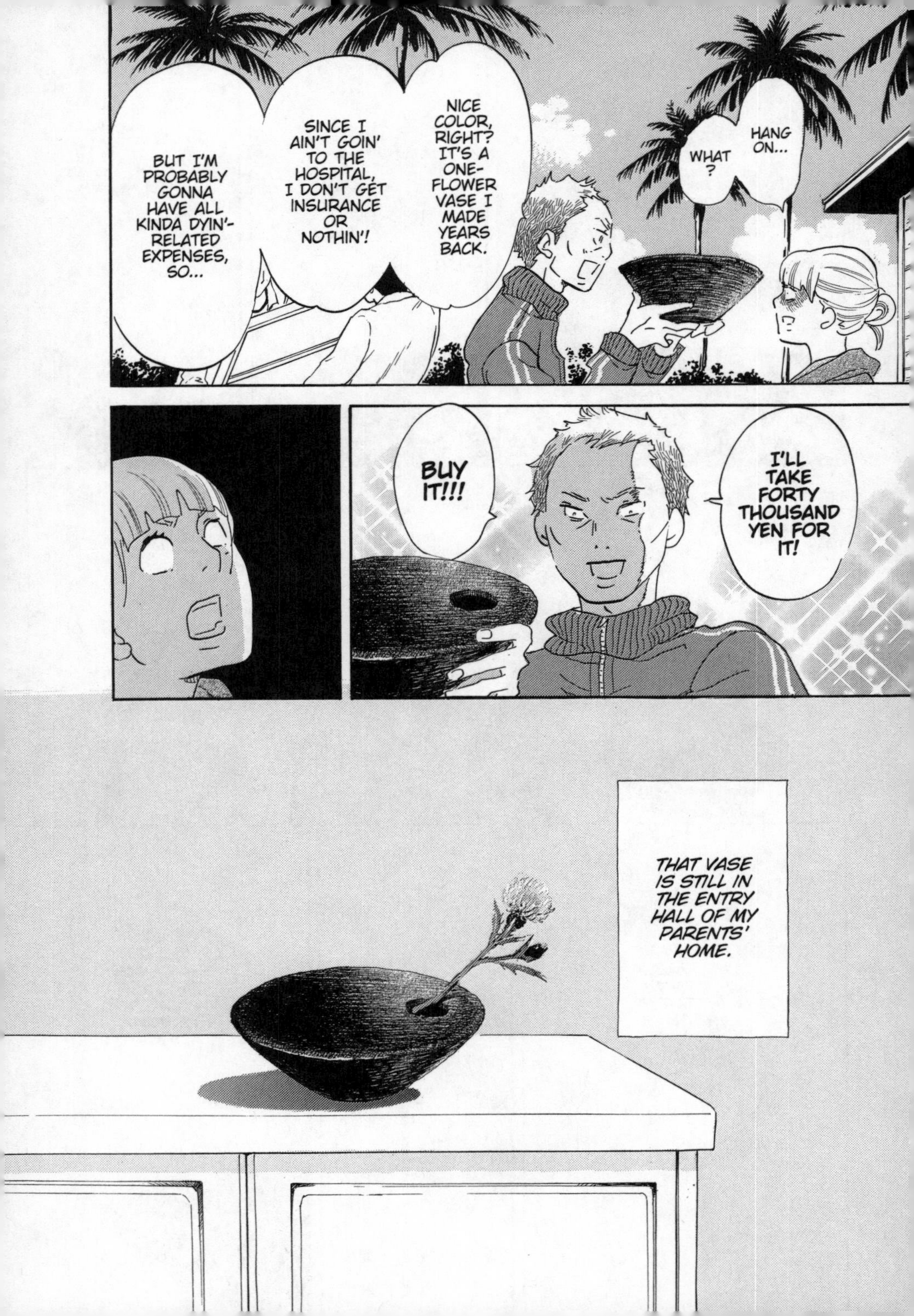
HANG ON...
WHAT?
NICE COLOR, RIGHT? IT'S A ONE-FLOWER VASE I MADE YEARS BACK.
SINCE I AIN'T GOIN' TO THE HOSPITAL, I DON'T GET INSURANCE OR NOTHIN'!
BUT I'M PROBABLY GONNA HAVE ALL KINDA DYIN'-RELATED EXPENSES, SO...
I'LL TAKE FORTY THOUSAND YEN FOR IT!
BUY IT!!!
THAT VASE IS STILL IN THE ENTRY HALL OF MY PARENTS' HOME.

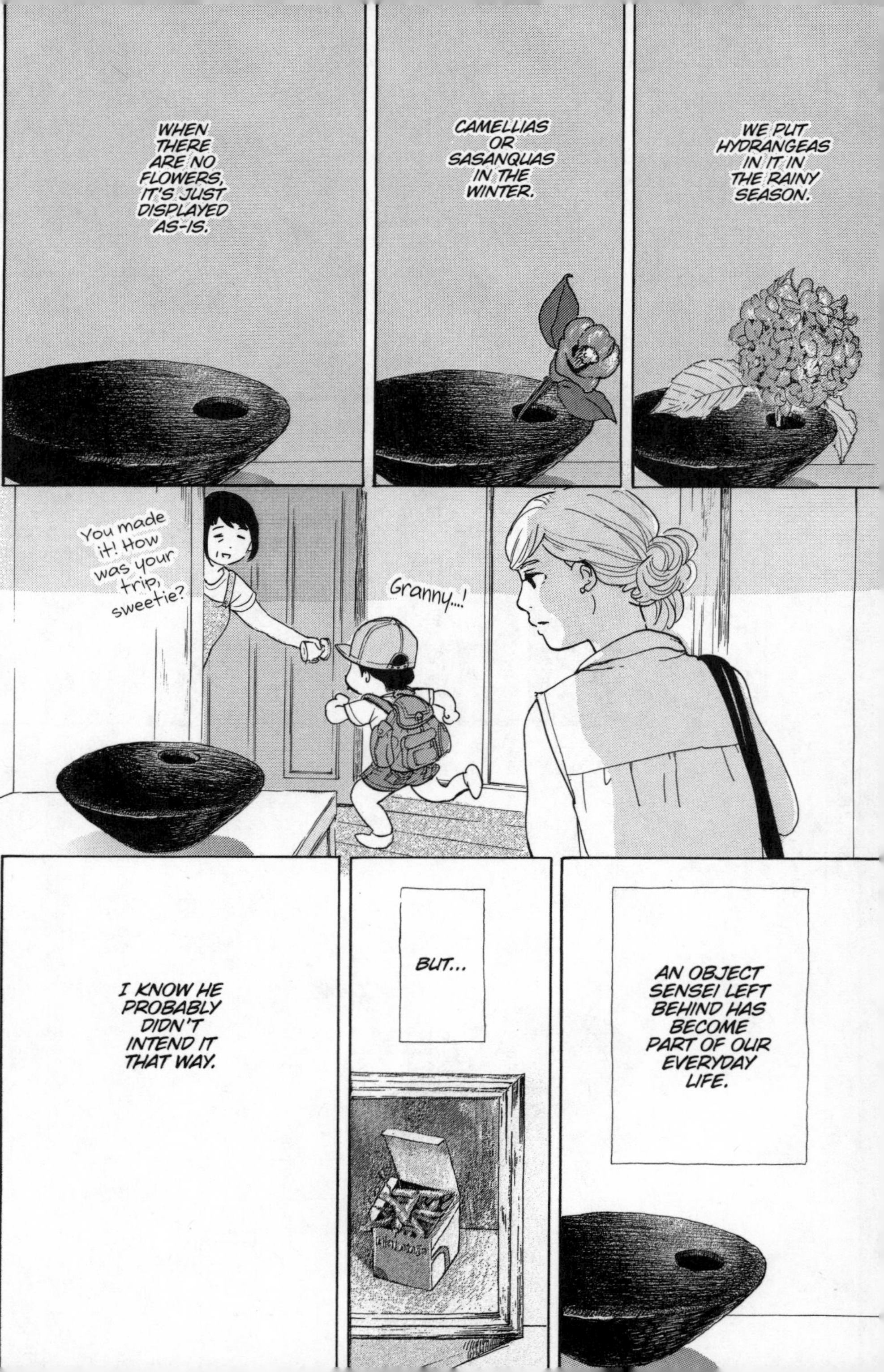
WE PUT HYDRANGEAS IN IT IN THE RAINY SEASON.
CAMELLIAS OR SASANQUAS IN THE WINTER.
WHEN THERE ARE NO FLOWERS, IT'S JUST DISPLAYED AS-IS.
Granny...!
You made it! How was your trip, sweetie?
AN OBJECT SENSEI LEFT BEHIND HAS BECOME PART OF OUR EVERYDAY LIFE.
BUT...
I KNOW HE PROBABLY DIDN'T INTEND IT THAT WAY.

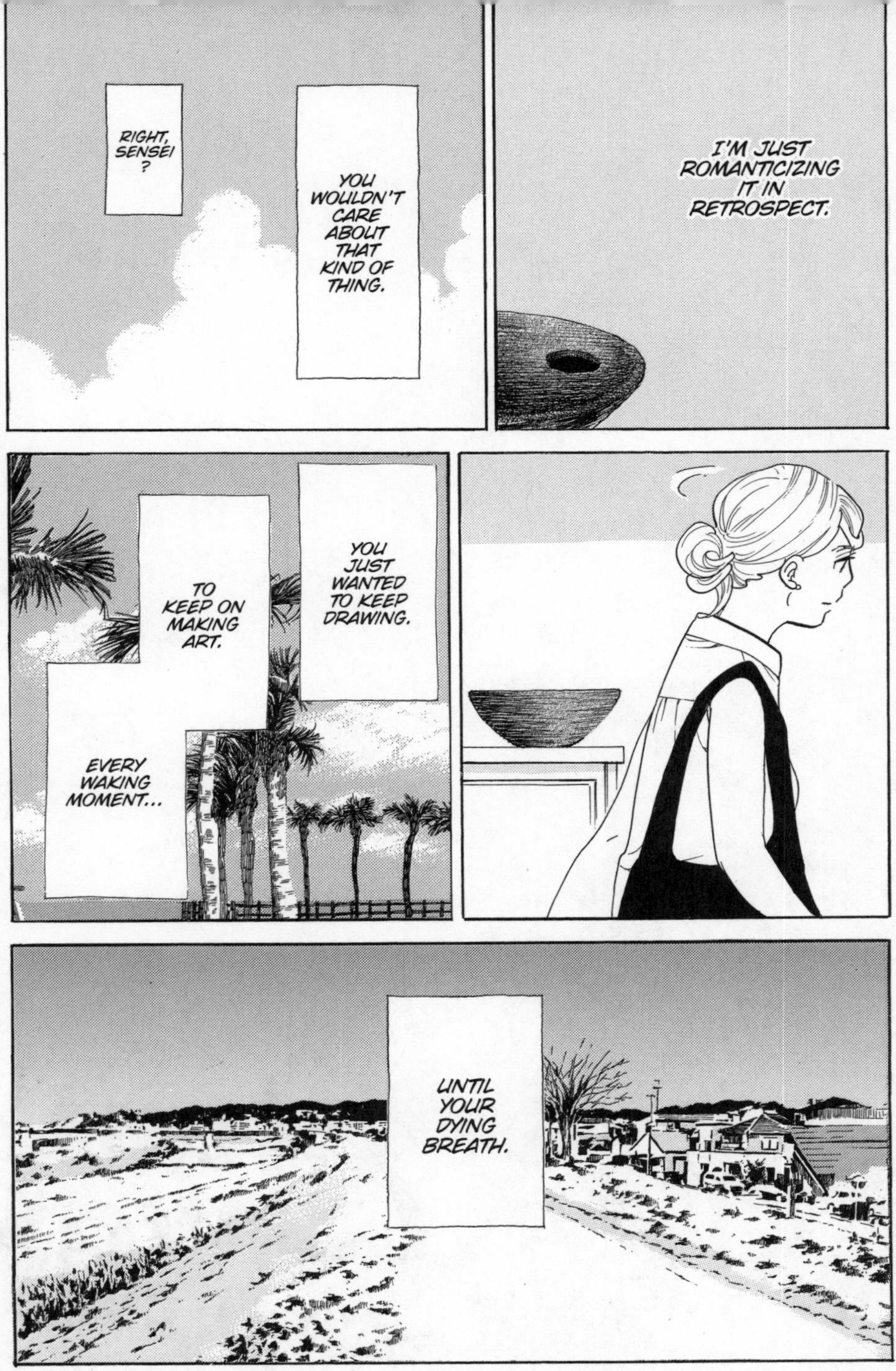
I'M JUST ROMANTICIZING IT IN RETROSPECT.
YOU WOULDN'T CARE ABOUT THAT KIND OF THING.
RIGHT, SENSEI?
YOU JUST WANTED TO KEEP DRAWING.
TO KEEP ON MAKING ART.
EVERY WAKING MOMENT...
UNTIL YOUR DYING BREATH.

Blank
Canvas
My So-Called
Artist's Journey

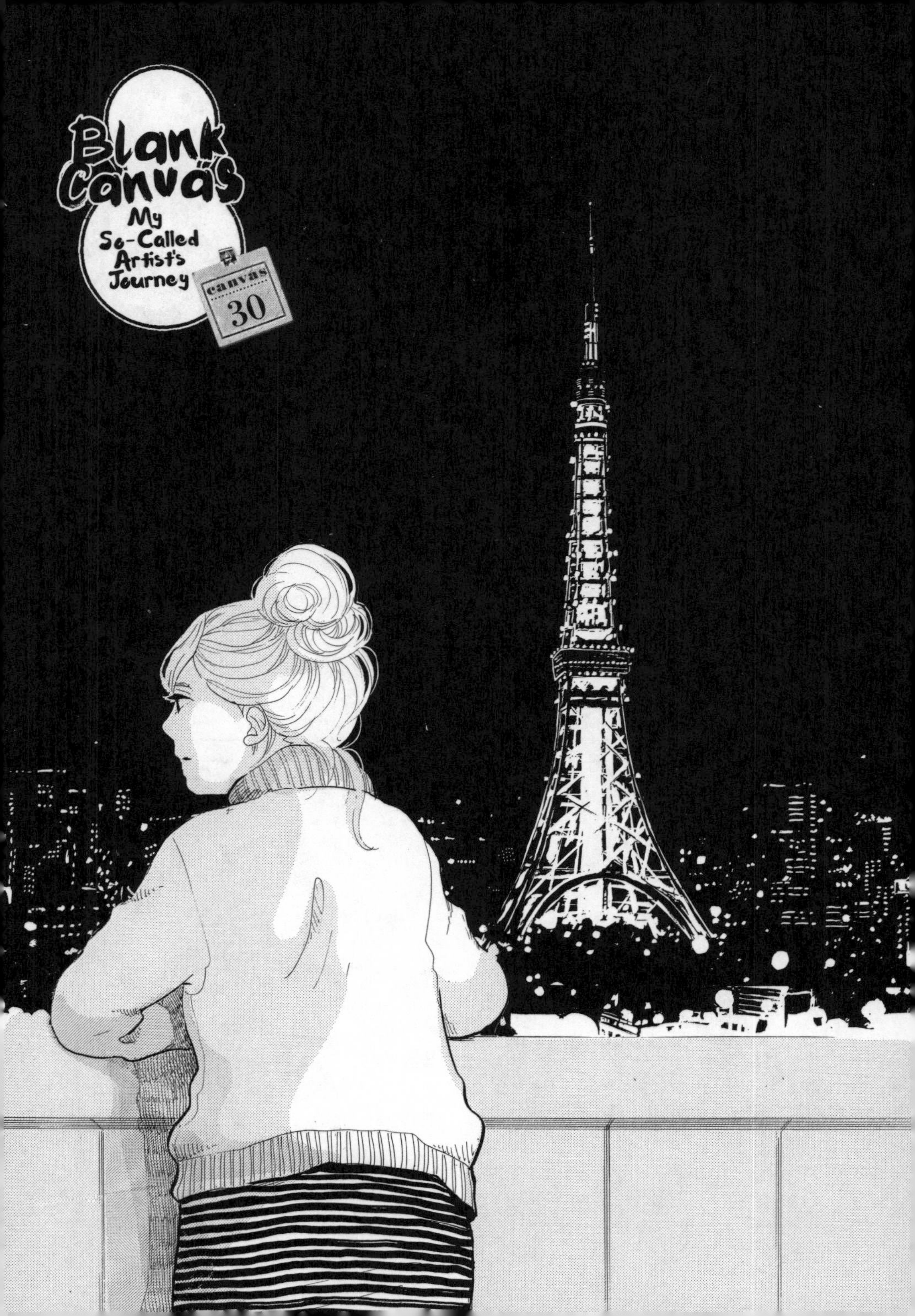
Blank Canvas
My So-Called Artist's Journey
canvas
30

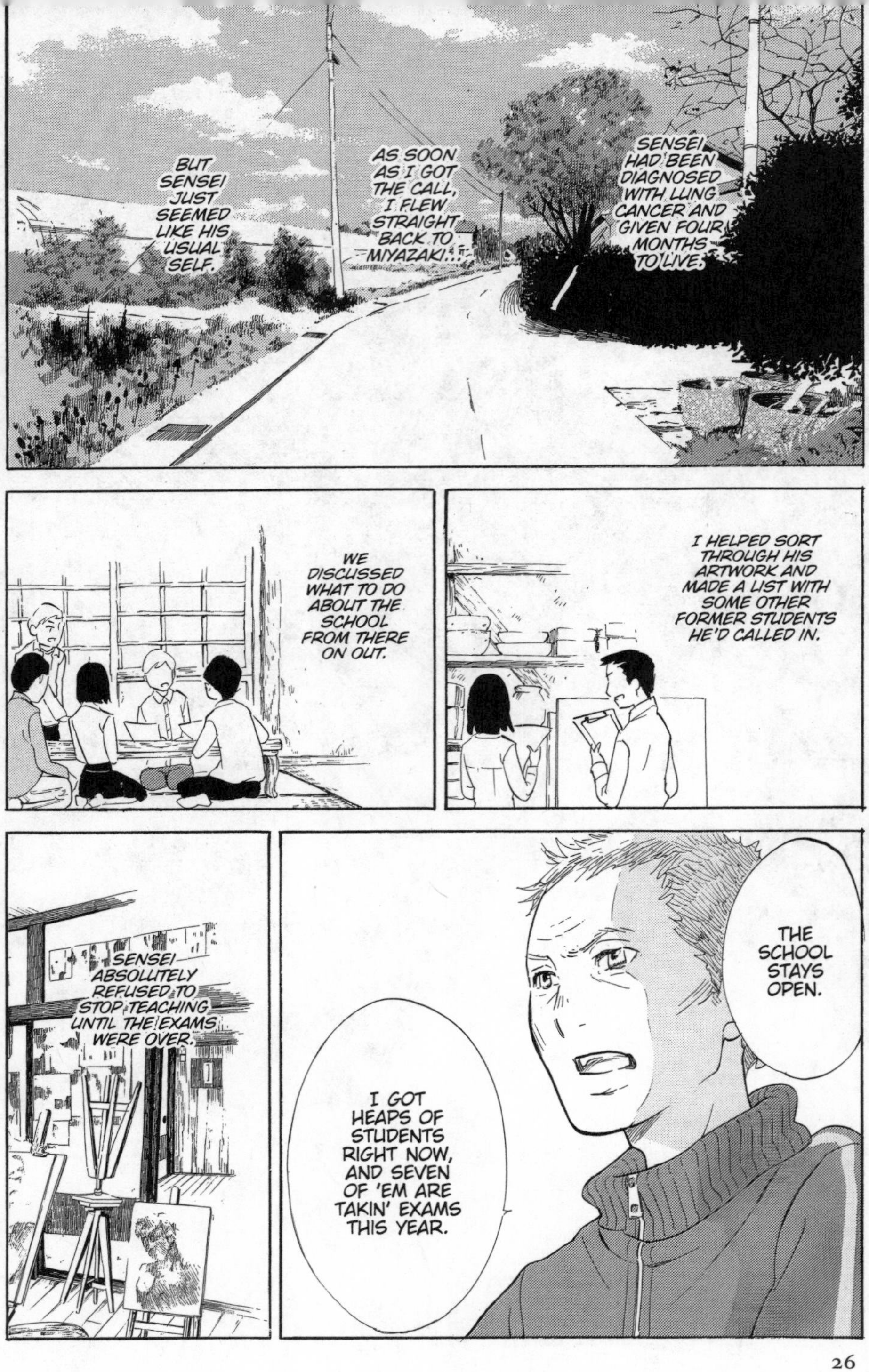
SENSEI HAD BEEN DIAGNOSED WITH LUNG CANCER AND GIVEN FOUR MONTHS TO LIVE.
AS SOON AS I GOT THE CALL, I FLEW STRAIGHT BACK TO MIYAZAKI...
BUT SENSEI JUST SEEMED LIKE HIS USUAL SELF.
I HELPED SORT THROUGH HIS ARTWORK AND MADE A LIST WITH SOME OTHER FORMER STUDENTS HE'D CALLED IN.
WE DISCUSSED WHAT TO DO ABOUT THE SCHOOL FROM THERE ON OUT.
THE SCHOOL STAYS OPEN.
I GOT HEAPS OF STUDENTS RIGHT NOW, AND SEVEN OF 'EM ARE TAKIN' EXAMS THIS YEAR.
SENSEI ABSOLUTELY REFUSED TO STOP TEACHING UNTIL THE EXAMS WERE OVER.

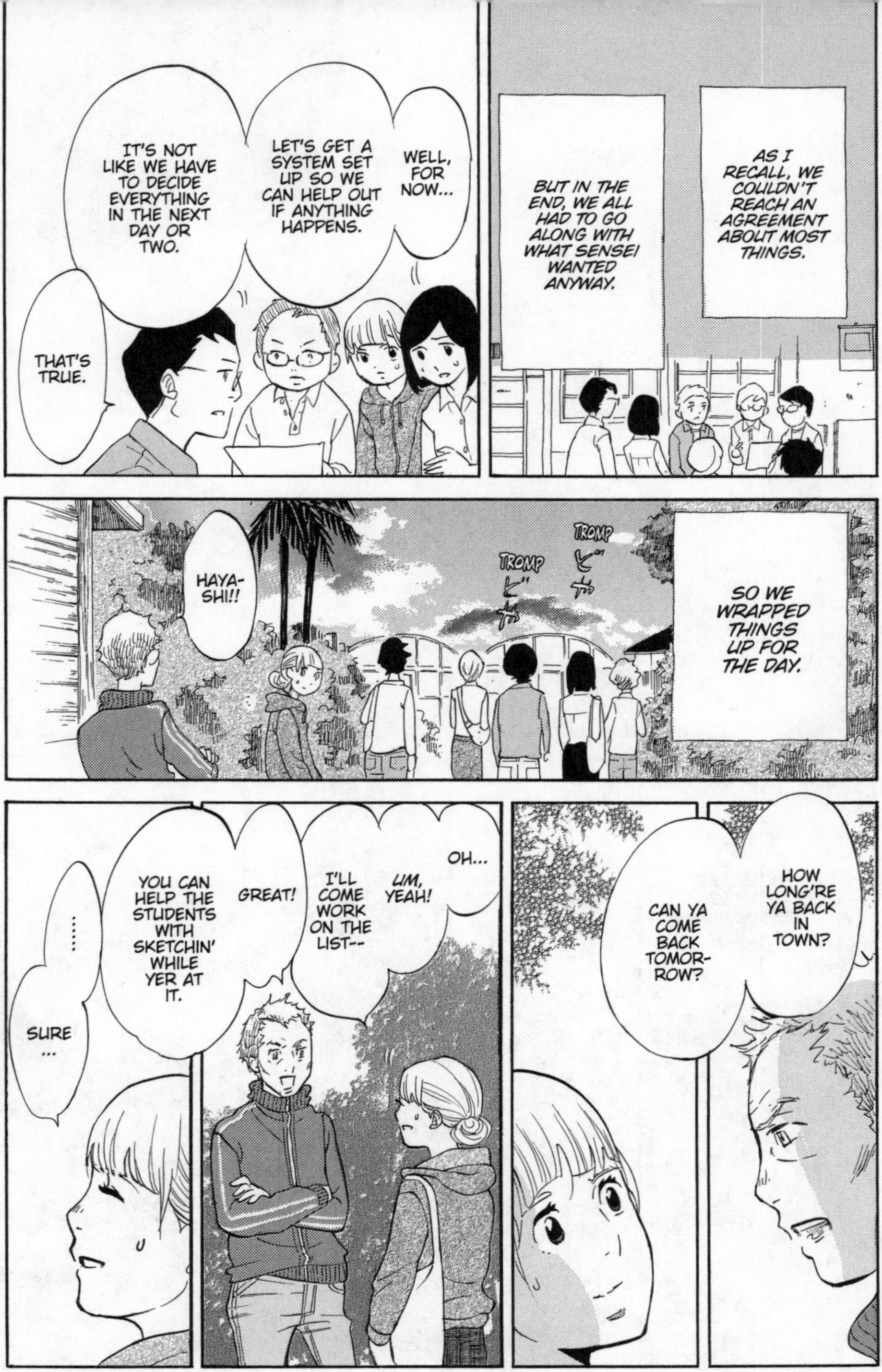
AS I RECALL, WE COULDN'T REACH AN AGREEMENT ABOUT MOST THINGS.
BUT IN THE END, WE ALL HAD TO GO ALONG WITH WHAT SENSEI WANTED ANYWAY.
WELL, FOR NOW...
LET'S GET A SYSTEM SET UP SO WE CAN HELP OUT IF ANYTHING HAPPENS.
IT'S NOT LIKE WE HAVE TO DECIDE EVERYTHING IN THE NEXT DAY OR TWO.
THAT'S TRUE.
SO WE WRAPPED THINGS UP FOR THE DAY.
TROMP
TROMP
HAYA-SHI!!
HOW LONG'RE YA BACK IN TOWN?
CAN YA COME BACK TOMOR-ROW?
OH...
UM, YEAH!
I'LL COME WORK ON THE LIST--
GREAT!
YOU CAN HELP THE STUDENTS WITH SKETCHIN' WHILE YER AT IT.
......
SURE ...

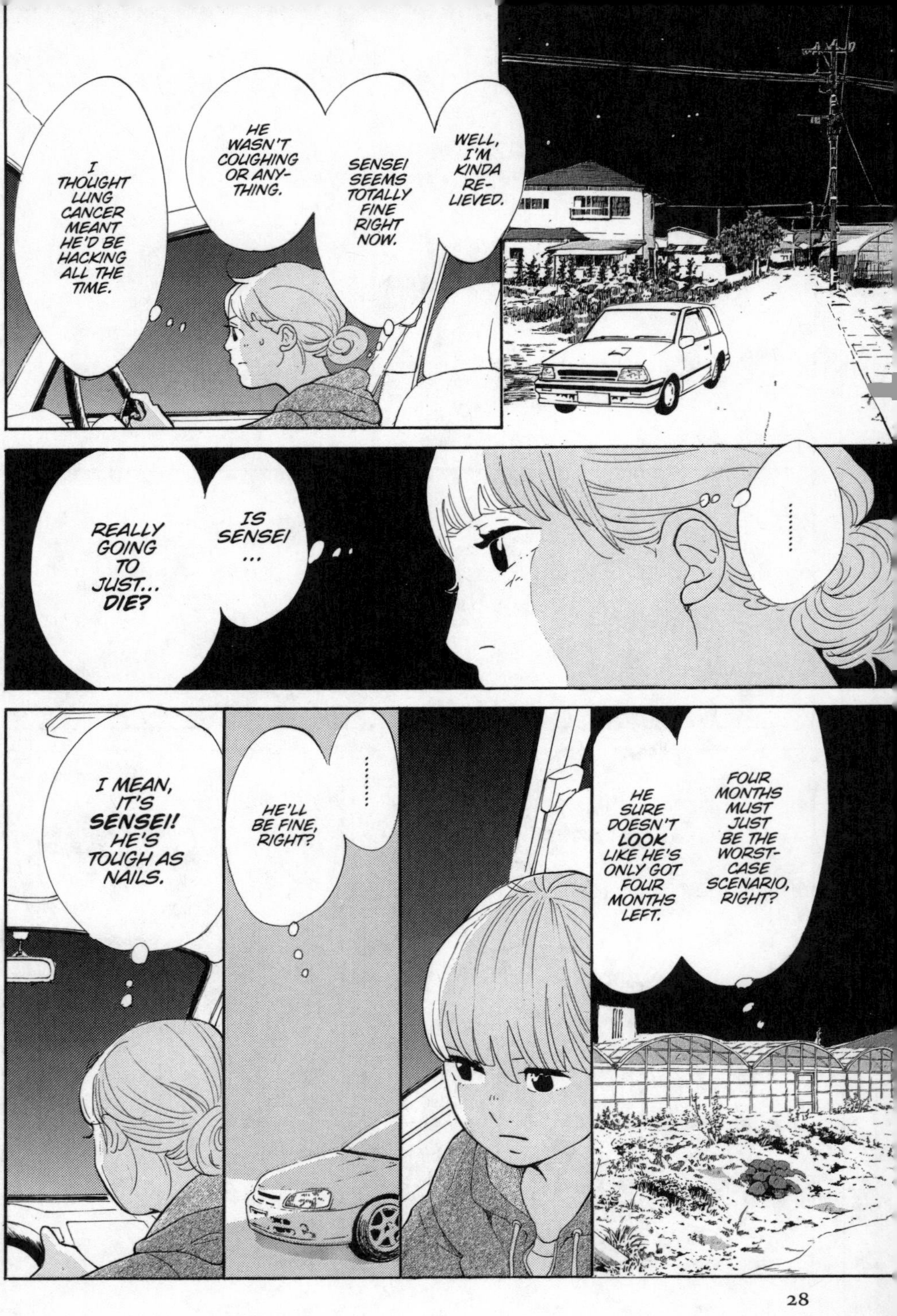
WELL, I'M KINDA RE-LIEVED.
SENSEI SEEMS TOTALLY FINE RIGHT NOW.
HE WASN'T COUGHING OR ANY-THING.
I THOUGHT LUNG CANCER MEANT HE'D BE HACKING ALL THE TIME.
......
IS SENSEI ...
REALLY GOING TO JUST... DIE?
FOUR MONTHS MUST JUST BE THE WORST-CASE SCENARIO, RIGHT?
HE SURE DOESN'T LOOK LIKE HE'S ONLY GOT FOUR MONTHS LEFT.
......
HE'LL BE FINE, RIGHT?
I MEAN, IT'S SENSEI! HE'S TOUGH AS NAILS.

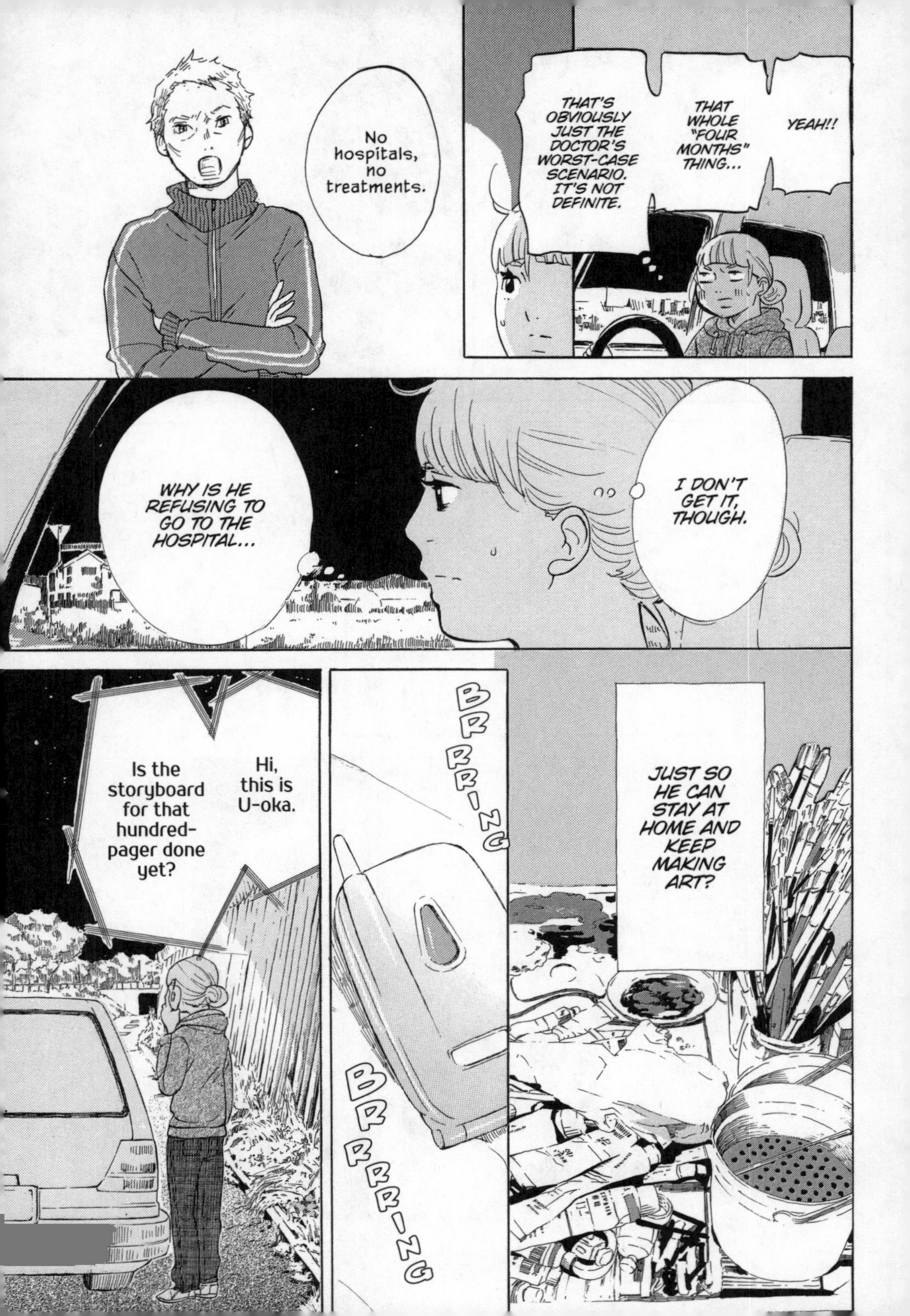
YEAH!!
THAT WHOLE "FOUR MONTHS" THING...
THAT'S OBVIOUSLY JUST THE DOCTOR'S WORST-CASE SCENARIO. IT'S NOT DEFINITE.
No hospitals, no treatments.
I DON'T GET IT, THOUGH.
WHY IS HE REFUSING TO GO TO THE HOSPITAL...
JUST SO HE CAN STAY AT HOME AND KEEP MAKING ART?
BRRRING
BRRRING
Hi, this is U-oka.
Is the storyboard for that hundred-pager done yet?

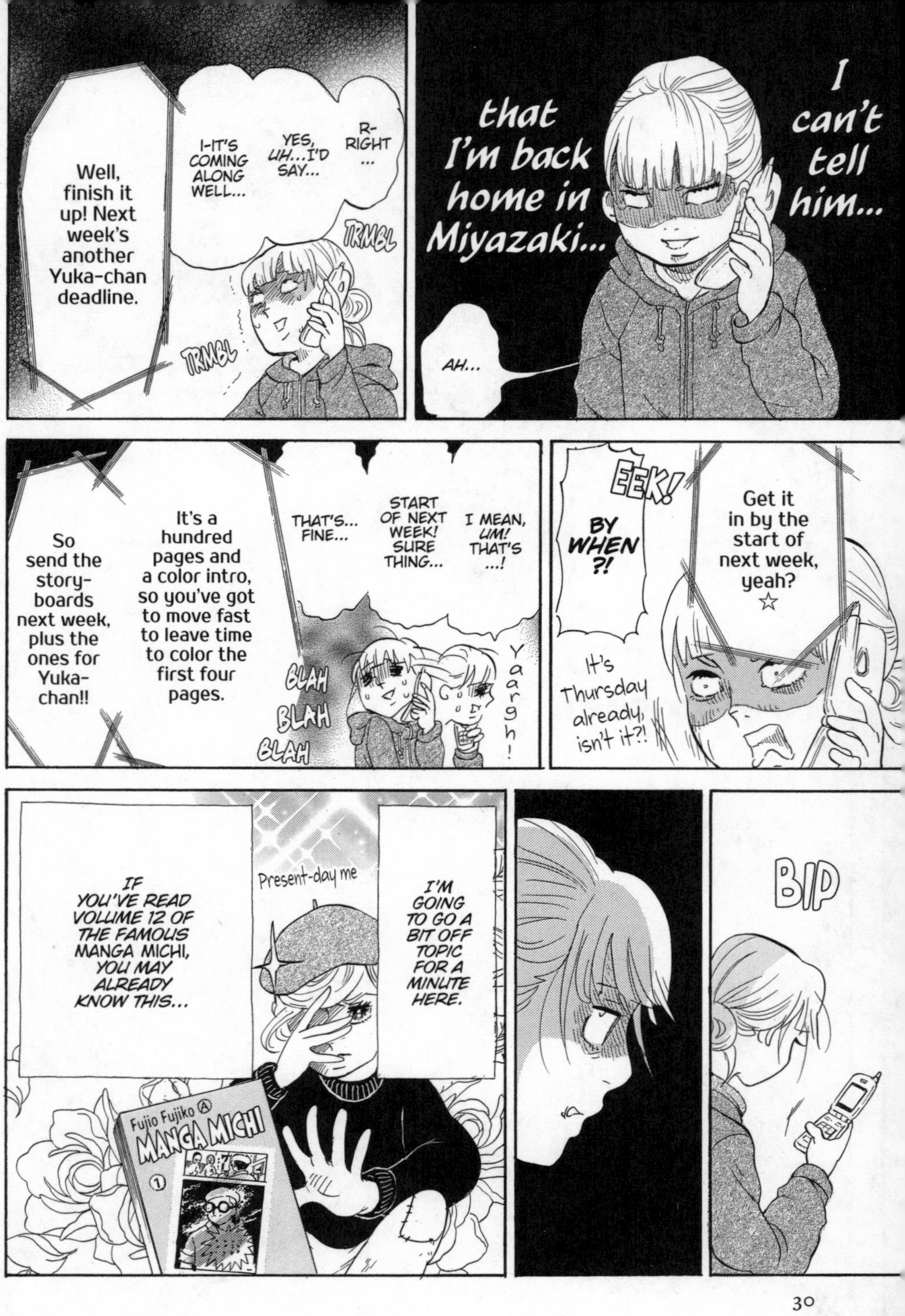
I can't tell him...
that I'm back home in Miyazaki...
AH...
R-RIGHT ...
YES, UH...I'D SAY...
I-IT'S COMING ALONG WELL...
Well, finish it up! Next week's another Yuka-chan deadline.
TRMBL
TRMBL
Get it in by the start of next week, yeah? ☆
EEK!
BY WHEN?!
It's Thursday already, isn't it?!
I MEAN, UM! THAT'S ...!
START OF NEXT WEEK! SURE THING...
THAT'S... FINE...
It's a hundred pages and a color intro, so you've got to move fast to leave time to color the first four pages.
So send the storyboards next week, plus the ones for Yuka-chan!!
Yaargh!
BLAH
BLAH
BLAH
BIP
I'M GOING TO GO A BIT OFF TOPIC FOR A MINUTE HERE.
Present-day me
IF YOU'VE READ VOLUME 12 OF THE FAMOUS MANGA MICHI, YOU MAY ALREADY KNOW THIS...
Fujio Fujiko Ⓐ
MANGA MICHI
1

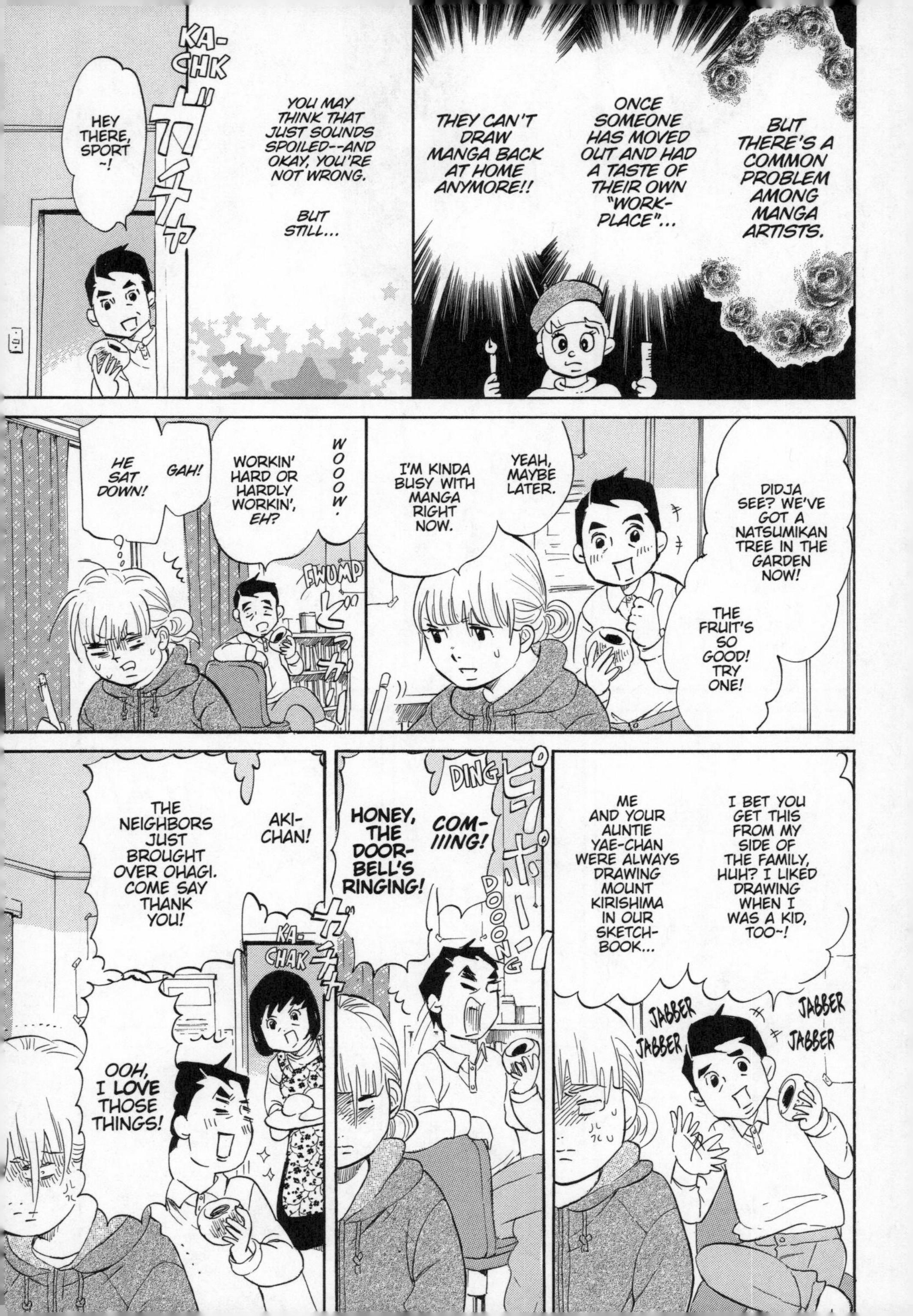
BUT THERE'S A COMMON PROBLEM AMONG MANGA ARTISTS.
ONCE SOMEONE HAS MOVED OUT AND HAD A TASTE OF THEIR OWN "WORK-PLACE"...
THEY CAN'T DRAW MANGA BACK AT HOME ANYMORE!!
YOU MAY THINK THAT JUST SOUNDS SPOILED--AND OKAY, YOU'RE NOT WRONG.
BUT STILL...
KA-CHK
HEY THERE, SPORT~!
DIDJA SEE? WE'VE GOT A NATSUMIKAN TREE IN THE GARDEN NOW!
THE FRUIT'S SO GOOD! TRY ONE!
YEAH, MAYBE LATER.
I'M KINDA BUSY WITH MANGA RIGHT NOW.
WOOOOW.
WORKIN' HARD OR HARDLY WORKIN', EH?
SWUMP
GAH!
HE SAT DOWN!
I BET YOU GET THIS FROM MY SIDE OF THE FAMILY, HUH? I LIKED DRAWING WHEN I WAS A KID, TOO~!
ME AND YOUR AUNTIE YAE-CHAN WERE ALWAYS DRAWING MOUNT KIRISHIMA IN OUR SKETCH-BOOK...
JABBER JABBER
JABBER JABBER
DING
DOOOONG
COM-IIING!
HONEY, THE DOOR-BELL'S RINGING!
KA-CHAK
AKI-CHAN!
THE NEIGHBORS JUST BROUGHT OVER OHAGI. COME SAY THANK YOU!
OOH, I LOVE THOSE THINGS!
...

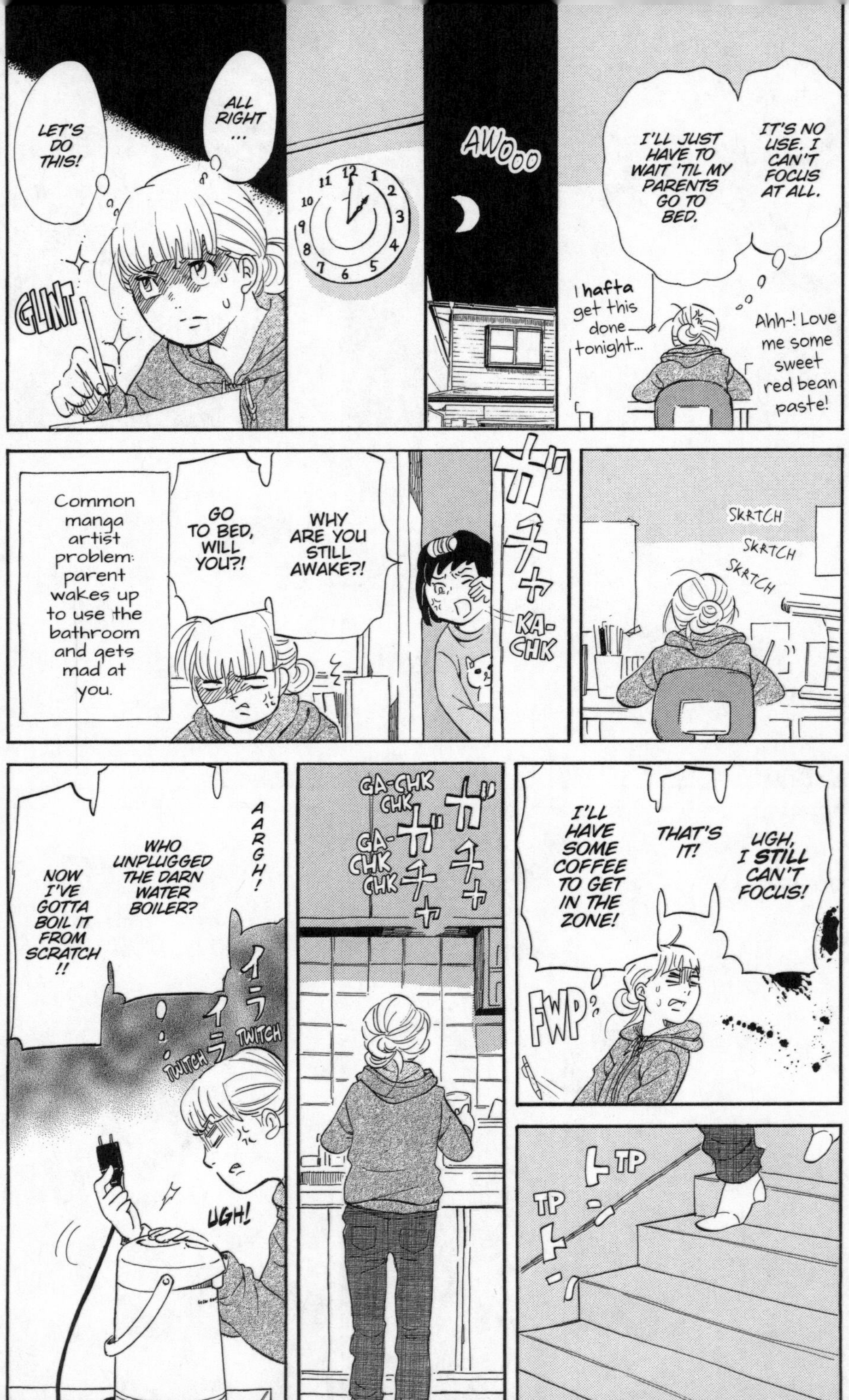
IT'S NO USE. I CAN'T FOCUS AT ALL.
I'LL JUST HAVE TO WAIT 'TIL MY PARENTS GO TO BED.
Ahh-! Love me some sweet red bean paste!
I hafta get this done tonight...
AWOooo
ALL RIGHT...
LET'S DO THIS!
GLINT
SKRTCH
SKRTCH
SKRTCH
ガチャ
KA-CHK
WHY ARE YOU STILL AWAKE?!
GO TO BED, WILL YOU?!
Common manga artist problem: parent wakes up to use the bathroom and gets mad at you.
UGH, I STILL CAN'T FOCUS!
THAT'S IT!
I'LL HAVE SOME COFFEE TO GET IN THE ZONE!
FWP
トー
TP
トー
TP
ガチャ
ガチャ
ガチャ
GA-CHK CHK
GA-CHK CHK
AARGH!
WHO UNPLUGGED THE DARN WATER BOILER?
NOW I'VE GOTTA BOIL IT FROM SCRATCH!!
イライラ
TWITCH
TWITCH
UGH!

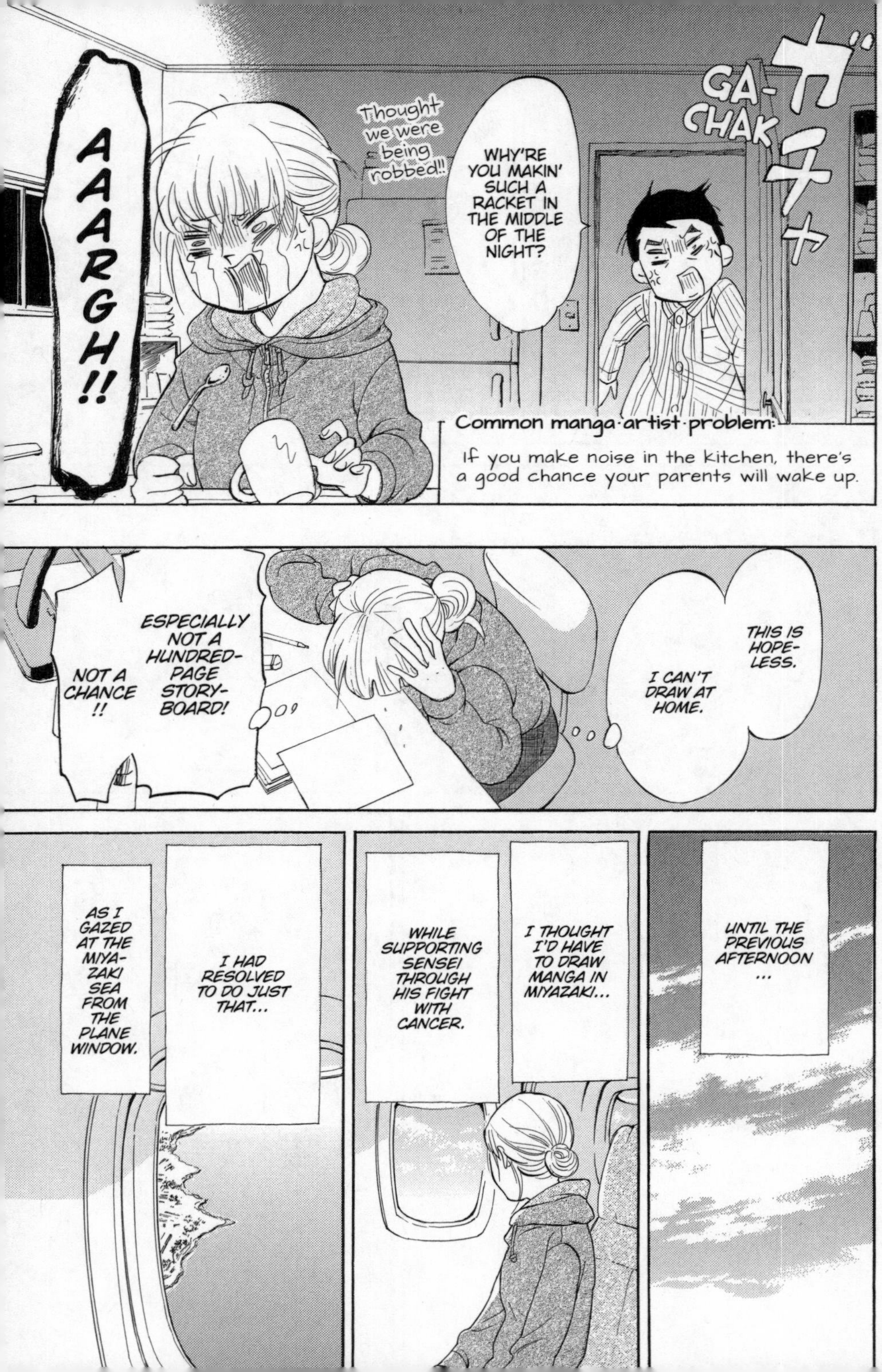

GA-CHAK ガチャ
WHY'RE YOU MAKIN' SUCH A RACKET IN THE MIDDLE OF THE NIGHT?
Thought we were being robbed!!
AAAARGH!!
Common manga artist problem:
If you make noise in the kitchen, there's a good chance your parents will wake up.
THIS IS HOPELESS.
I CAN'T DRAW AT HOME.
ESPECIALLY NOT A HUNDRED-PAGE STORYBOARD!
NOT A CHANCE!!
UNTIL THE PREVIOUS AFTERNOON...
I THOUGHT I'D HAVE TO DRAW MANGA IN MIYAZAKI...
WHILE SUPPORTING SENSEI THROUGH HIS FIGHT WITH CANCER.
I HAD RESOLVED TO DO JUST THAT...
AS I GAZED AT THE MIYAZAKI SEA FROM THE PLANE WINDOW.

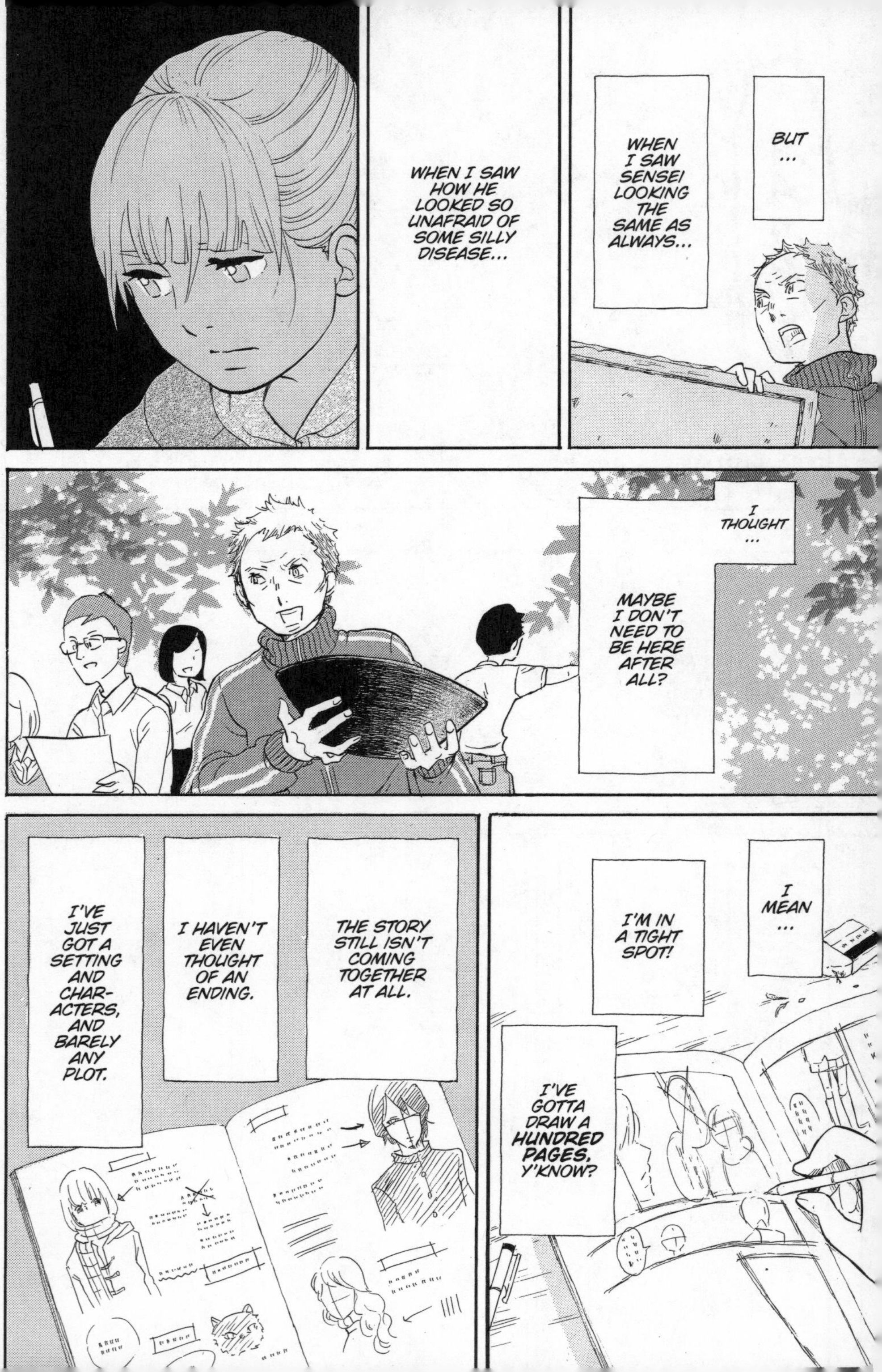
BUT ...
WHEN I SAW SENSEI LOOKING THE SAME AS ALWAYS...
WHEN I SAW HOW HE LOOKED SO UNAFRAID OF SOME SILLY DISEASE...
I THOUGHT ...
MAYBE I DON'T NEED TO BE HERE AFTER ALL?
I MEAN ...
I'M IN A TIGHT SPOT!
I'VE GOTTA DRAW A **HUNDRED PAGES**, Y'KNOW?
THE STORY STILL ISN'T COMING TOGETHER AT ALL.
I HAVEN'T EVEN THOUGHT OF AN ENDING.
I'VE JUST GOT A SETTING AND CHAR-ACTERS, AND BARELY ANY PLOT.

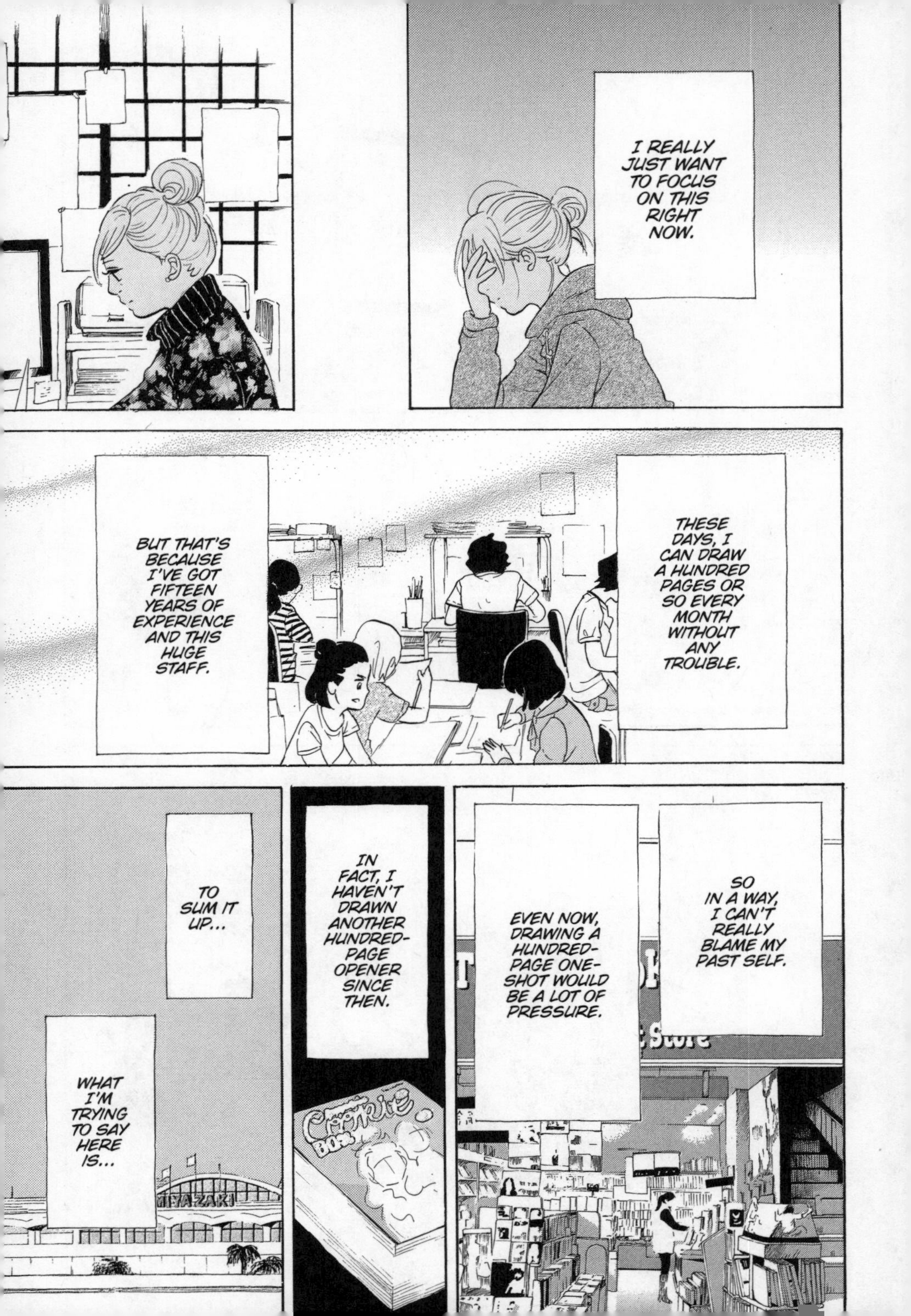
I REALLY JUST WANT TO FOCUS ON THIS RIGHT NOW.
THESE DAYS, I CAN DRAW A HUNDRED PAGES OR SO EVERY MONTH WITHOUT ANY TROUBLE.
BUT THAT'S BECAUSE I'VE GOT FIFTEEN YEARS OF EXPERIENCE AND THIS HUGE STAFF.
SO IN A WAY, I CAN'T REALLY BLAME MY PAST SELF.
EVEN NOW, DRAWING A HUNDRED-PAGE ONE-SHOT WOULD BE A LOT OF PRESSURE.
IN FACT, I HAVEN'T DRAWN ANOTHER HUNDRED-PAGE OPENER SINCE THEN.
TO SUM IT UP...
WHAT I'M TRYING TO SAY HERE IS...
MIYAZAKI

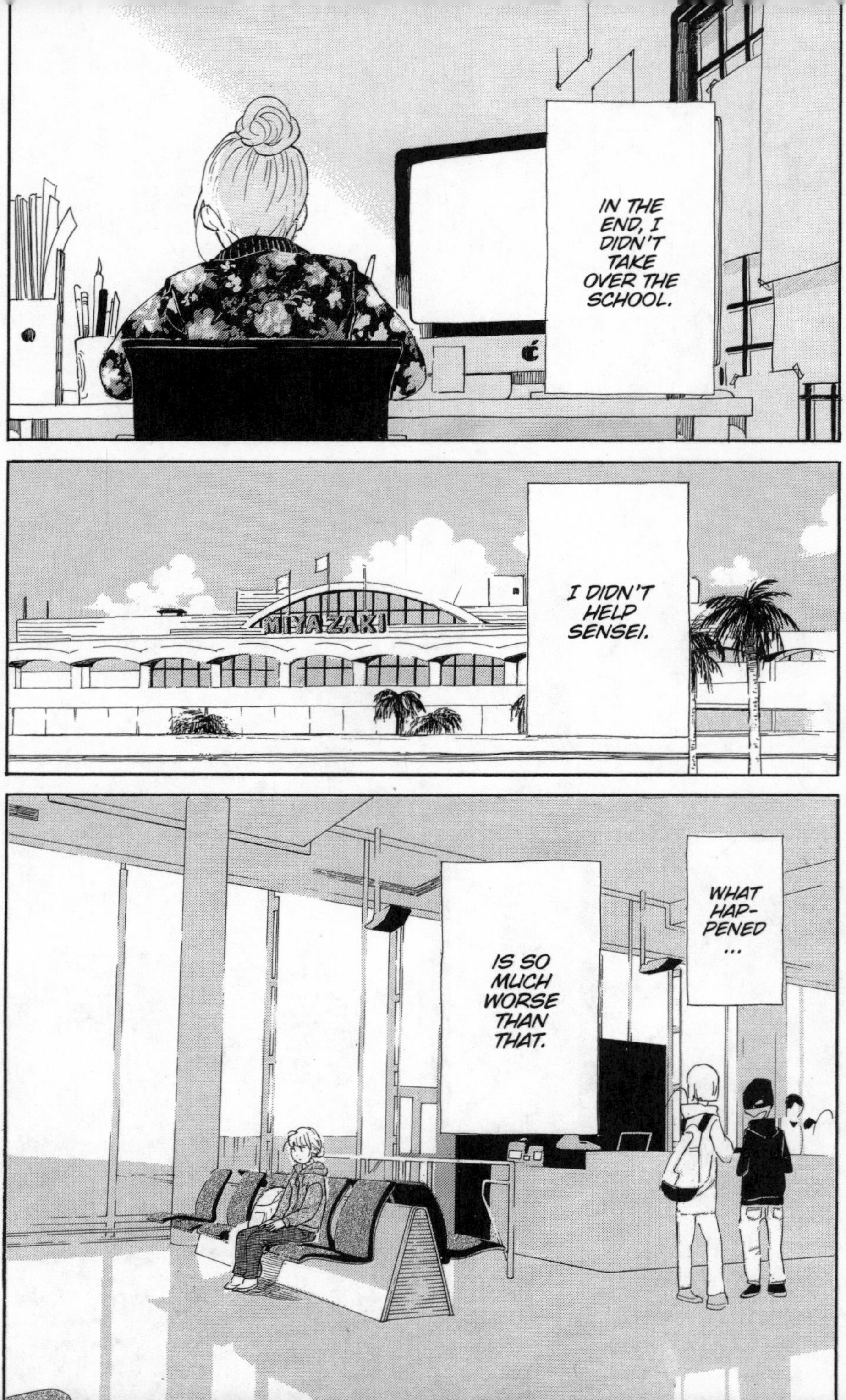
IN THE END, I DIDN'T TAKE OVER THE SCHOOL.
MIYAZAKI
I DIDN'T HELP SENSEI.
WHAT HAP-PENED ...
IS SO MUCH WORSE THAN THAT.

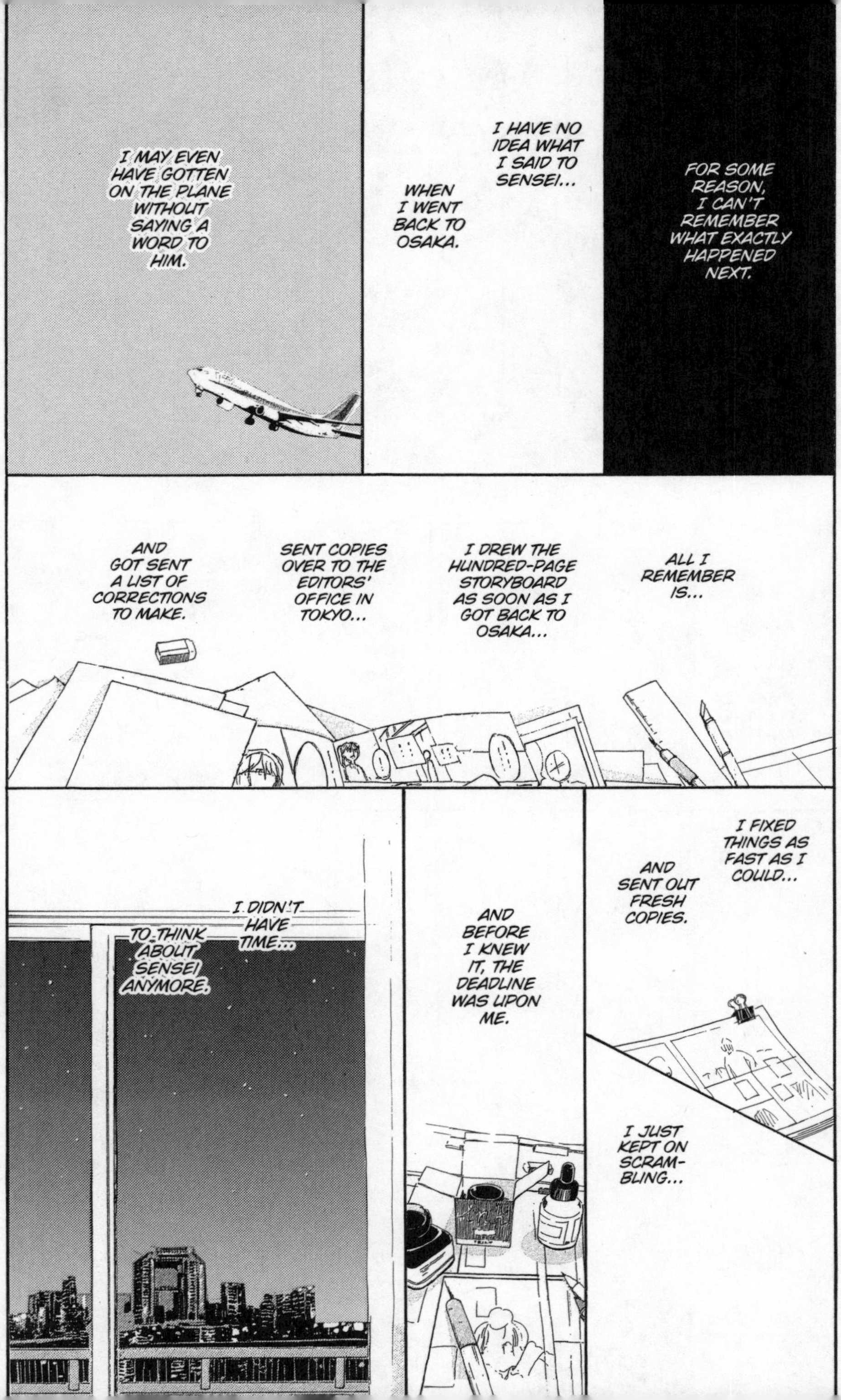
FOR SOME REASON, I CAN'T REMEMBER WHAT EXACTLY HAPPENED NEXT.
I HAVE NO IDEA WHAT I SAID TO SENSEI...
WHEN I WENT BACK TO OSAKA.
I MAY EVEN HAVE GOTTEN ON THE PLANE WITHOUT SAYING A WORD TO HIM.
ALL I REMEMBER IS...
I DREW THE HUNDRED-PAGE STORYBOARD AS SOON AS I GOT BACK TO OSAKA...
SENT COPIES OVER TO THE EDITORS' OFFICE IN TOKYO...
AND GOT SENT A LIST OF CORRECTIONS TO MAKE.
I FIXED THINGS AS FAST AS I COULD...
AND SENT OUT FRESH COPIES.
I JUST KEPT ON SCRAMBLING...
AND BEFORE I KNEW IT, THE DEADLINE WAS UPON ME.
I DIDN'T HAVE TIME...
TO THINK ABOUT SENSEI ANYMORE.

SKRTCH
SKRTCH
SKRTCH

PLUS I'VE NEVER DONE IT BEFORE, SO I WOULDN'T KNOW WHAT TO TELL THEM ANYWAY!

I'M TOO BROKE TO HIRE ASSISTANTS!!

WAAAH!

It's just like you said, Ishida-sensei!

YEAH, NO KIDDING!!

Never seems to end, am I right?

Hey, Akiko-haaan~! How's the hundred-pager?

Assistants	Assistants	Me	BY THE WAY, THESE DAYS...
SPOT BLACKS, TONES, ETC.	BACK-GROUNDS, MOBS, ETC.	SKETCH AND INK THE CHARACTERS.	

MOB = CROWDS OF PEOPLE IN THE BACKGROUND.

THE PEOPLE, THE BACK-GROUNDS, THE MOBS-- ALL OF IT!!

I JUST GOTTA DRAW IT ALL MYSELF!!

Huff! SKTCH
Huff!

CRONCH
CRONCH

STAARE

I sit around eating snacks and stuff.

Watching YouTube or whatever.

Good work, everyone!!

IT'S DONE, I GUESS.

Assistants: wiped out.

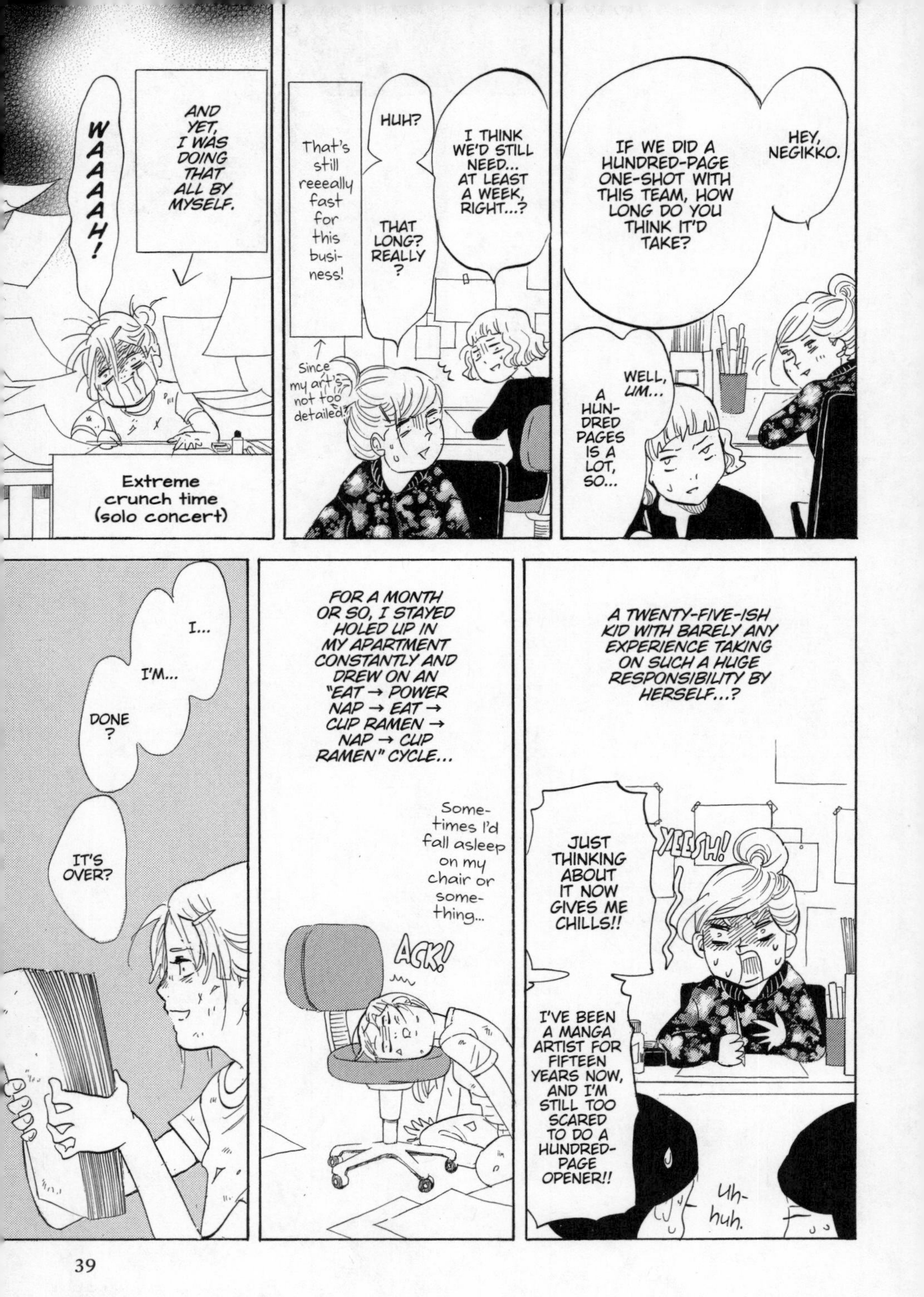
HEY, NEGIKKO.
IF WE DID A HUNDRED-PAGE ONE-SHOT WITH THIS TEAM, HOW LONG DO YOU THINK IT'D TAKE?
WELL, UM...
A HUNDRED PAGES IS A LOT, SO...
I THINK WE'D STILL NEED... AT LEAST A WEEK, RIGHT...?
HUH?
THAT LONG? REALLY?
That's still reeeally fast for this business!
Since my art's not too detailed?
AND YET, I WAS DOING THAT ALL BY MYSELF.
WAAAAAH!
Extreme crunch time (solo concert)
A TWENTY-FIVE-ISH KID WITH BARELY ANY EXPERIENCE TAKING ON SUCH A HUGE RESPONSIBILITY BY HERSELF...?
YEESH!
JUST THINKING ABOUT IT NOW GIVES ME CHILLS!!
I'VE BEEN A MANGA ARTIST FOR FIFTEEN YEARS NOW, AND I'M STILL TOO SCARED TO DO A HUNDRED-PAGE OPENER!!
Uh-huh.
FOR A MONTH OR SO, I STAYED HOLED UP IN MY APARTMENT CONSTANTLY AND DREW ON AN "EAT → POWER NAP → EAT → CUP RAMEN → NAP → CUP RAMEN" CYCLE...
Sometimes I'd fall asleep on my chair or something...
ACK!
I...
I'M...
DONE?
IT'S OVER?

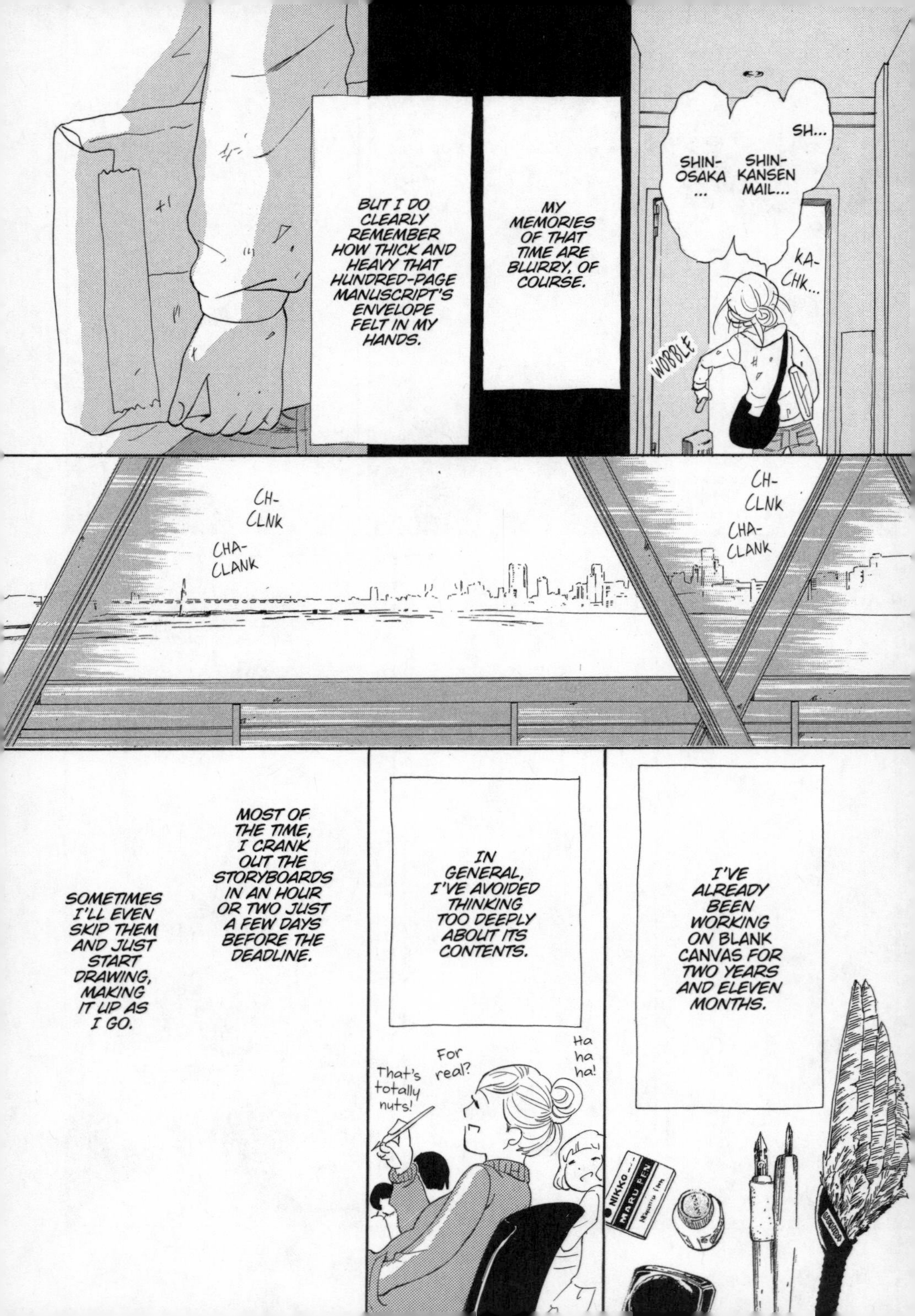
SH...
SHIN-KANSEN MAIL...
SHIN-OSAKA ...
KA-CHK...
WOBBLE
MY MEMORIES OF THAT TIME ARE BLURRY, OF COURSE.
BUT I DO CLEARLY REMEMBER HOW THICK AND HEAVY THAT HUNDRED-PAGE MANUSCRIPT'S ENVELOPE FELT IN MY HANDS.
CH-CLNk
CHA-CLANK
CH-CLNk
CHA-CLANK
I'VE ALREADY BEEN WORKING ON BLANK CANVAS FOR TWO YEARS AND ELEVEN MONTHS.
IN GENERAL, I'VE AVOIDED THINKING TOO DEEPLY ABOUT ITS CONTENTS.
Ha ha ha!
For real?
That's totally nuts!
MOST OF THE TIME, I CRANK OUT THE STORYBOARDS IN AN HOUR OR TWO JUST A FEW DAYS BEFORE THE DEADLINE.
SOMETIMES I'LL EVEN SKIP THEM AND JUST START DRAWING, MAKING IT UP AS I GO.

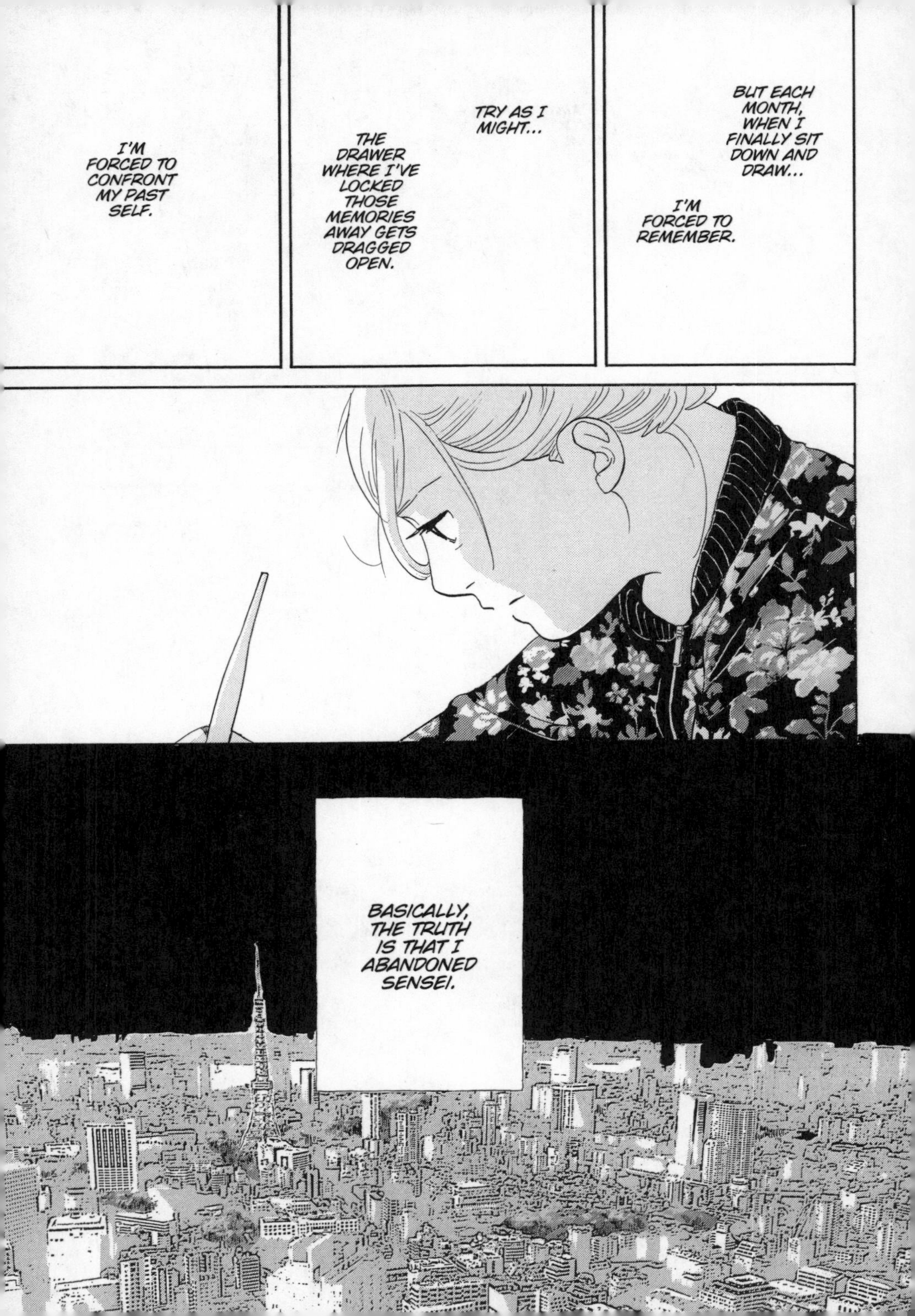
BUT EACH MONTH, WHEN I FINALLY SIT DOWN AND DRAW...
I'M FORCED TO REMEMBER.
TRY AS I MIGHT...
THE DRAWER WHERE I'VE LOCKED THOSE MEMORIES AWAY GETS DRAGGED OPEN.
I'M FORCED TO CONFRONT MY PAST SELF.
BASICALLY, THE TRUTH IS THAT I ABANDONED SENSEI.

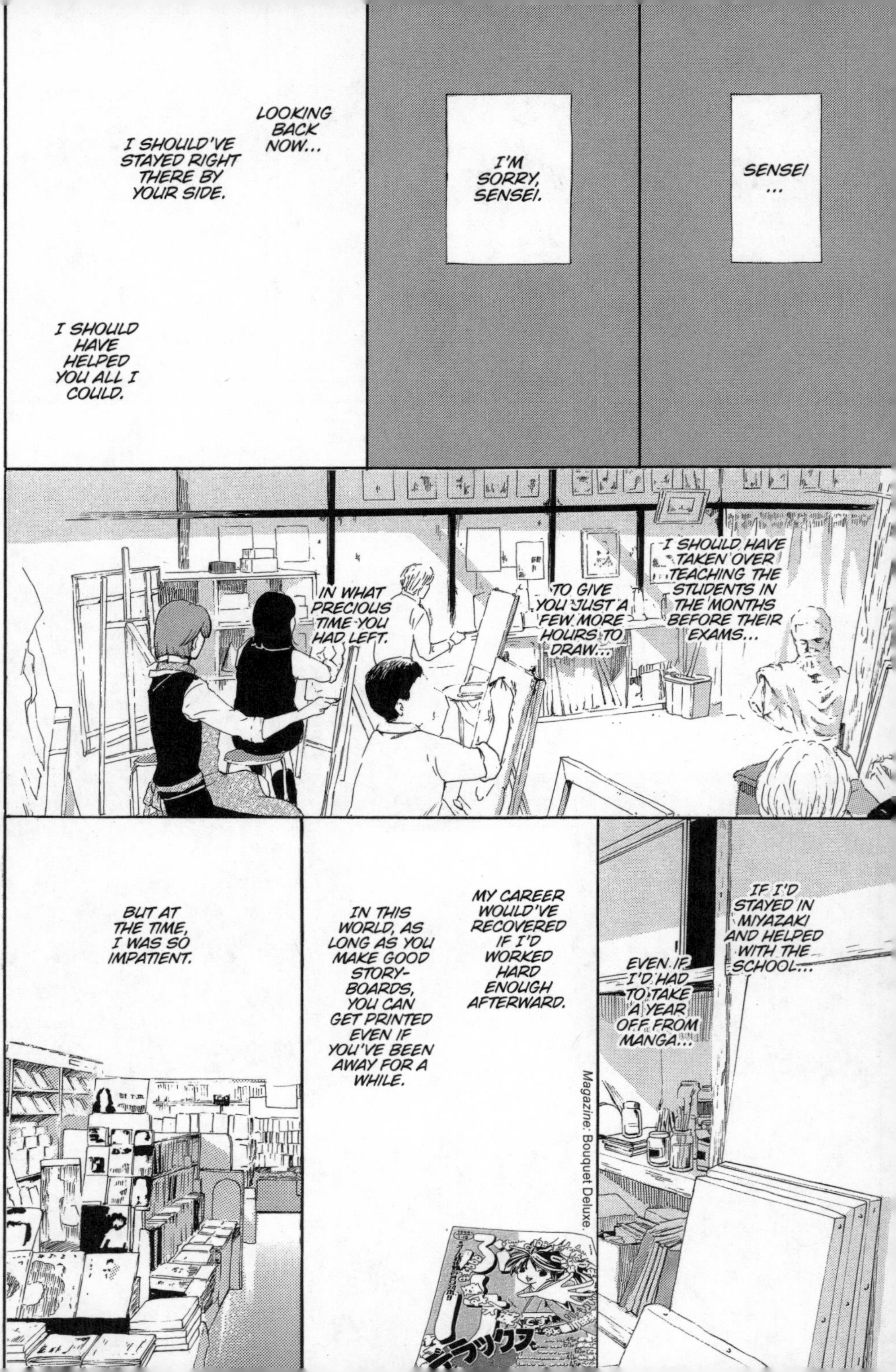
SENSEI ...
I'M SORRY, SENSEI.
LOOKING BACK NOW...
I SHOULD'VE STAYED RIGHT THERE BY YOUR SIDE.
I SHOULD HAVE HELPED YOU ALL I COULD.
I SHOULD HAVE TAKEN OVER TEACHING THE STUDENTS IN THE MONTHS BEFORE THEIR EXAMS...
TO GIVE YOU JUST A FEW MORE HOURS TO DRAW...
IN WHAT PRECIOUS TIME YOU HAD LEFT.
IF I'D STAYED IN MIYAZAKI AND HELPED WITH THE SCHOOL...
EVEN IF I'D HAD TO TAKE A YEAR OFF FROM MANGA...
MY CAREER WOULD'VE RECOVERED IF I'D WORKED HARD ENOUGH AFTERWARD.
IN THIS WORLD, AS LONG AS YOU MAKE GOOD STORY-BOARDS, YOU CAN GET PRINTED EVEN IF YOU'VE BEEN AWAY FOR A WHILE.
Magazine: Bouquet Deluxe.
BUT AT THE TIME, I WAS SO IMPATIENT.

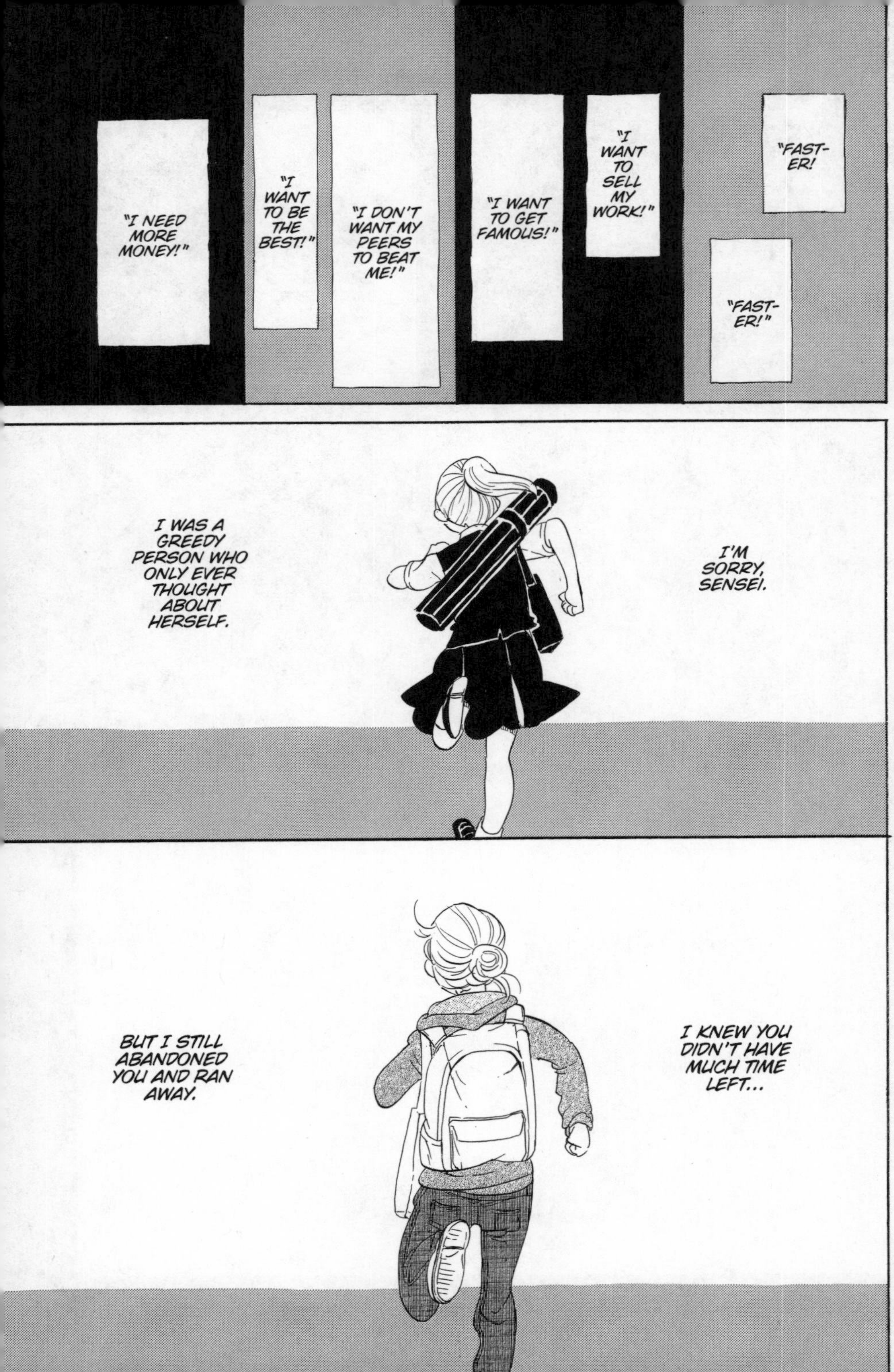
"FAST-ER!
"FAST-ER!"
"I WANT TO SELL MY WORK!"
"I WANT TO GET FAMOUS!"
"I DON'T WANT MY PEERS TO BEAT ME!"
"I WANT TO BE THE BEST!"
"I NEED MORE MONEY!"
I'M SORRY, SENSEI.
I WAS A GREEDY PERSON WHO ONLY EVER THOUGHT ABOUT HERSELF.
I KNEW YOU DIDN'T HAVE MUCH TIME LEFT...
BUT I STILL ABANDONED YOU AND RAN AWAY.

ONLY THE WORST KIND OF SCUM WOULD DO SOMETHING LIKE THAT.

I'M SORRY.

I'M SORRY, SENSEI...

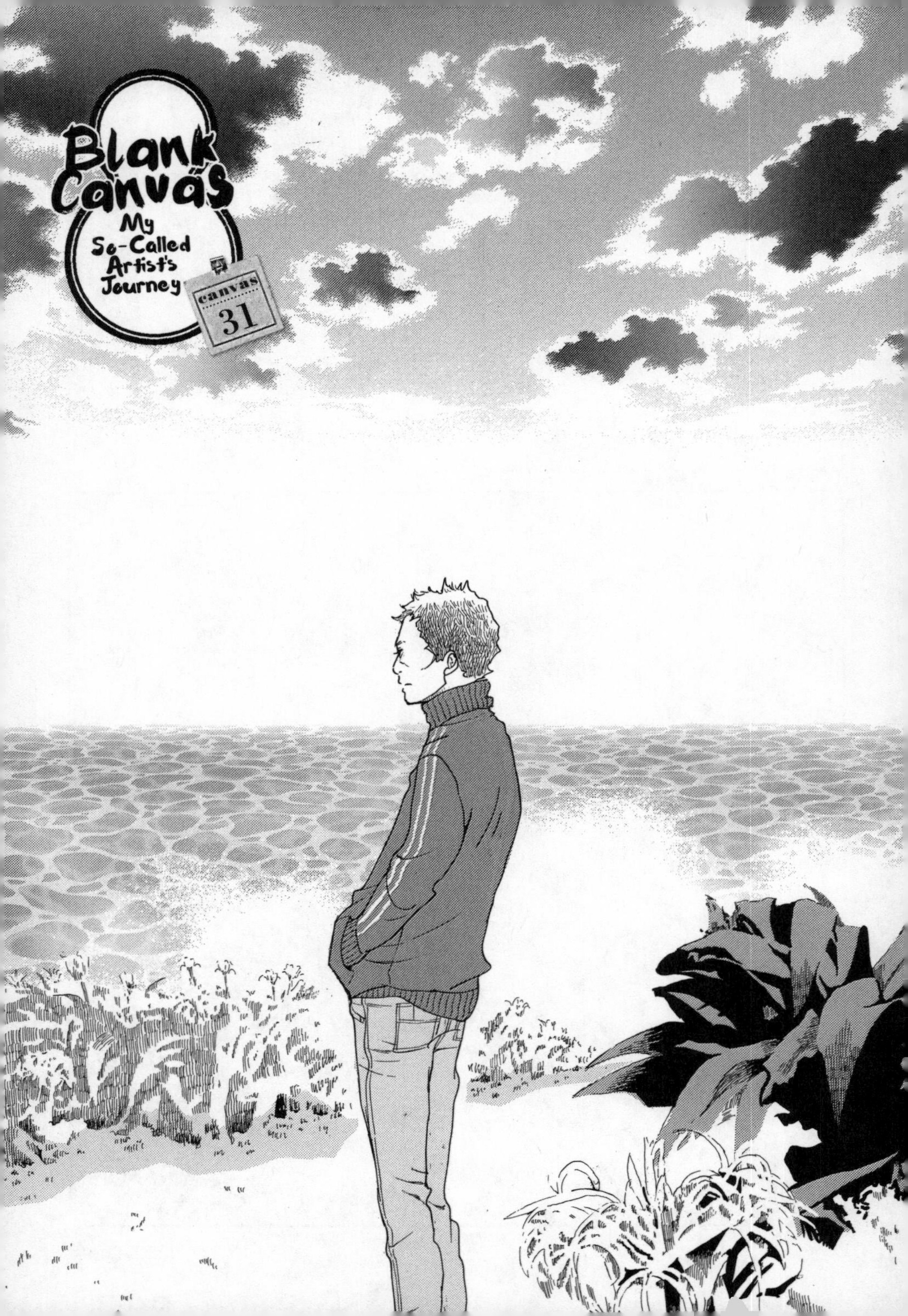
Blank Canvas
My So-Called Artist's Journey
canvas
31

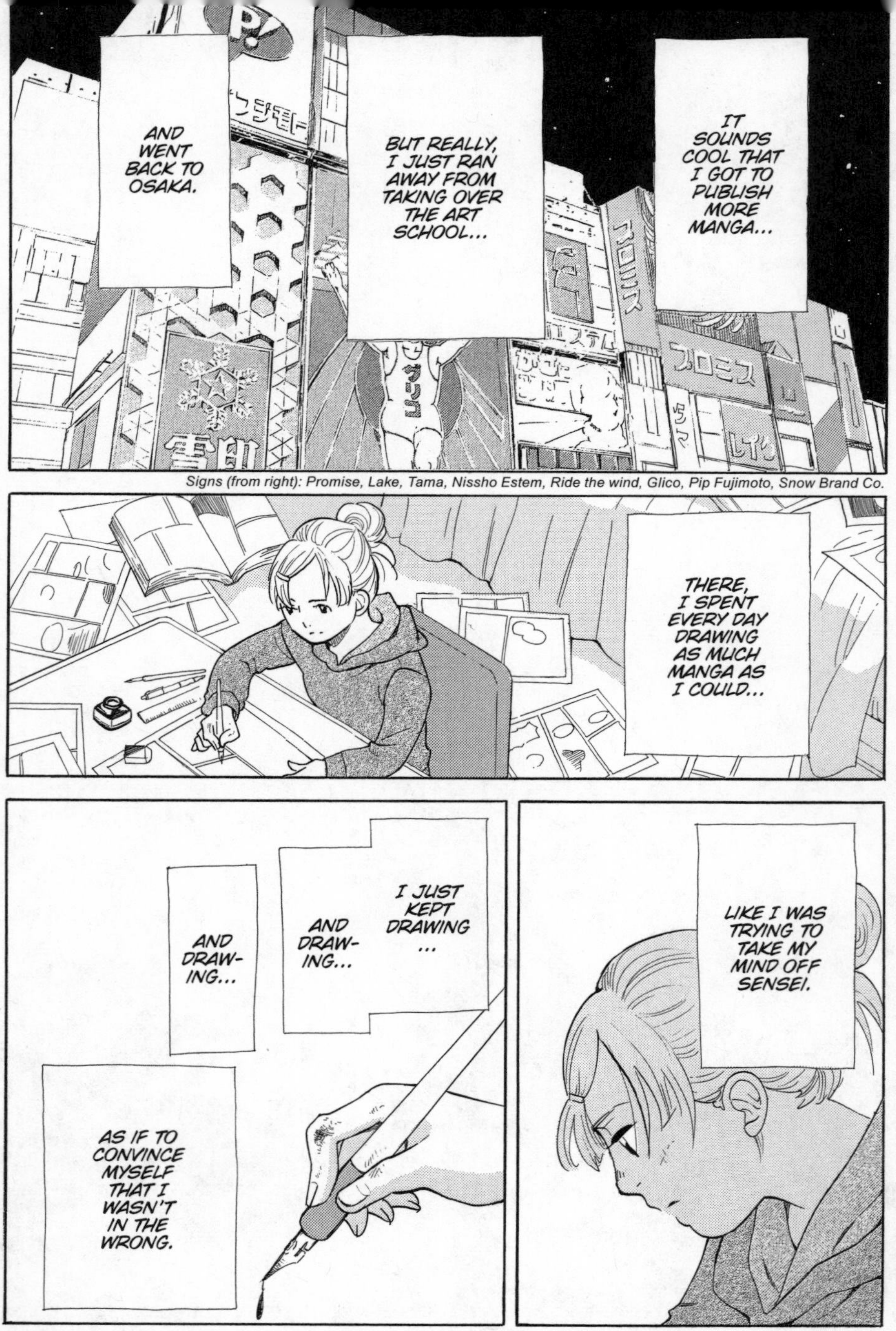
IT SOUNDS COOL THAT I GOT TO PUBLISH MORE MANGA...
BUT REALLY, I JUST RAN AWAY FROM TAKING OVER THE ART SCHOOL...
AND WENT BACK TO OSAKA.
THERE, I SPENT EVERY DAY DRAWING AS MUCH MANGA AS I COULD...
LIKE I WAS TRYING TO TAKE MY MIND OFF SENSEI.
I JUST KEPT DRAWING ...
AND DRAW-ING...
AND DRAW-ING...
AS IF TO CONVINCE MYSELF THAT I WASN'T IN THE WRONG.
Signs (from right): Promise, Lake, Tama, Nissho Estem, Ride the wind, Glico, Pip Fujimoto, Snow Brand Co.

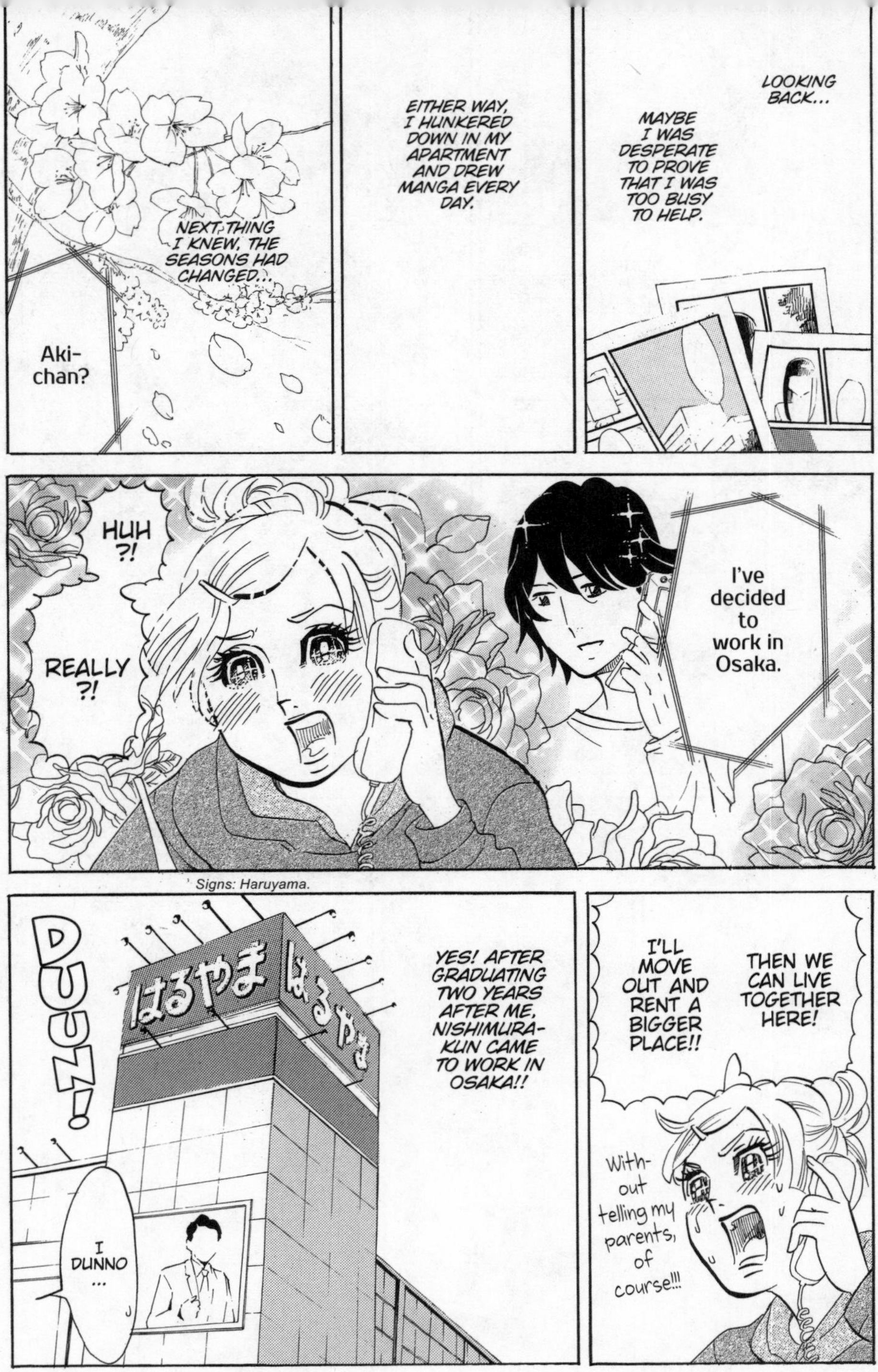
LOOKING BACK...
MAYBE I WAS DESPERATE TO PROVE THAT I WAS TOO BUSY TO HELP.
EITHER WAY, I HUNKERED DOWN IN MY APARTMENT AND DREW MANGA EVERY DAY.
NEXT THING I KNEW, THE SEASONS HAD CHANGED...
Aki-chan?
I've decided to work in Osaka.
HUH?!
REALLY?!
Signs: Haruyama.
I'LL MOVE OUT AND RENT A BIGGER PLACE!!
THEN WE CAN LIVE TOGETHER HERE!
Without telling my parents, of course!!!
YES! AFTER GRADUATING TWO YEARS AFTER ME, NISHIMURA-KUN CAME TO WORK IN OSAKA!!
はるやま はるやま
DUUN!
I DUNNO...

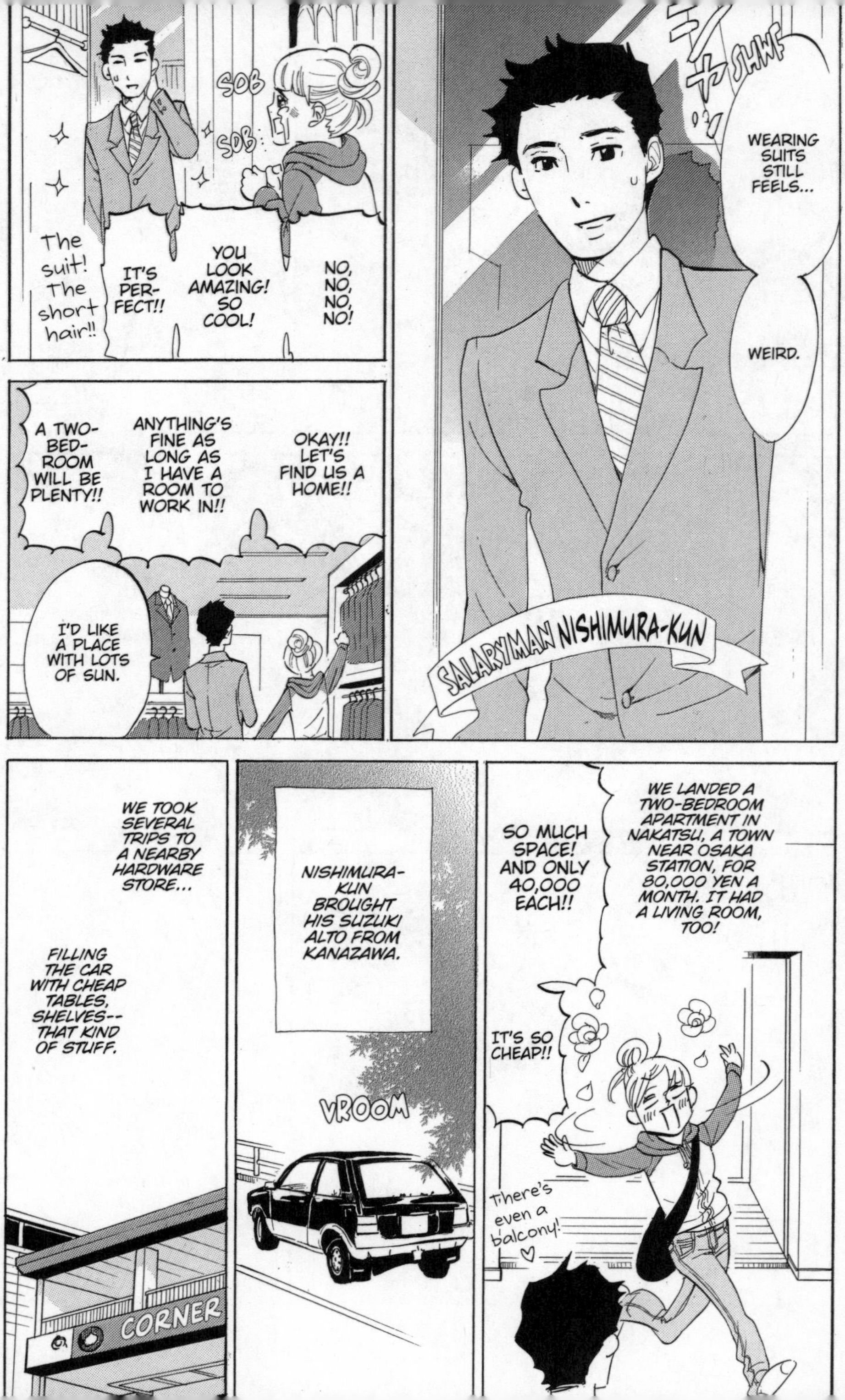
SHAWF
WEARING SUITS STILL FEELS...
WEIRD.
SALARYMAN NISHIMURA-KUN
SOB
SOB
NO, NO, NO, NO!
YOU LOOK AMAZING! SO COOL!
IT'S PERFECT!!
The suit! The short hair!!
OKAY!! LET'S FIND US A HOME!!
ANYTHING'S FINE AS LONG AS I HAVE A ROOM TO WORK IN!!
A TWO-BEDROOM WILL BE PLENTY!!
I'D LIKE A PLACE WITH LOTS OF SUN.
WE LANDED A TWO-BEDROOM APARTMENT IN NAKATSU, A TOWN NEAR OSAKA STATION, FOR 80,000 YEN A MONTH. IT HAD A LIVING ROOM, TOO!
SO MUCH SPACE! AND ONLY 40,000 EACH!!
IT'S SO CHEAP!!
There's even a balcony! ♥
NISHIMURA-KUN BROUGHT HIS SUZUKI ALTO FROM KANAZAWA.
VROOM
WE TOOK SEVERAL TRIPS TO A NEARBY HARDWARE STORE...
FILLING THE CAR WITH CHEAP TABLES, SHELVES--THAT KIND OF STUFF.
CORNER

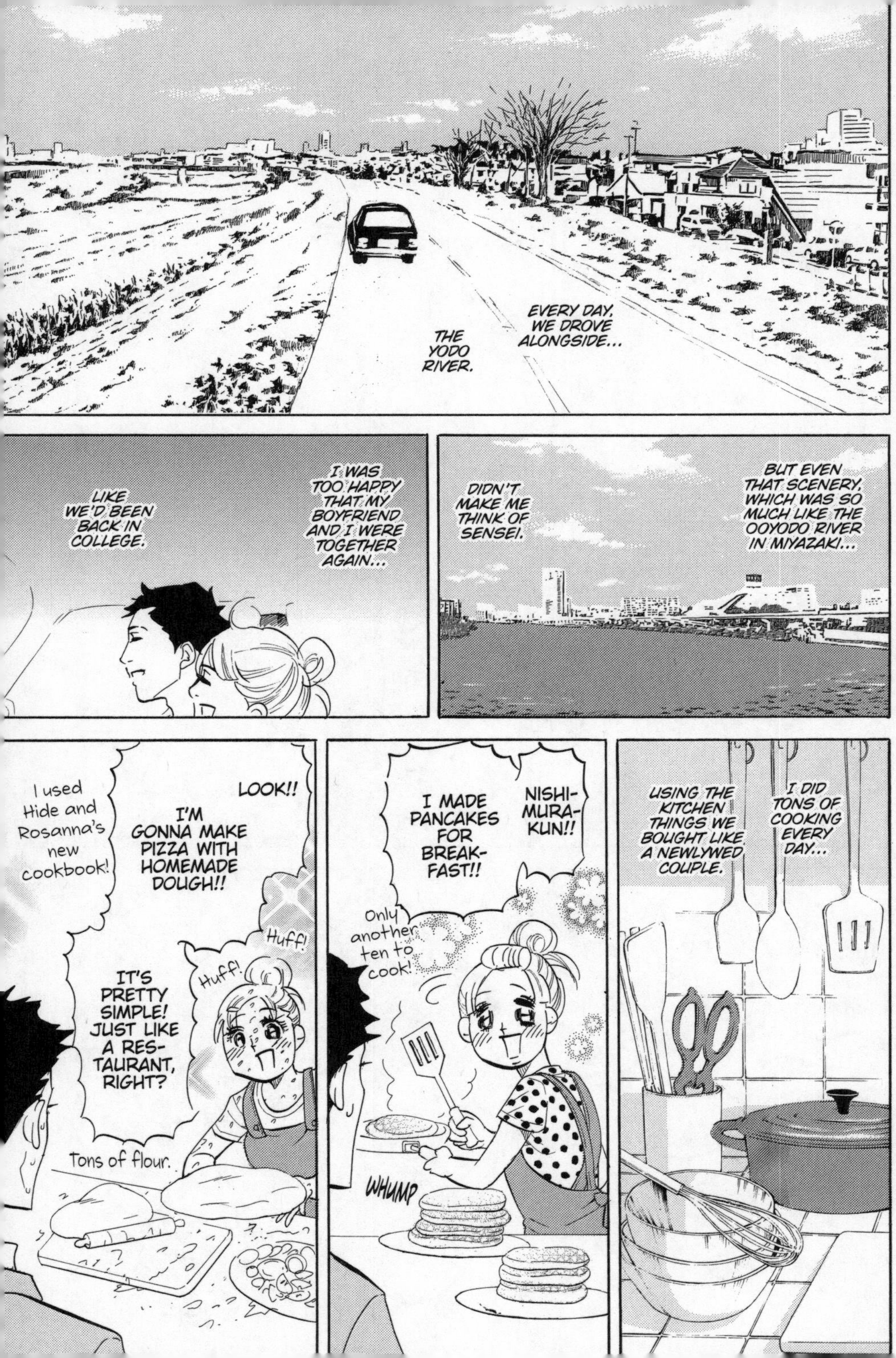
EVERY DAY, WE DROVE ALONGSIDE...
THE YODO RIVER.
BUT EVEN THAT SCENERY, WHICH WAS SO MUCH LIKE THE OOYODO RIVER IN MIYAZAKI...
DIDN'T MAKE ME THINK OF SENSEI.
I WAS TOO HAPPY THAT MY BOYFRIEND AND I WERE TOGETHER AGAIN...
LIKE WE'D BEEN BACK IN COLLEGE.
I DID TONS OF COOKING EVERY DAY...
USING THE KITCHEN THINGS WE BOUGHT LIKE A NEWLYWED COUPLE.
NISHI-MURA-KUN!!
I MADE PANCAKES FOR BREAK-FAST!!
Only another ten to cook!
WHUMP
LOOK!!
I'M GONNA MAKE PIZZA WITH HOMEMADE DOUGH!!
I used Hide and Rosanna's new cookbook!
Huff!
Huff!
IT'S PRETTY SIMPLE! JUST LIKE A RES-TAURANT, RIGHT?
Tons of flour.

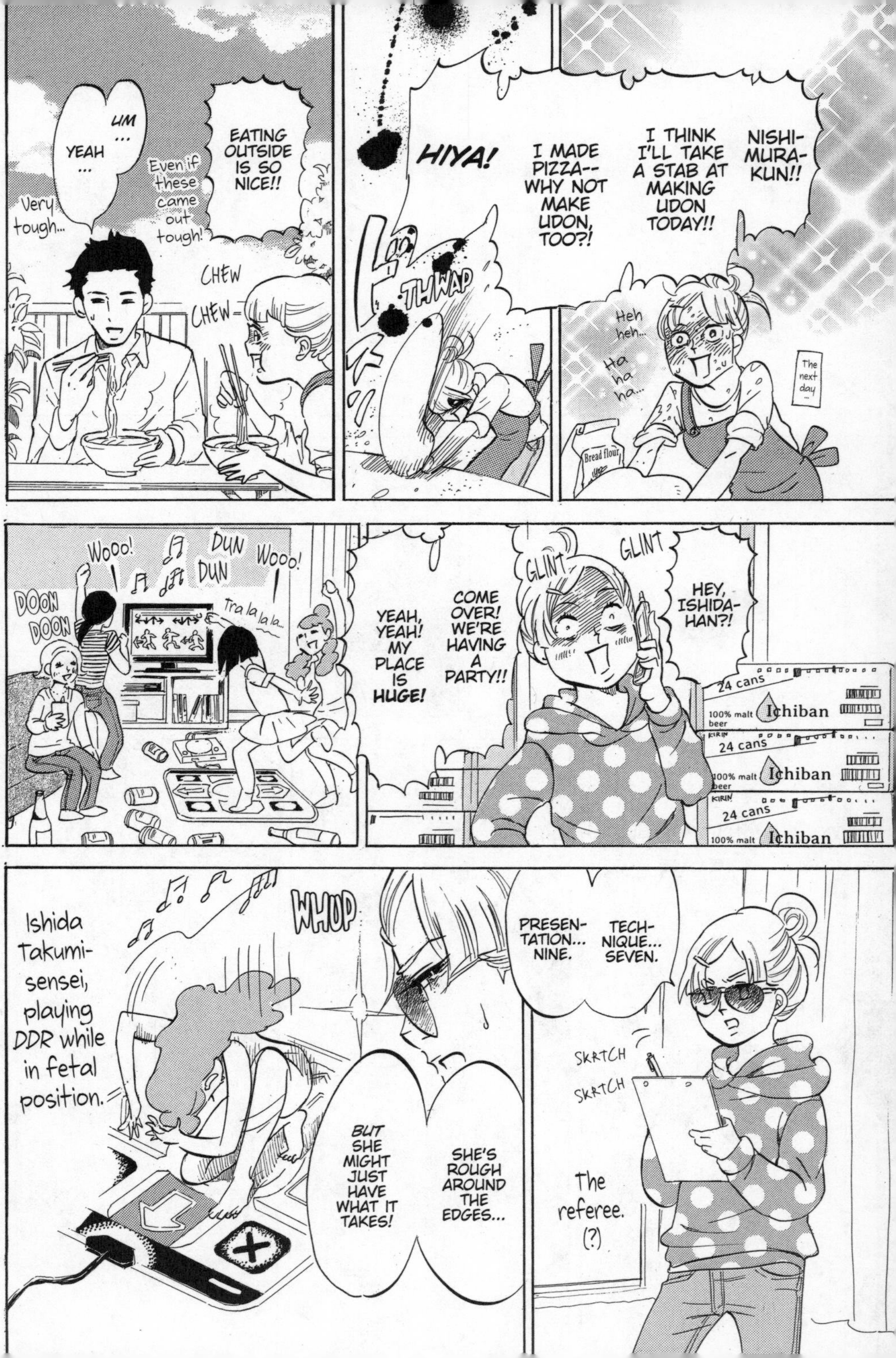
The next day...
NISHI-MURA-KUN!!
I THINK I'LL TAKE A STAB AT MAKING UDON TODAY!!
Heh heh...
Ha ha ha...
Bread flour
I MADE PIZZA--WHY NOT MAKE UDON, TOO?!
HIYA!
THWAP
EATING OUTSIDE IS SO NICE!!
Even if these came out tough!
UM ...
YEAH ...
Very tough...
CHEW
CHEW
HEY, ISHIDA-HAN?!
GLINT
GLINT
COME OVER! WE'RE HAVING A PARTY!!
YEAH, YEAH! MY PLACE IS HUGE!
24 cans
100% malt beer
Ichiban
KIRIN
24 cans
100% malt beer
Ichiban
KIRIN
24 cans
100% malt
Ichiban
Wooo!
DUN DUN
Wooo!
DOON DOON
Tra la la la...
TECH-NIQUE... SEVEN.
PRESEN-TATION... NINE.
SKRTCH
SKRTCH
The referee. (?)
SHE'S ROUGH AROUND THE EDGES...
BUT SHE MIGHT JUST HAVE WHAT IT TAKES!
WHOP
Ishida Takumi-sensei, playing DDR while in fetal position.

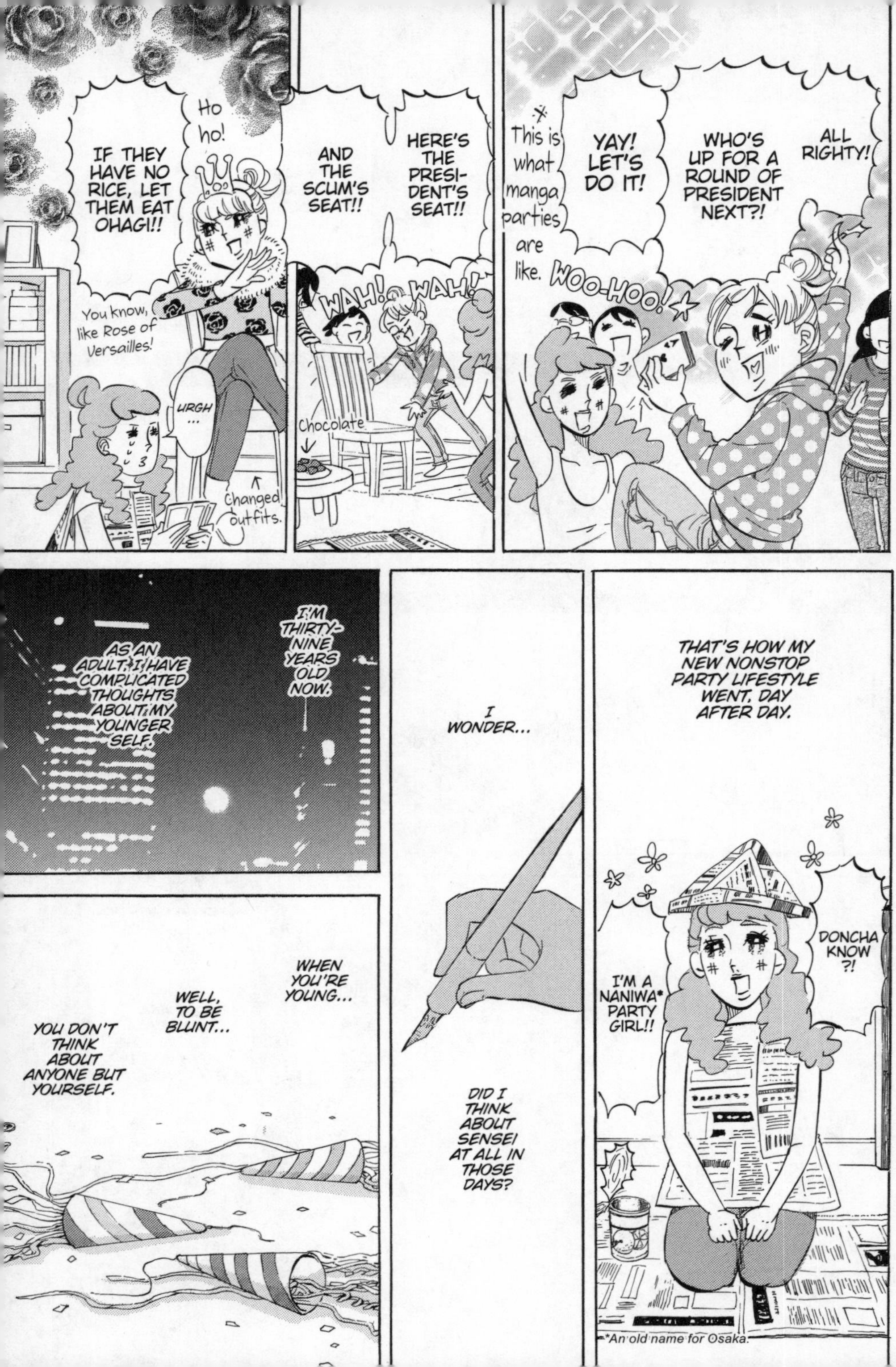
ALL RIGHTY!
WHO'S UP FOR A ROUND OF PRESIDENT NEXT?!
YAY! LET'S DO IT!
*This is what manga parties are like.
WOO-HOO!
HERE'S THE PRESIDENT'S SEAT!!
AND THE SCUM'S SEAT!!
WAH! WAH!
Chocolate
Ho ho!
IF THEY HAVE NO RICE, LET THEM EAT OHAGI!!
You know, like Rose of Versailles!
URGH...
Changed outfits.
THAT'S HOW MY NEW NONSTOP PARTY LIFESTYLE WENT, DAY AFTER DAY.
DONCHA KNOW?!
I'M A NANIWA* PARTY GIRL!!
I WONDER...
DID I THINK ABOUT SENSEI AT ALL IN THOSE DAYS?
I'M THIRTY-NINE YEARS OLD NOW.
AS AN ADULT, I HAVE COMPLICATED THOUGHTS ABOUT MY YOUNGER SELF.
WHEN YOU'RE YOUNG...
WELL, TO BE BLUNT...
YOU DON'T THINK ABOUT ANYONE BUT YOURSELF.

*An old name for Osaka.

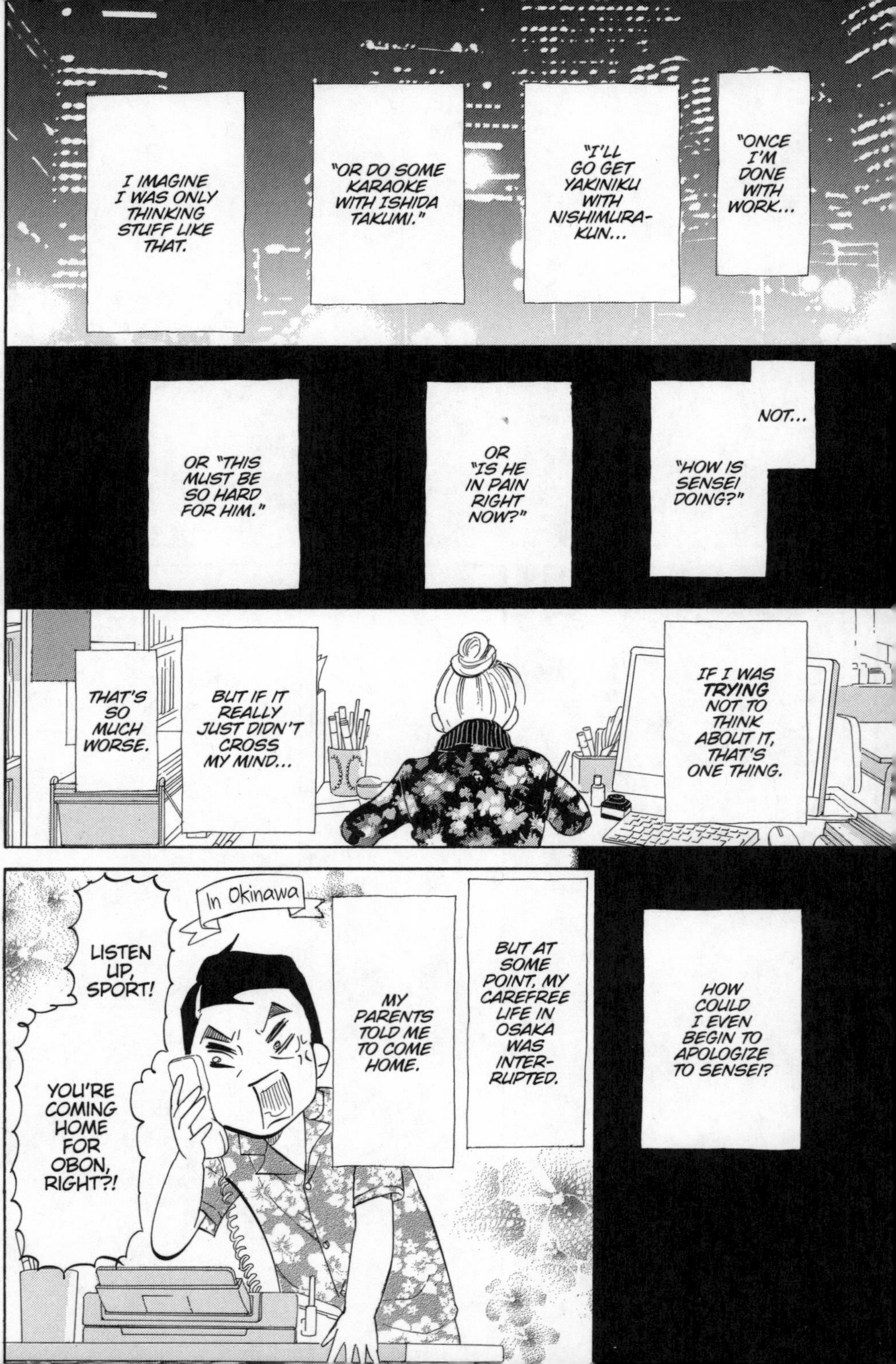
"ONCE I'M DONE WITH WORK...
"I'LL GO GET YAKINIKU WITH NISHIMURA-KUN...
"OR DO SOME KARAOKE WITH ISHIDA TAKUMI."
I IMAGINE I WAS ONLY THINKING STUFF LIKE THAT.
NOT...
"HOW IS SENSEI DOING?"
OR "IS HE IN PAIN RIGHT NOW?"
OR "THIS MUST BE SO HARD FOR HIM."
IF I WAS TRYING NOT TO THINK ABOUT IT, THAT'S ONE THING.
BUT IF IT REALLY JUST DIDN'T CROSS MY MIND...
THAT'S SO MUCH WORSE.
HOW COULD I EVEN BEGIN TO APOLOGIZE TO SENSEI?
BUT AT SOME POINT, MY CAREFREE LIFE IN OSAKA WAS INTER-RUPTED.
MY PARENTS TOLD ME TO COME HOME.
In Okinawa
LISTEN UP, SPORT!
YOU'RE COMING HOME FOR OBON, RIGHT?!

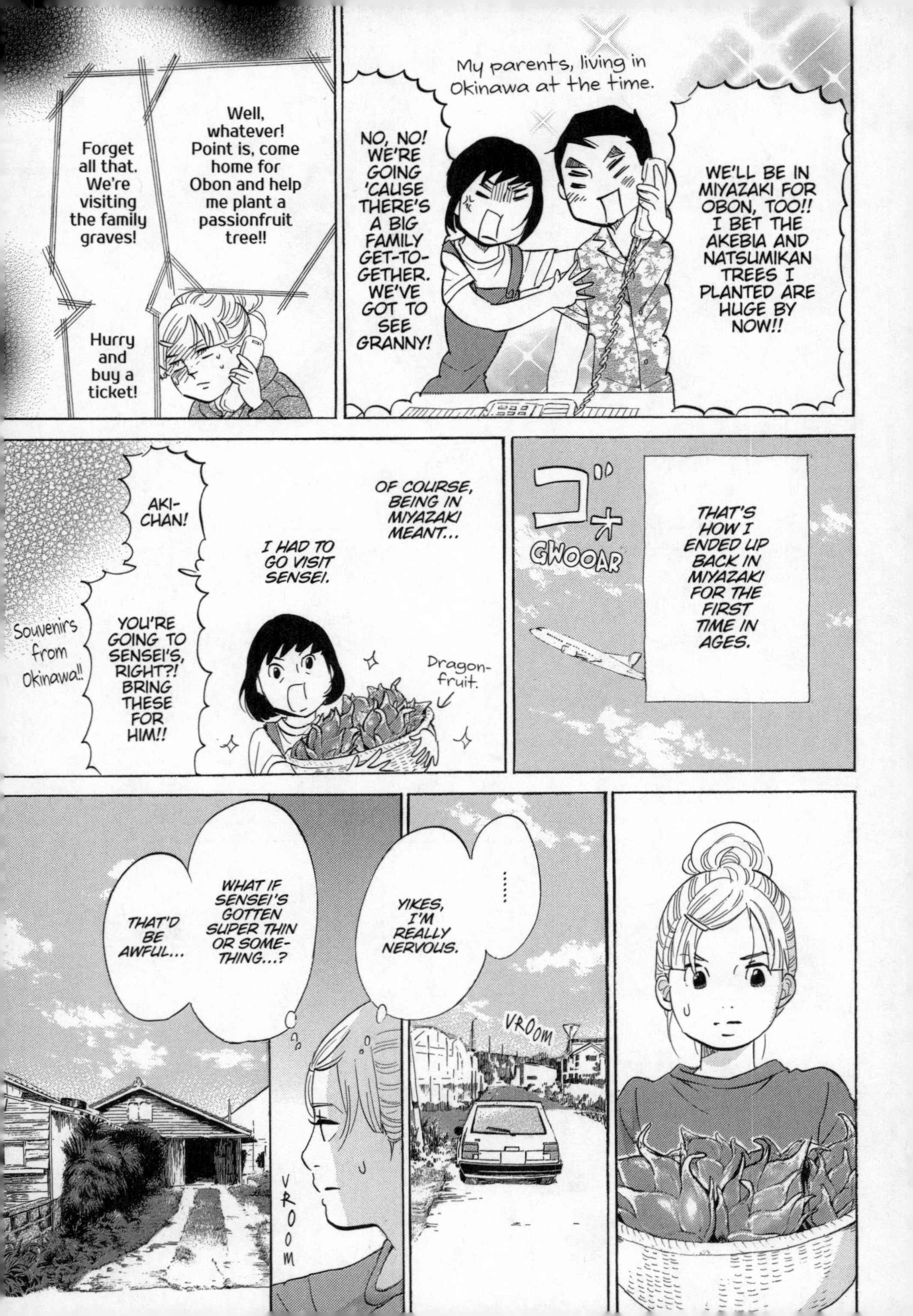
My parents, living in Okinawa at the time.
WE'LL BE IN MIYAZAKI FOR OBON, TOO!! I BET THE AKEBIA AND NATSUMIKAN TREES I PLANTED ARE HUGE BY NOW!!
NO, NO! WE'RE GOING 'CAUSE THERE'S A BIG FAMILY GET-TO-GETHER. WE'VE GOT TO SEE GRANNY!
Well, whatever! Point is, come home for Obon and help me plant a passionfruit tree!!
Forget all that. We're visiting the family graves!
Hurry and buy a ticket!
GWOOAR
THAT'S HOW I ENDED UP BACK IN MIYAZAKI FOR THE FIRST TIME IN AGES.
OF COURSE, BEING IN MIYAZAKI MEANT...
I HAD TO GO VISIT SENSEI.
AKI-CHAN!
YOU'RE GOING TO SENSEI'S, RIGHT?! BRING THESE FOR HIM!!
Dragon-fruit.
Souvenirs from Okinawa!!
VROOM
......
YIKES, I'M REALLY NERVOUS.
WHAT IF SENSEI'S GOTTEN SUPER THIN OR SOME-THING...?
THAT'D BE AWFUL...
VROOM

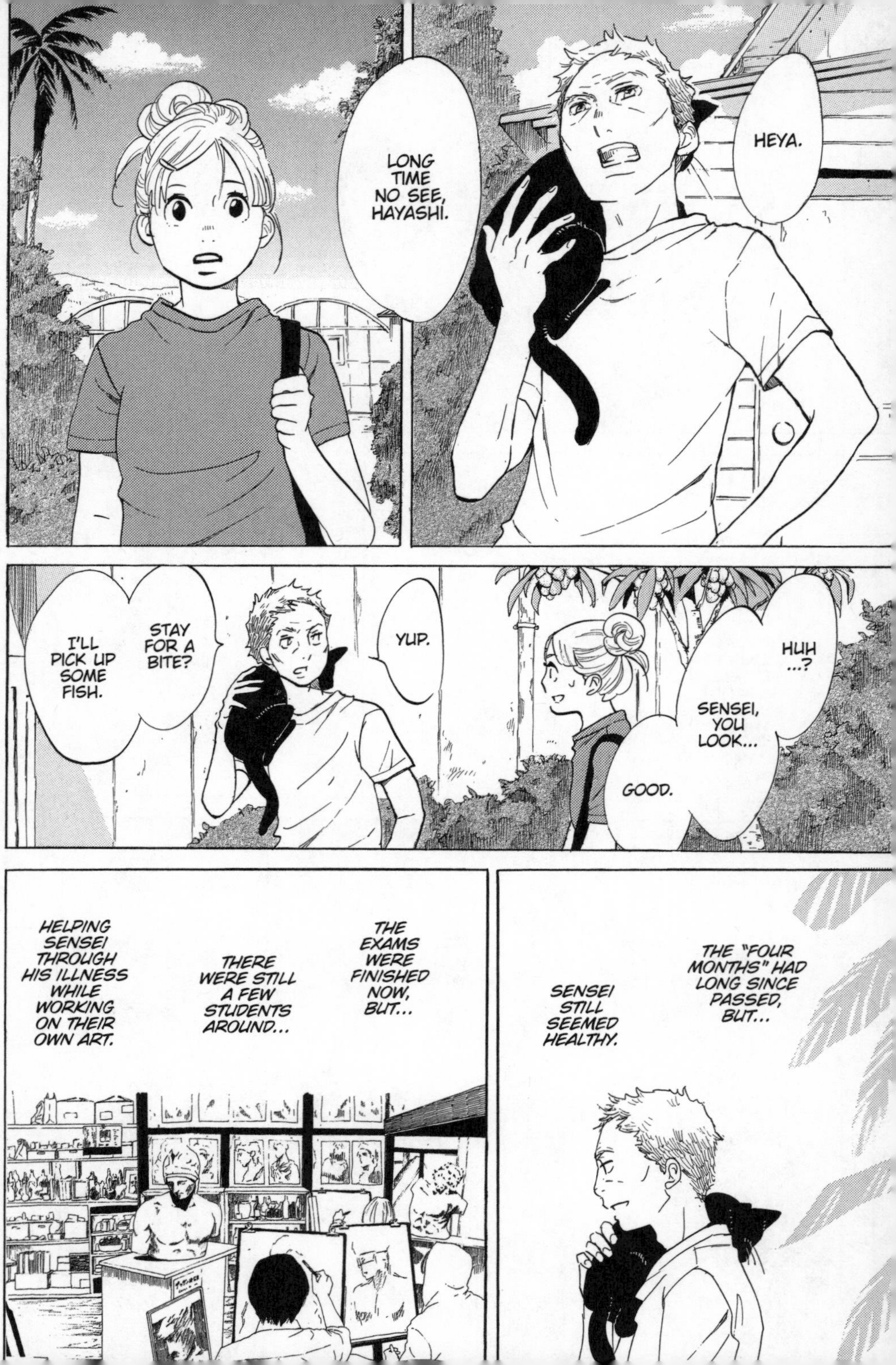
HEYA.
LONG TIME NO SEE, HAYASHI.
HUH ...?
SENSEI, YOU LOOK...
GOOD.
YUP.
STAY FOR A BITE?
I'LL PICK UP SOME FISH.
THE "FOUR MONTHS" HAD LONG SINCE PASSED, BUT...
SENSEI STILL SEEMED HEALTHY.
THE EXAMS WERE FINISHED NOW, BUT...
THERE WERE STILL A FEW STUDENTS AROUND...
HELPING SENSEI THROUGH HIS ILLNESS WHILE WORKING ON THEIR OWN ART.

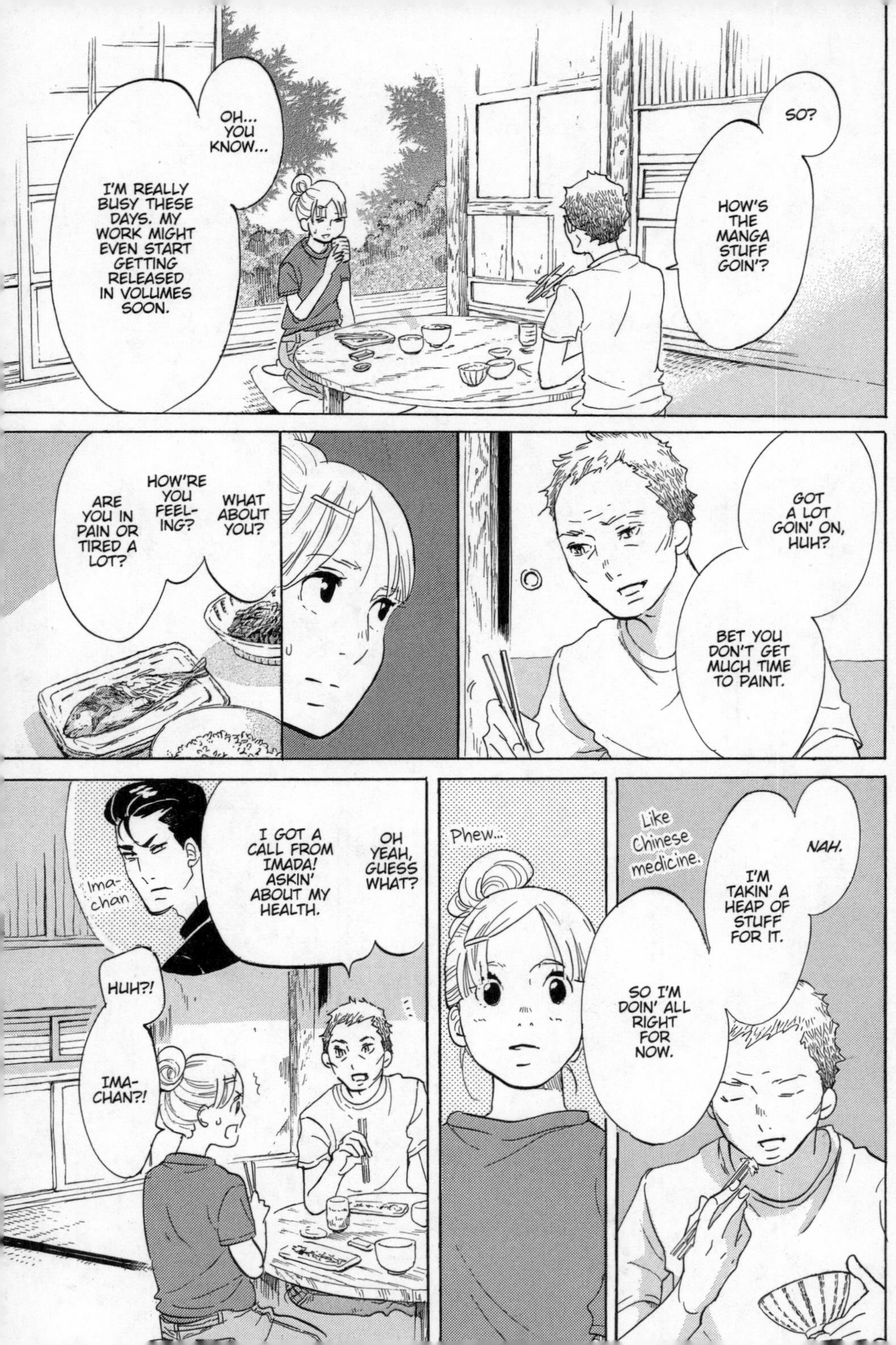
SO?
HOW'S THE MANGA STUFF GOIN'?
OH... YOU KNOW...
I'M REALLY BUSY THESE DAYS. MY WORK MIGHT EVEN START GETTING RELEASED IN VOLUMES SOON.
GOT A LOT GOIN' ON, HUH?
BET YOU DON'T GET MUCH TIME TO PAINT.
WHAT ABOUT YOU?
HOW'RE YOU FEELING?
ARE YOU IN PAIN OR TIRED A LOT?
NAH.
I'M TAKIN' A HEAP OF STUFF FOR IT.
Like Chinese medicine.
SO I'M DOIN' ALL RIGHT FOR NOW.
Phew...
OH YEAH, GUESS WHAT?
I GOT A CALL FROM IMADA! ASKIN' ABOUT MY HEALTH.
Ima-chan
HUH?!
IMA-CHAN?!

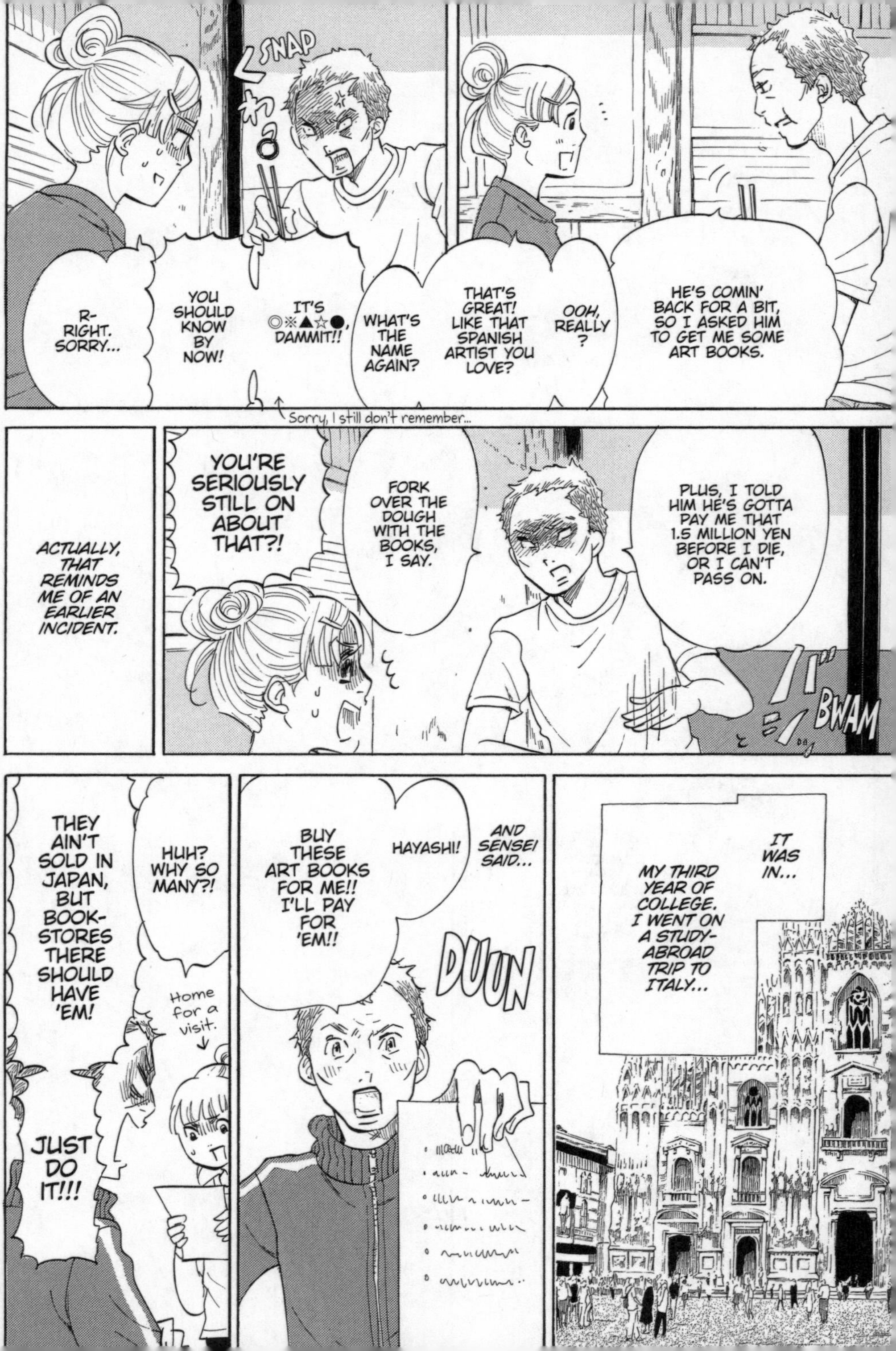
HE'S COMIN' BACK FOR A BIT, SO I ASKED HIM TO GET ME SOME ART BOOKS.
OOH, REALLY?
THAT'S GREAT! LIKE THAT SPANISH ARTIST YOU LOVE?
WHAT'S THE NAME AGAIN?
SNAP
IT'S ◎※▲☆●, DAMMIT!!
YOU SHOULD KNOW BY NOW!
R-RIGHT. SORRY...
Sorry, I still don't remember...
PLUS, I TOLD HIM HE'S GOTTA PAY ME THAT 1.5 MILLION YEN BEFORE I DIE, OR I CAN'T PASS ON.
BWAM
FORK OVER THE DOUGH WITH THE BOOKS, I SAY.
YOU'RE SERIOUSLY STILL ON ABOUT THAT?!
ACTUALLY, THAT REMINDS ME OF AN EARLIER INCIDENT.
IT WAS IN...
MY THIRD YEAR OF COLLEGE. I WENT ON A STUDY-ABROAD TRIP TO ITALY...
AND SENSEI SAID...
HAYASHI!
BUY THESE ART BOOKS FOR ME!! I'LL PAY FOR 'EM!!
DUUN
HUH? WHY SO MANY?!
THEY AIN'T SOLD IN JAPAN, BUT BOOK-STORES THERE SHOULD HAVE 'EM!
Home for a visit.
JUST DO IT!!!

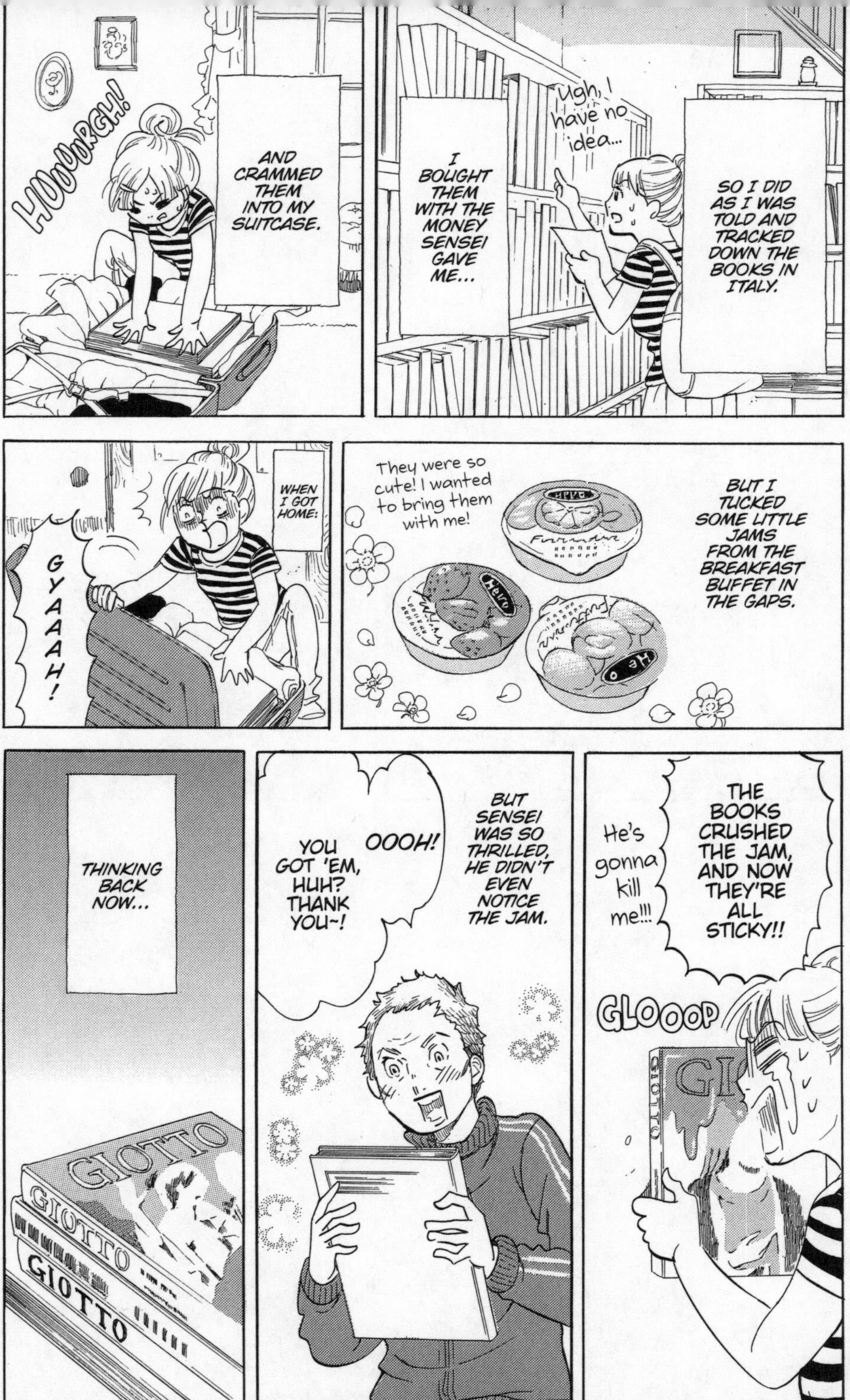
SO I DID AS I WAS TOLD AND TRACKED DOWN THE BOOKS IN ITALY.
Ugh, I have no idea...
I BOUGHT THEM WITH THE MONEY SENSEI GAVE ME...
AND CRAMMED THEM INTO MY SUITCASE.
HUUUURGH!
BUT I TUCKED SOME LITTLE JAMS FROM THE BREAKFAST BUFFET IN THE GAPS.
They were so cute! I wanted to bring them with me!
WHEN I GOT HOME:
GYAAAAH!
THE BOOKS CRUSHED THE JAM, AND NOW THEY'RE ALL STICKY!!
He's gonna kill me!!!
GLOOOP
BUT SENSEI WAS SO THRILLED, HE DIDN'T EVEN NOTICE THE JAM.
OOOH!
YOU GOT 'EM, HUH? THANK YOU~!
THINKING BACK NOW...
GIOTTO
GIOTTO
GIOTTO
GIOTTO

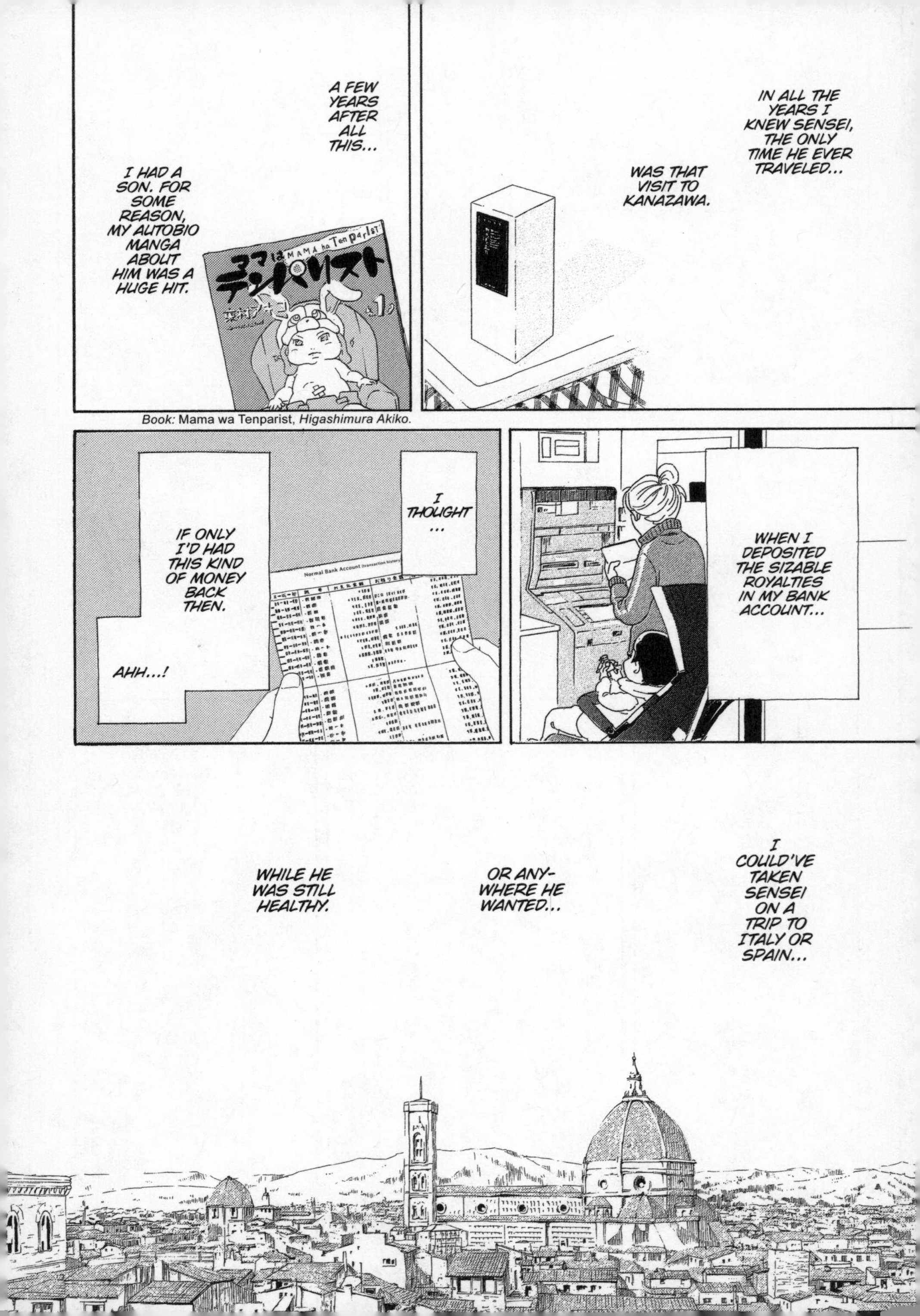
IN ALL THE YEARS I KNEW SENSEI, THE ONLY TIME HE EVER TRAVELED...
WAS THAT VISIT TO KANAZAWA.
A FEW YEARS AFTER ALL THIS...
I HAD A SON. FOR SOME REASON, MY AUTOBIO MANGA ABOUT HIM WAS A HUGE HIT.
WHEN I DEPOSITED THE SIZABLE ROYALTIES IN MY BANK ACCOUNT...
I THOUGHT...
IF ONLY I'D HAD THIS KIND OF MONEY BACK THEN.
Normal Bank Account (transaction history)
AHH...!
I COULD'VE TAKEN SENSEI ON A TRIP TO ITALY OR SPAIN...
OR ANY-WHERE HE WANTED...
WHILE HE WAS STILL HEALTHY.
Book: Mama wa Tenparist, *Higashimura Akiko.*

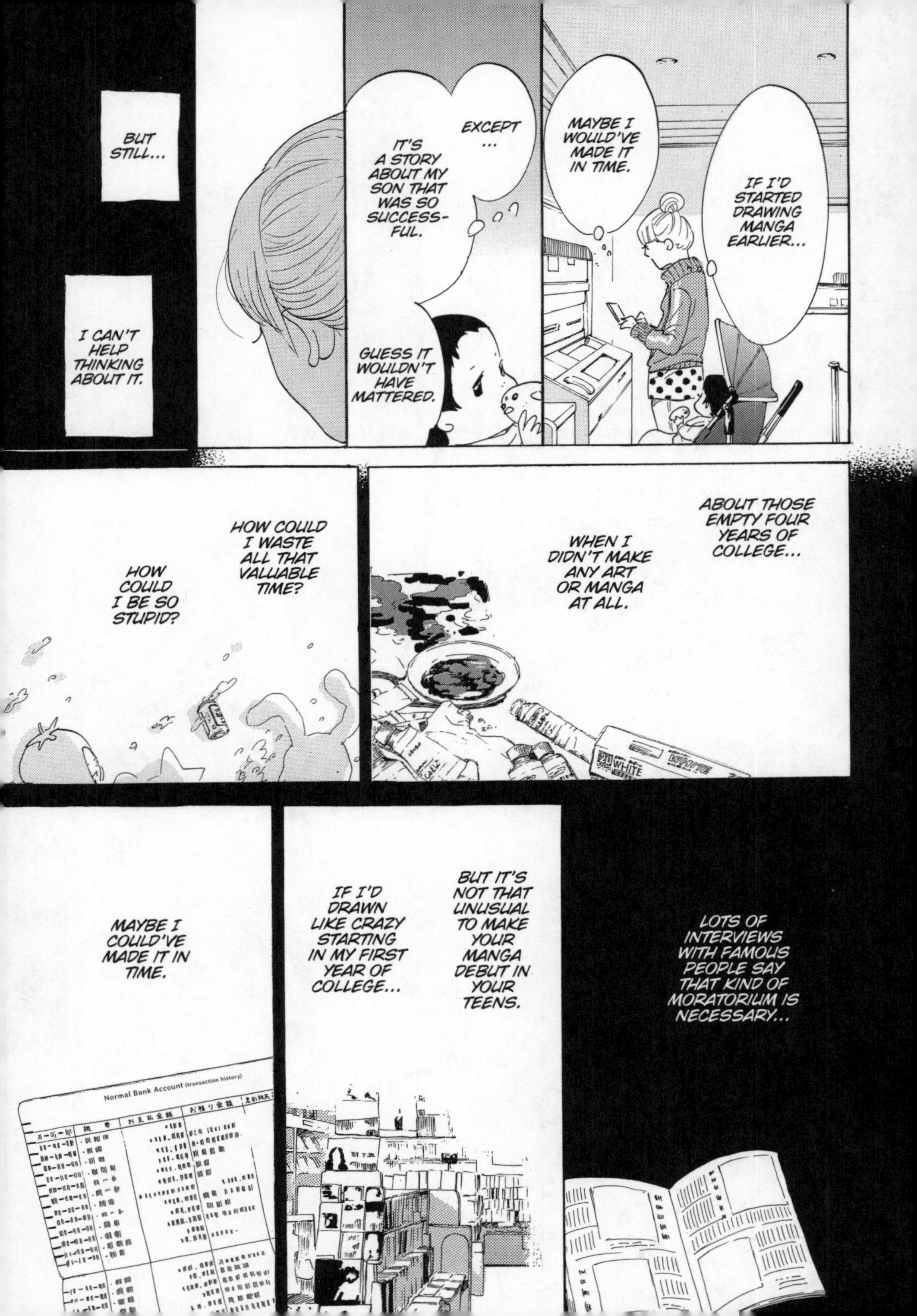
IF I'D STARTED DRAWING MANGA EARLIER...
MAYBE I WOULD'VE MADE IT IN TIME.
EXCEPT...
IT'S A STORY ABOUT MY SON THAT WAS SO SUCCESSFUL.
GUESS IT WOULDN'T HAVE MATTERED.
BUT STILL...
I CAN'T HELP THINKING ABOUT IT.
ABOUT THOSE EMPTY FOUR YEARS OF COLLEGE...
WHEN I DIDN'T MAKE ANY ART OR MANGA AT ALL.
WHITE
HOW COULD I WASTE ALL THAT VALUABLE TIME?
HOW COULD I BE SO STUPID?
LOTS OF INTERVIEWS WITH FAMOUS PEOPLE SAY THAT KIND OF MORATORIUM IS NECESSARY...
BUT IT'S NOT THAT UNUSUAL TO MAKE YOUR MANGA DEBUT IN YOUR TEENS.
IF I'D DRAWN LIKE CRAZY STARTING IN MY FIRST YEAR OF COLLEGE...
MAYBE I COULD'VE MADE IT IN TIME.
Normal Bank Account (transaction history)

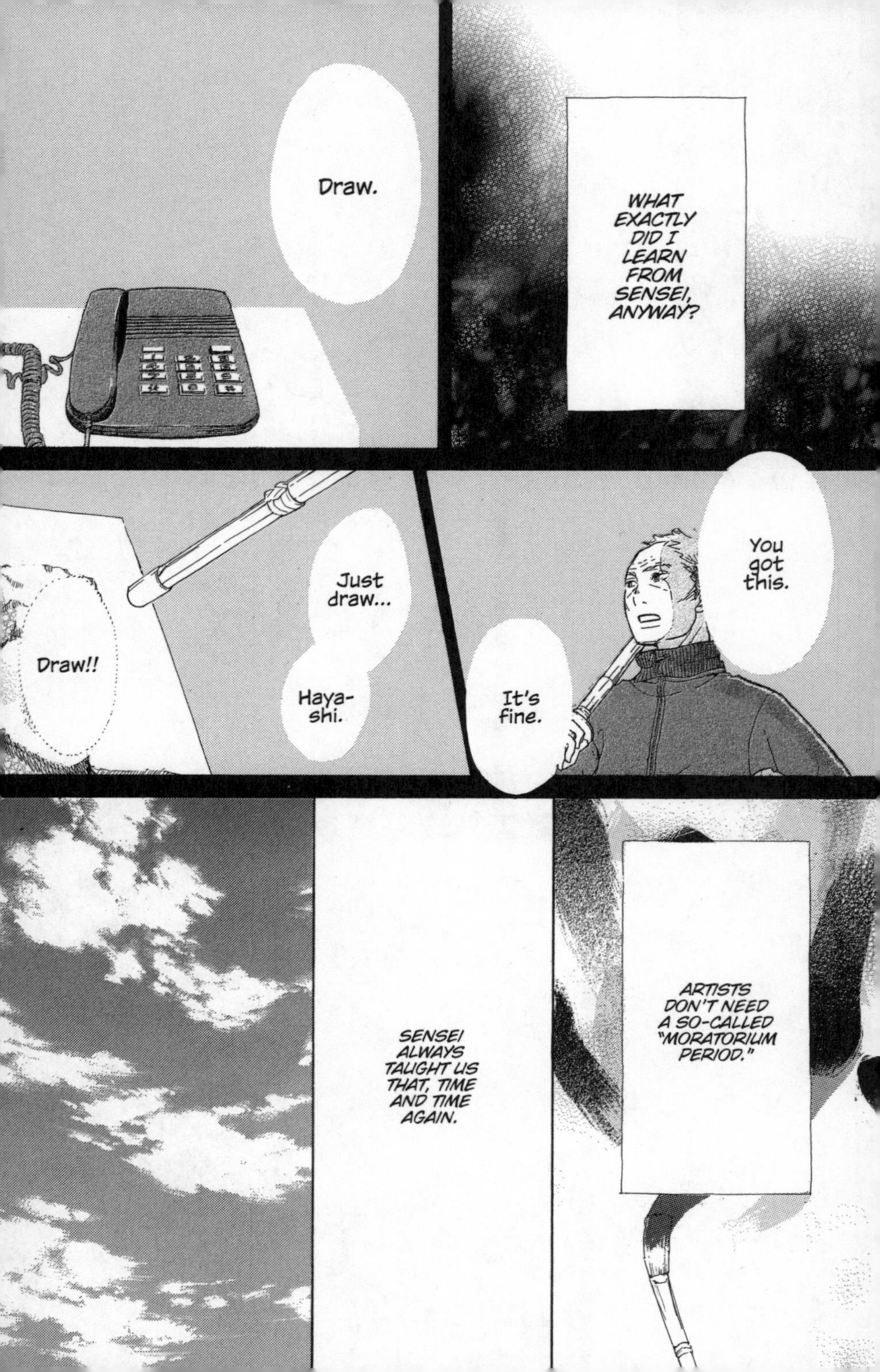
WHAT EXACTLY DID I LEARN FROM SENSEI, ANYWAY?
Draw.
You got this.
It's fine.
Just draw...
Haya-shi.
Draw!!
ARTISTS DON'T NEED A SO-CALLED "MORATORIUM PERIOD."
SENSEI ALWAYS TAUGHT US THAT, TIME AND TIME AGAIN.

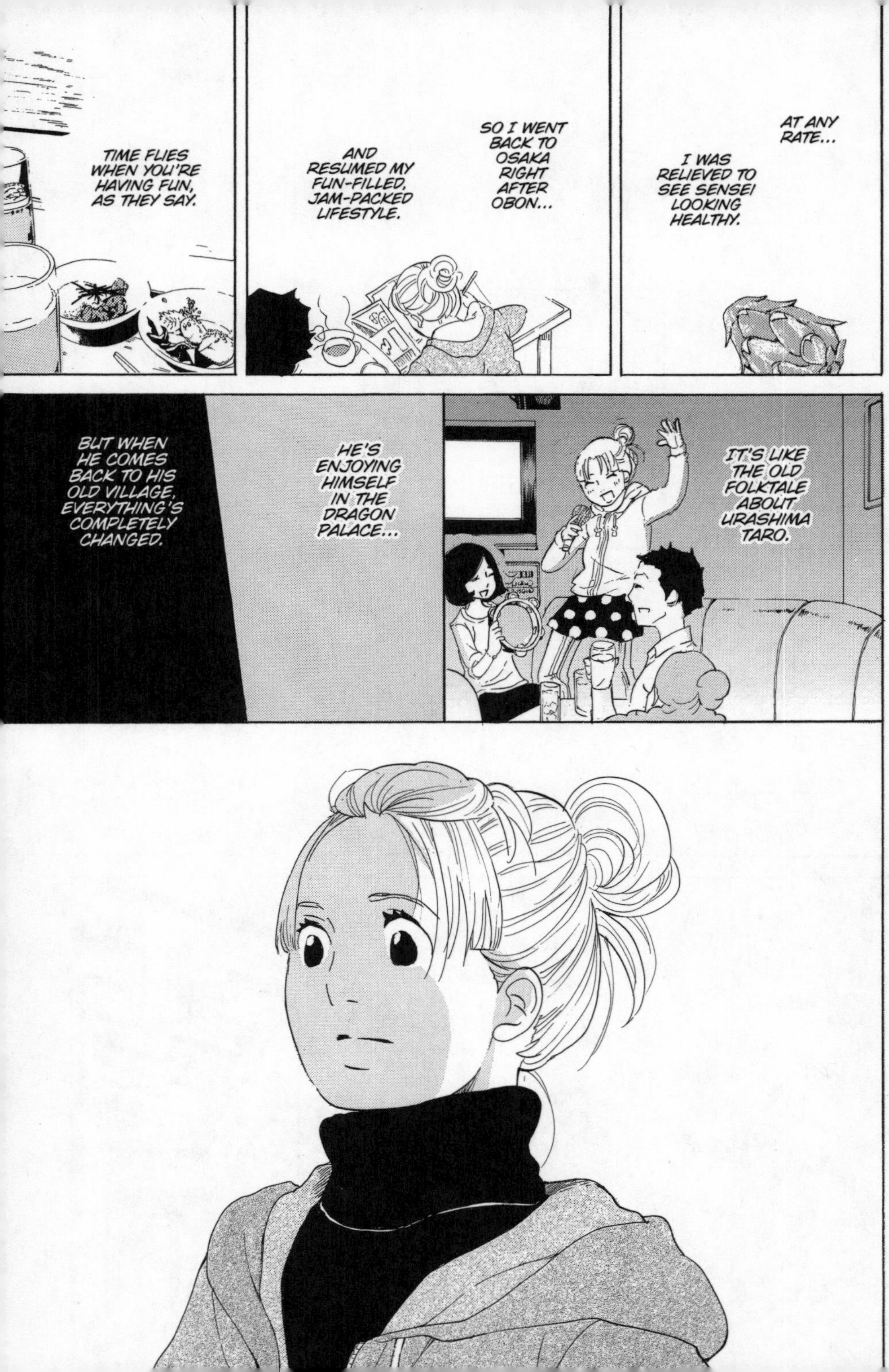
AT ANY RATE...
I WAS RELIEVED TO SEE SENSEI LOOKING HEALTHY.
SO I WENT BACK TO OSAKA RIGHT AFTER OBON...
AND RESUMED MY FUN-FILLED, JAM-PACKED LIFESTYLE.
TIME FLIES WHEN YOU'RE HAVING FUN, AS THEY SAY.
IT'S LIKE THE OLD FOLKTALE ABOUT URASHIMA TARO.
HE'S ENJOYING HIMSELF IN THE DRAGON PALACE...
BUT WHEN HE COMES BACK TO HIS OLD VILLAGE, EVERYTHING'S COMPLETELY CHANGED.

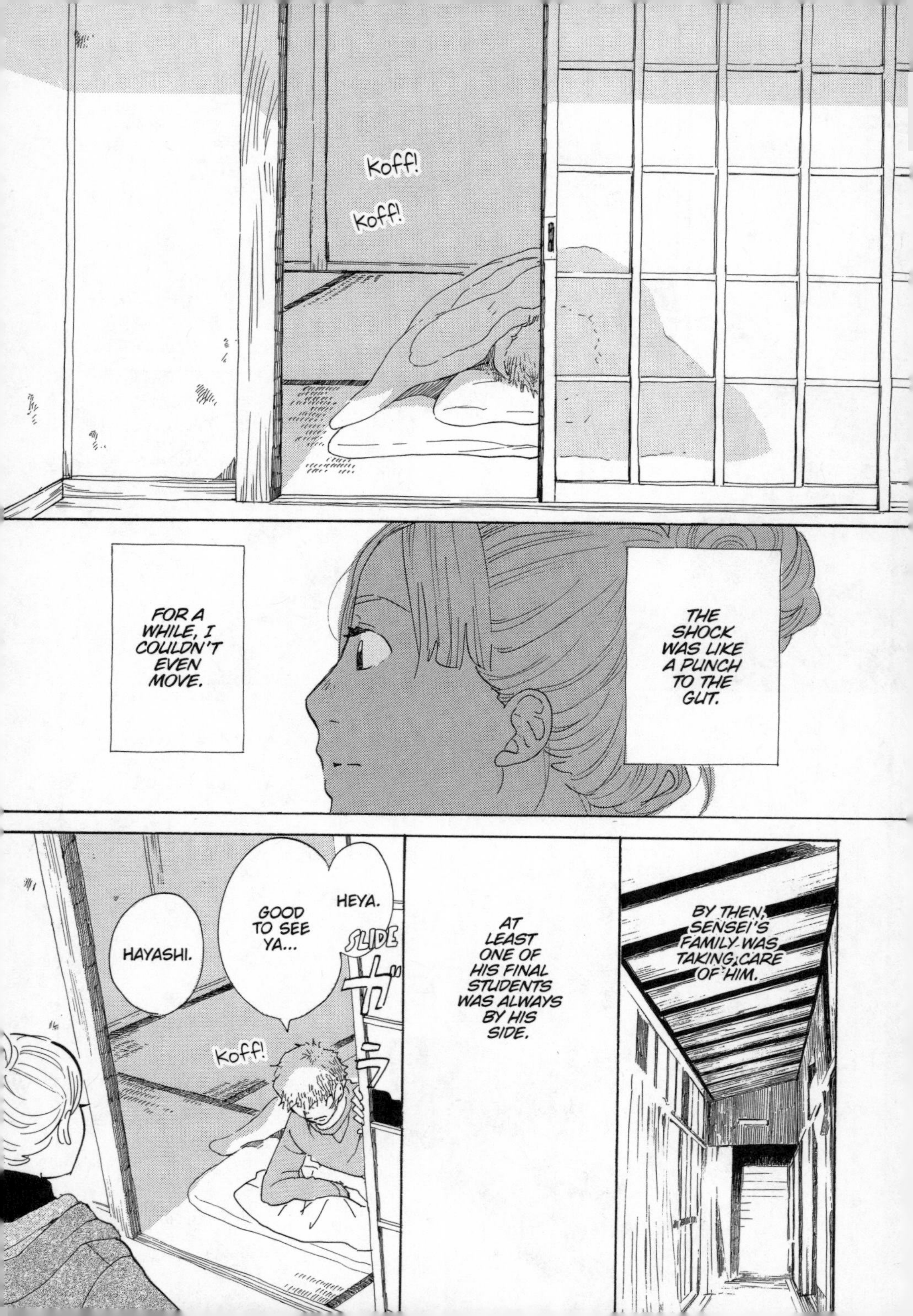
Koff!
Koff!
THE SHOCK WAS LIKE A PUNCH TO THE GUT.
FOR A WHILE, I COULDN'T EVEN MOVE.
BY THEN, SENSEI'S FAMILY WAS TAKING CARE OF HIM.
AT LEAST ONE OF HIS FINAL STUDENTS WAS ALWAYS BY HIS SIDE.
SLIDE
HEYA.
GOOD TO SEE YA...
HAYASHI.
Koff!

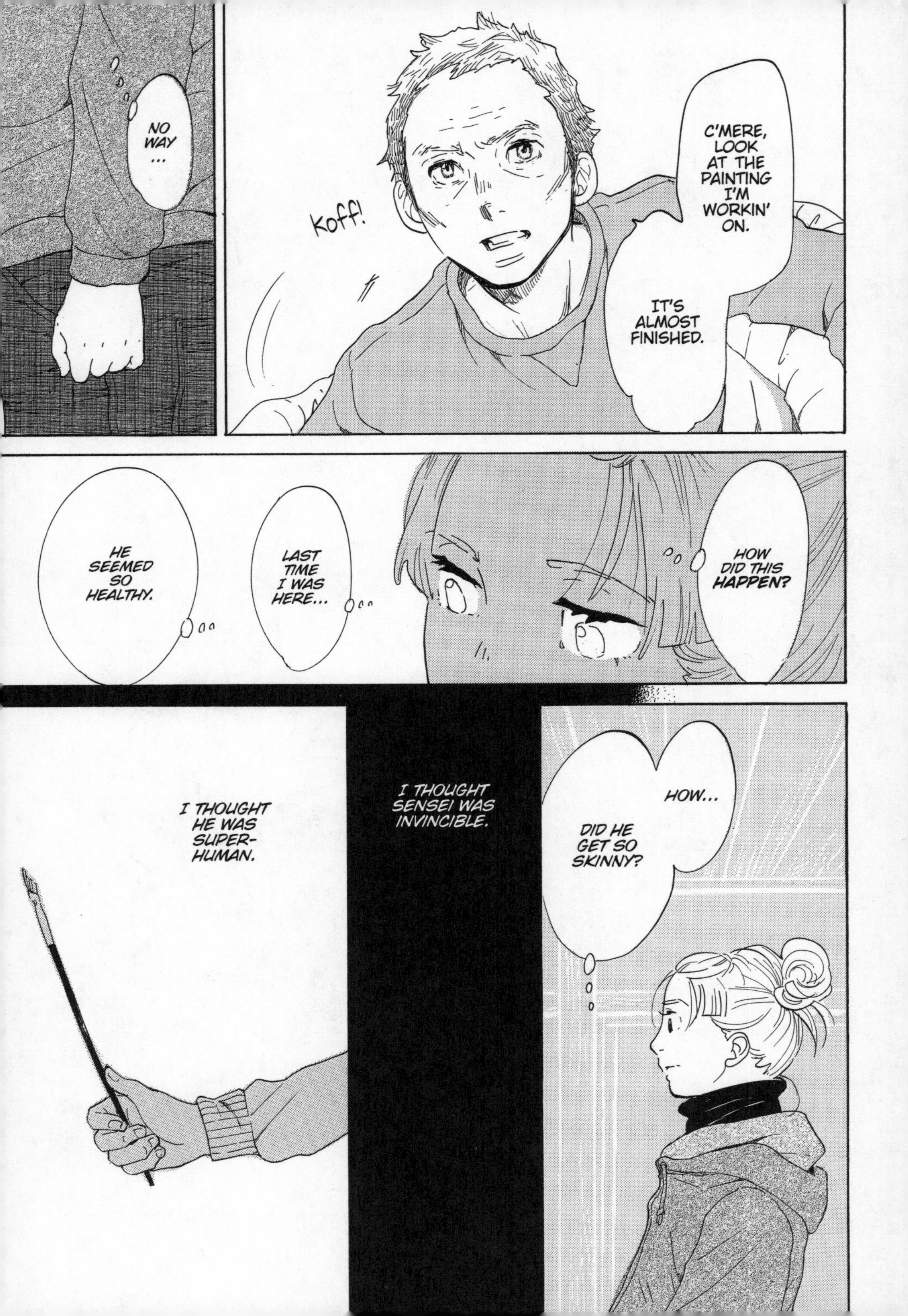
Koff!
C'MERE, LOOK AT THE PAINTING I'M WORKIN' ON.
IT'S ALMOST FINISHED.
NO WAY...
HOW DID THIS HAPPEN?
LAST TIME I WAS HERE...
HE SEEMED SO HEALTHY.
HOW...
DID HE GET SO SKINNY?
I THOUGHT SENSEI WAS INVINCIBLE.
I THOUGHT HE WAS SUPER-HUMAN.

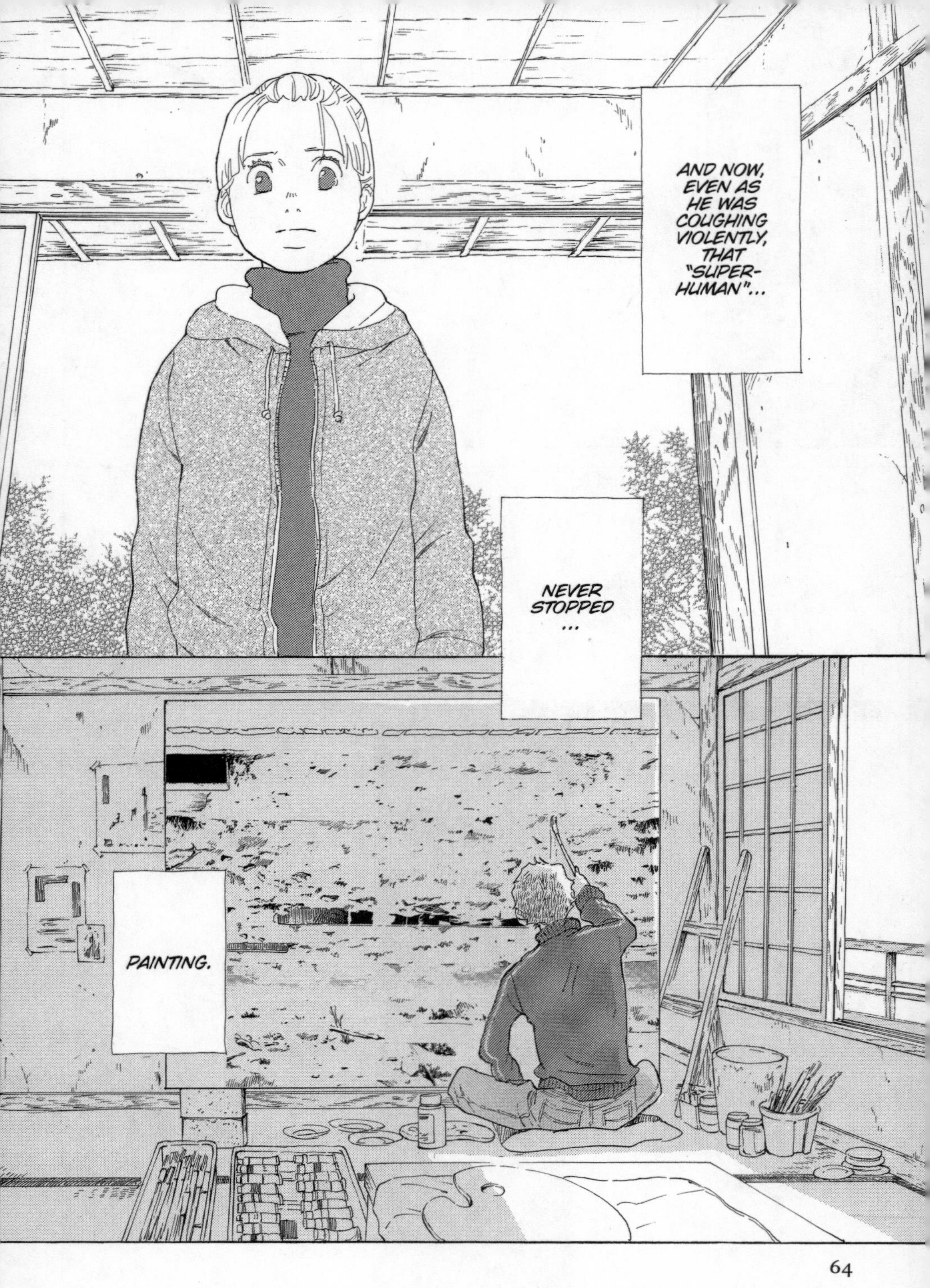
AND NOW, EVEN AS HE WAS COUGHING VIOLENTLY, THAT "SUPER-HUMAN"...
NEVER STOPPED ...
PAINTING.

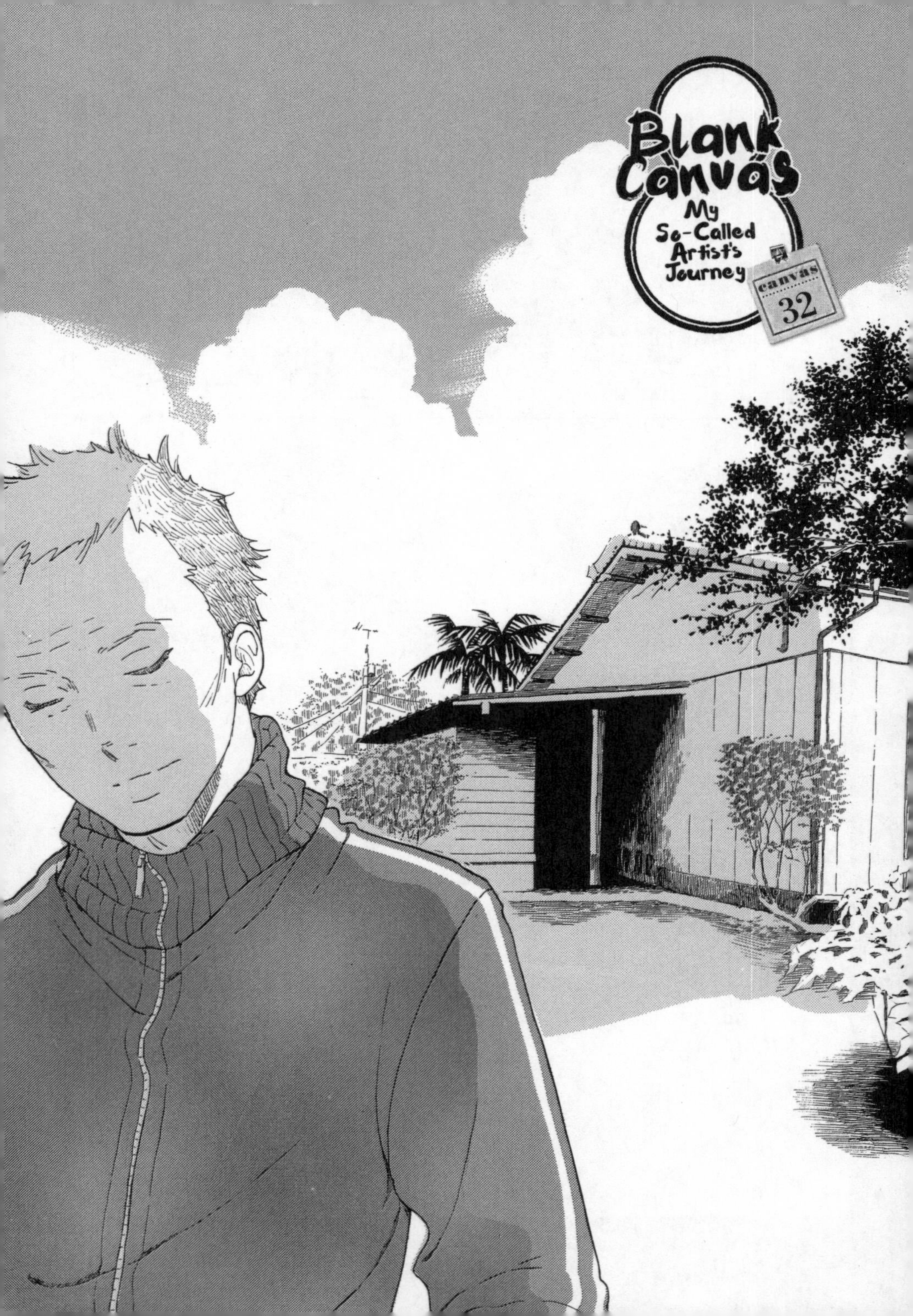
Blank Canvas
My So-Called Artist's Journey
canvas
32

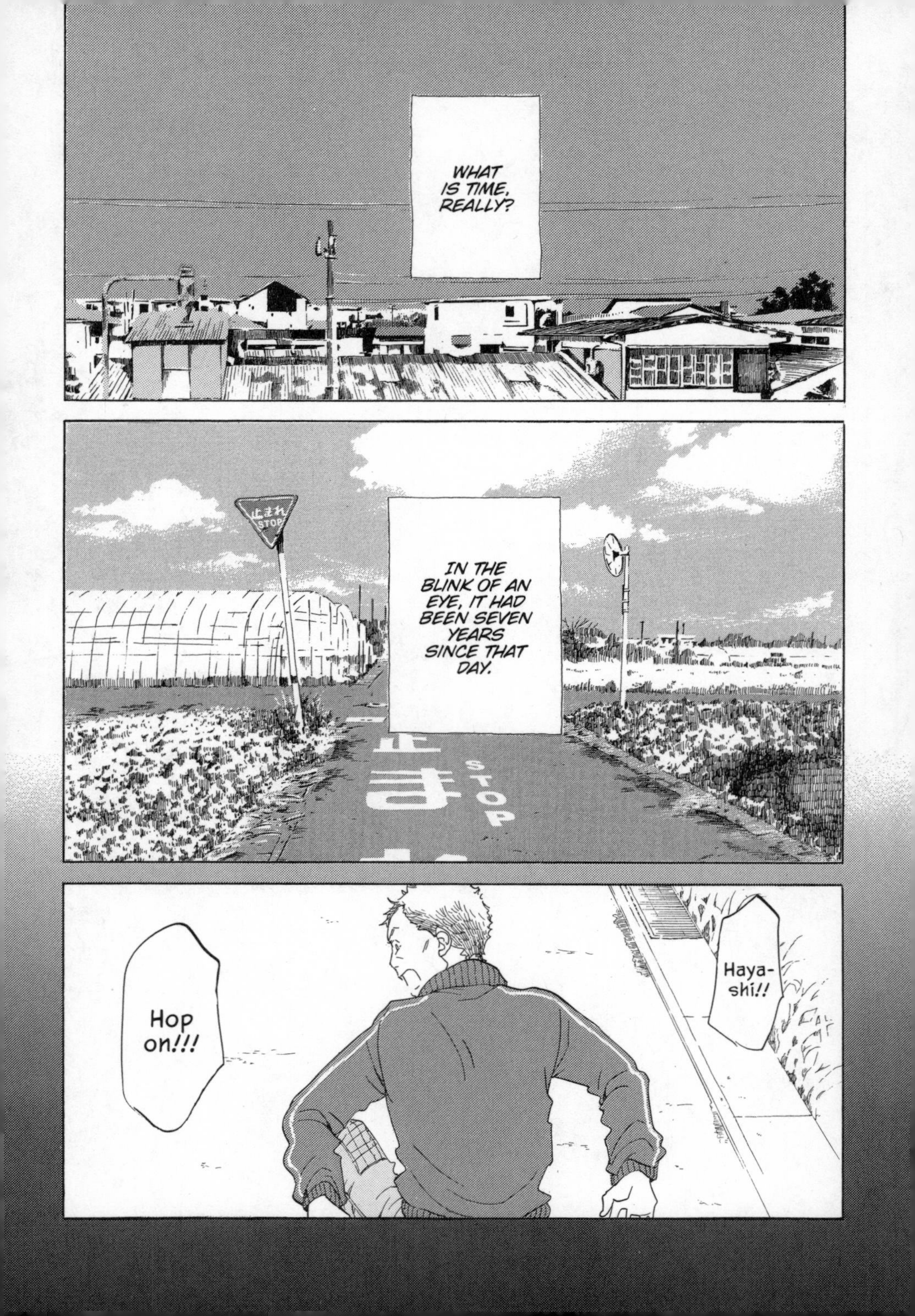
WHAT IS TIME, REALLY?
止まれ STOP
IN THE BLINK OF AN EYE, IT HAD BEEN SEVEN YEARS SINCE THAT DAY.
STOP
Haya-shi!!
Hop on!!!

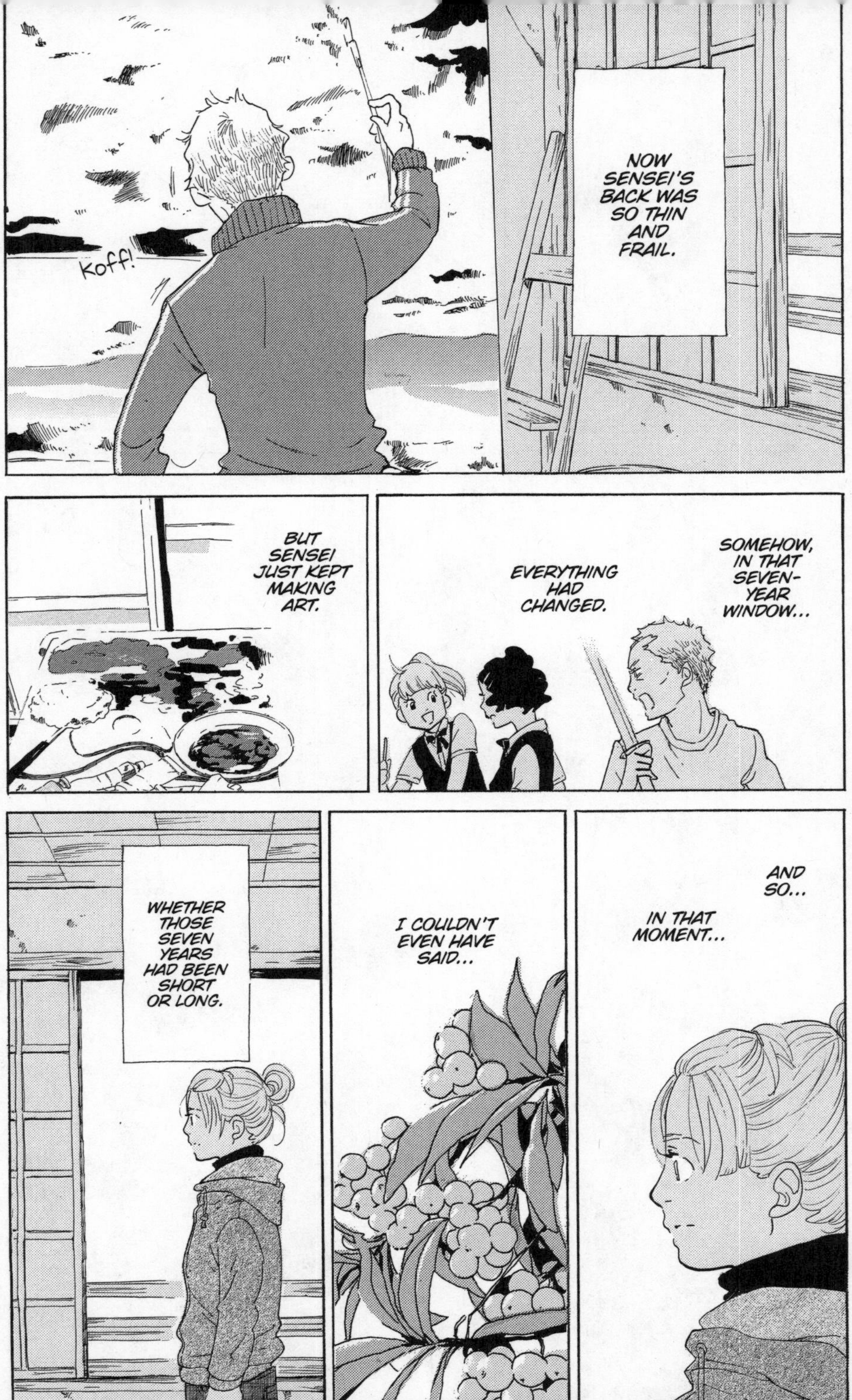
NOW SENSEI'S BACK WAS SO THIN AND FRAIL.
Koff!
SOMEHOW, IN THAT SEVEN-YEAR WINDOW...
EVERYTHING HAD CHANGED.
BUT SENSEI JUST KEPT MAKING ART.
AND SO...
IN THAT MOMENT...
I COULDN'T EVEN HAVE SAID...
WHETHER THOSE SEVEN YEARS HAD BEEN SHORT OR LONG.

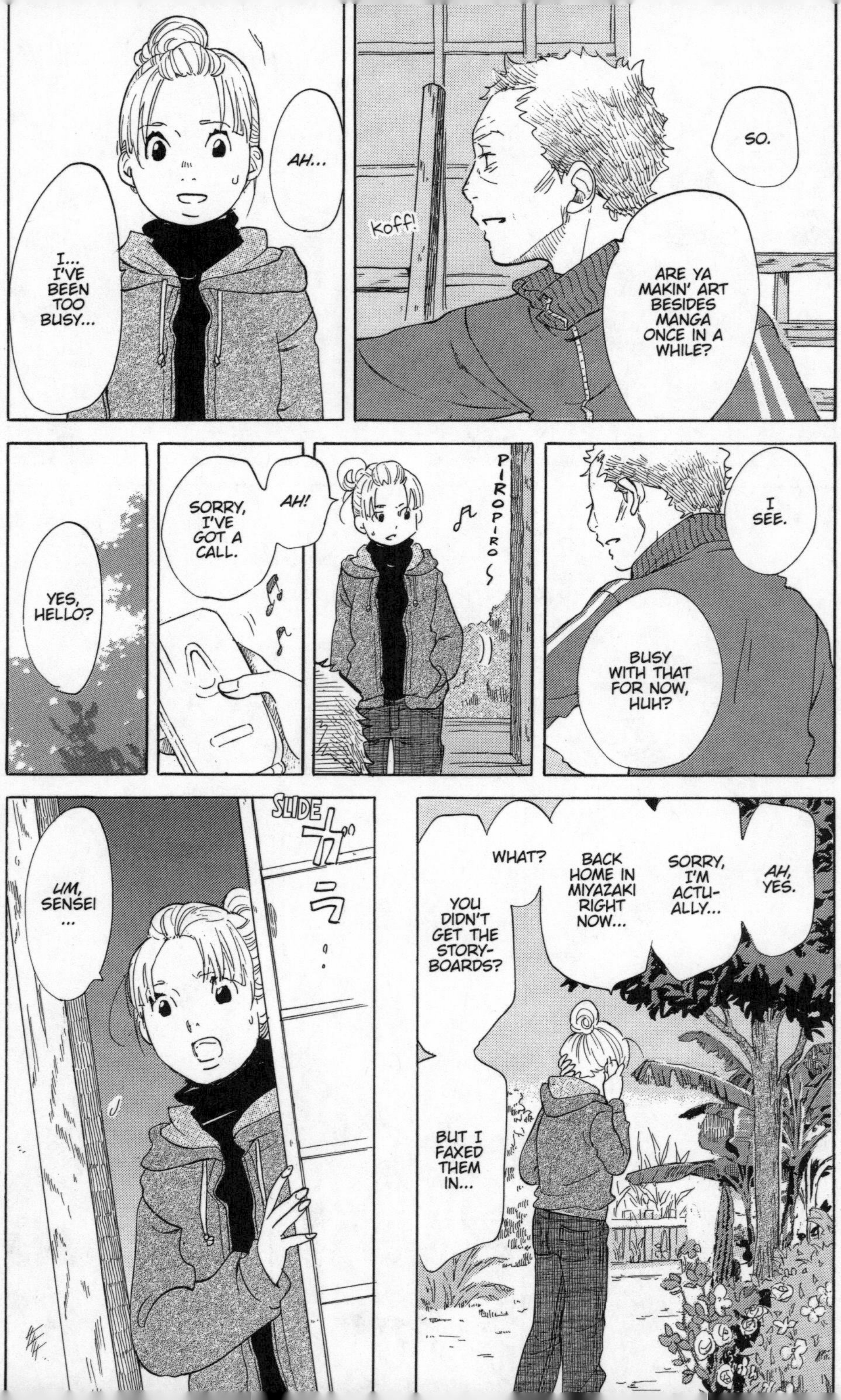
SO.
koff!
ARE YA MAKIN' ART BESIDES MANGA ONCE IN A WHILE?
AH...
I... I'VE BEEN TOO BUSY...
I SEE.
BUSY WITH THAT FOR NOW, HUH?
PIROPIRO
AH!
SORRY, I'VE GOT A CALL.
YES, HELLO?
AH, YES.
SORRY, I'M ACTU-ALLY...
BACK HOME IN MIYAZAKI RIGHT NOW...
WHAT?
YOU DIDN'T GET THE STORY-BOARDS?
BUT I FAXED THEM IN...
SLIDE
UM, SENSEI ...

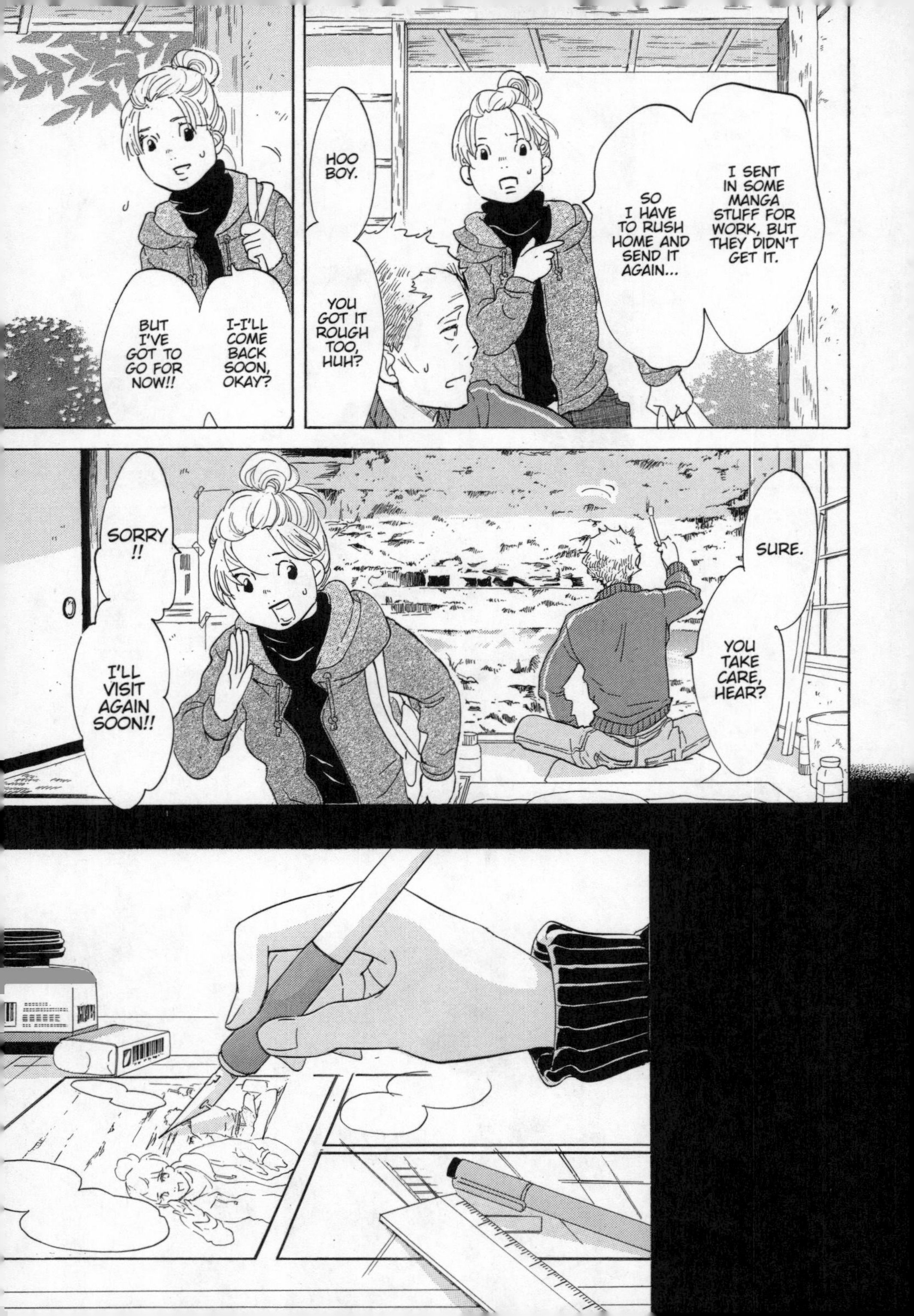
I SENT IN SOME MANGA STUFF FOR WORK, BUT THEY DIDN'T GET IT.
SO I HAVE TO RUSH HOME AND SEND IT AGAIN...
HOO BOY.
YOU GOT IT ROUGH TOO, HUH?
I-I'LL COME BACK SOON, OKAY?
BUT I'VE GOT TO GO FOR NOW!!
SURE.
YOU TAKE CARE, HEAR?
SORRY!!
I'LL VISIT AGAIN SOON!!

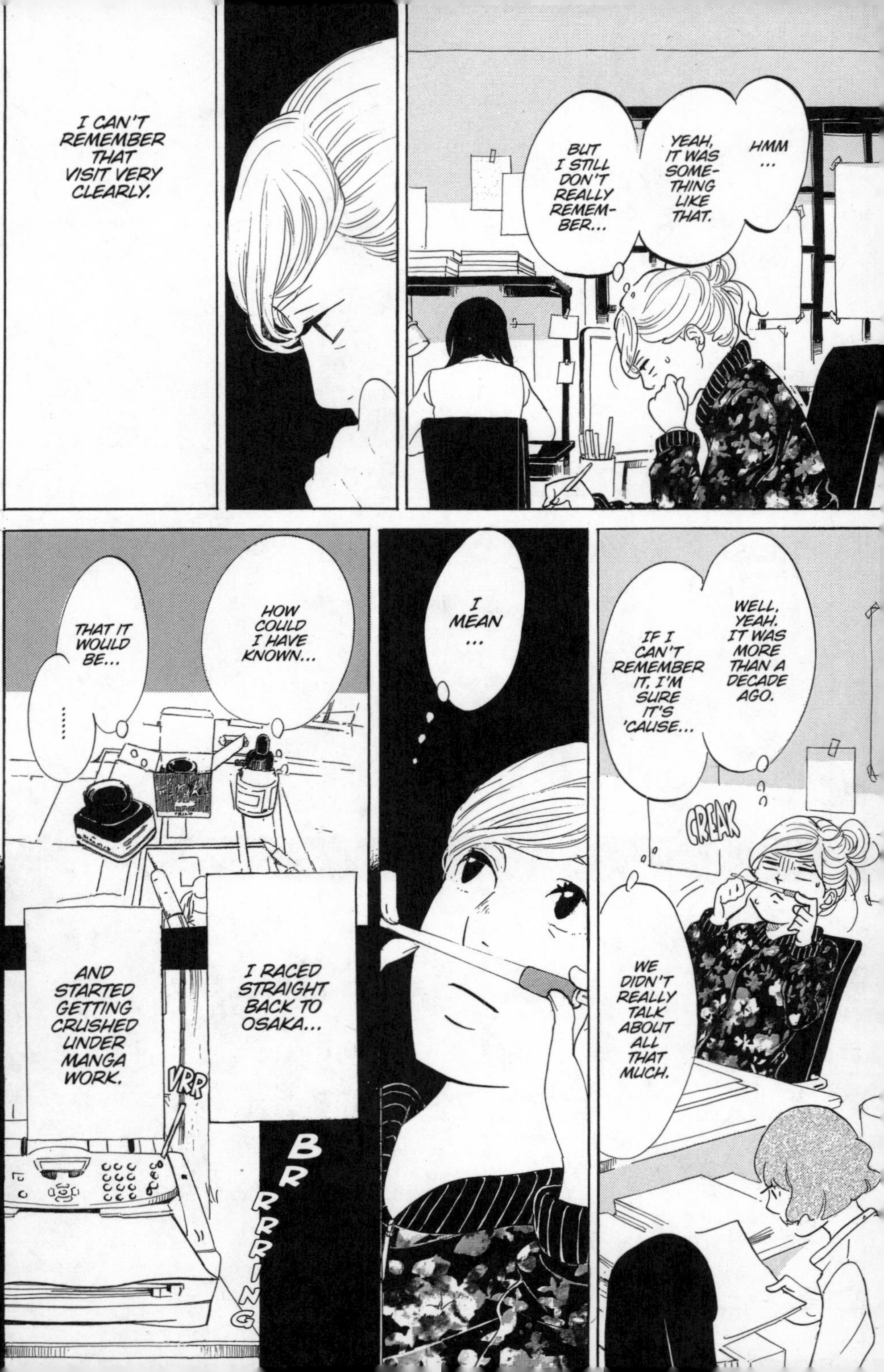
HMM ...
YEAH, IT WAS SOME-THING LIKE THAT.
BUT I STILL DON'T REALLY REMEM-BER...
I CAN'T REMEMBER THAT VISIT VERY CLEARLY.
WELL, YEAH. IT WAS MORE THAN A DECADE AGO.
IF I CAN'T REMEMBER IT, I'M SURE IT'S 'CAUSE...
CREAK
WE DIDN'T REALLY TALK ABOUT ALL THAT MUCH.
I MEAN ...
BRRRRING
HOW COULD I HAVE KNOWN...
THAT IT WOULD BE...
......
I RACED STRAIGHT BACK TO OSAKA...
AND STARTED GETTING CRUSHED UNDER MANGA WORK.
VRR

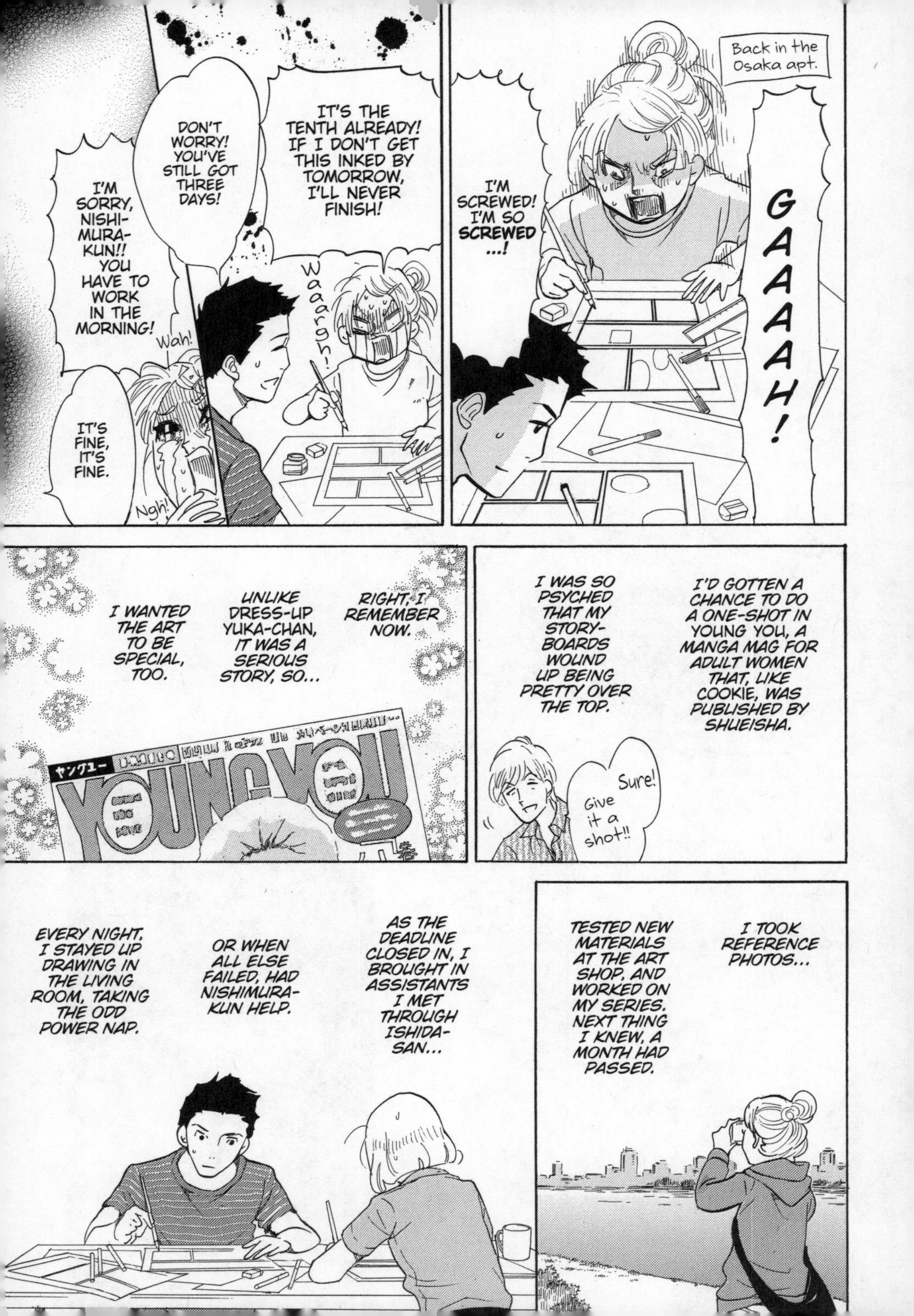
Back in the Osaka apt.
I'M SCREWED! I'M SO SCREWED...!
GAAAAAH!
IT'S THE TENTH ALREADY! IF I DON'T GET THIS INKED BY TOMORROW, I'LL NEVER FINISH!
DON'T WORRY! YOU'VE STILL GOT THREE DAYS!
I'M SORRY, NISHIMURA-KUN!! YOU HAVE TO WORK IN THE MORNING!
Waaargh!
Wah!
IT'S FINE, IT'S FINE.
Ngh!
I'D GOTTEN A CHANCE TO DO A ONE-SHOT IN YOUNG YOU, A MANGA MAG FOR ADULT WOMEN THAT, LIKE COOKIE, WAS PUBLISHED BY SHUEISHA.
I WAS SO PSYCHED THAT MY STORY-BOARDS WOUND UP BEING PRETTY OVER THE TOP.
Sure!
Give it a shot!!
RIGHT, I REMEMBER NOW.
UNLIKE DRESS-UP YUKA-CHAN, IT WAS A SERIOUS STORY, SO...
I WANTED THE ART TO BE SPECIAL, TOO.
ヤングユー
YOUNG YOU
I TOOK REFERENCE PHOTOS...
TESTED NEW MATERIALS AT THE ART SHOP, AND WORKED ON MY SERIES. NEXT THING I KNEW, A MONTH HAD PASSED.
AS THE DEADLINE CLOSED IN, I BROUGHT IN ASSISTANTS I MET THROUGH ISHIDA-SAN...
OR WHEN ALL ELSE FAILED, HAD NISHIMURA-KUN HELP.
EVERY NIGHT, I STAYED UP DRAWING IN THE LIVING ROOM, TAKING THE ODD POWER NAP.

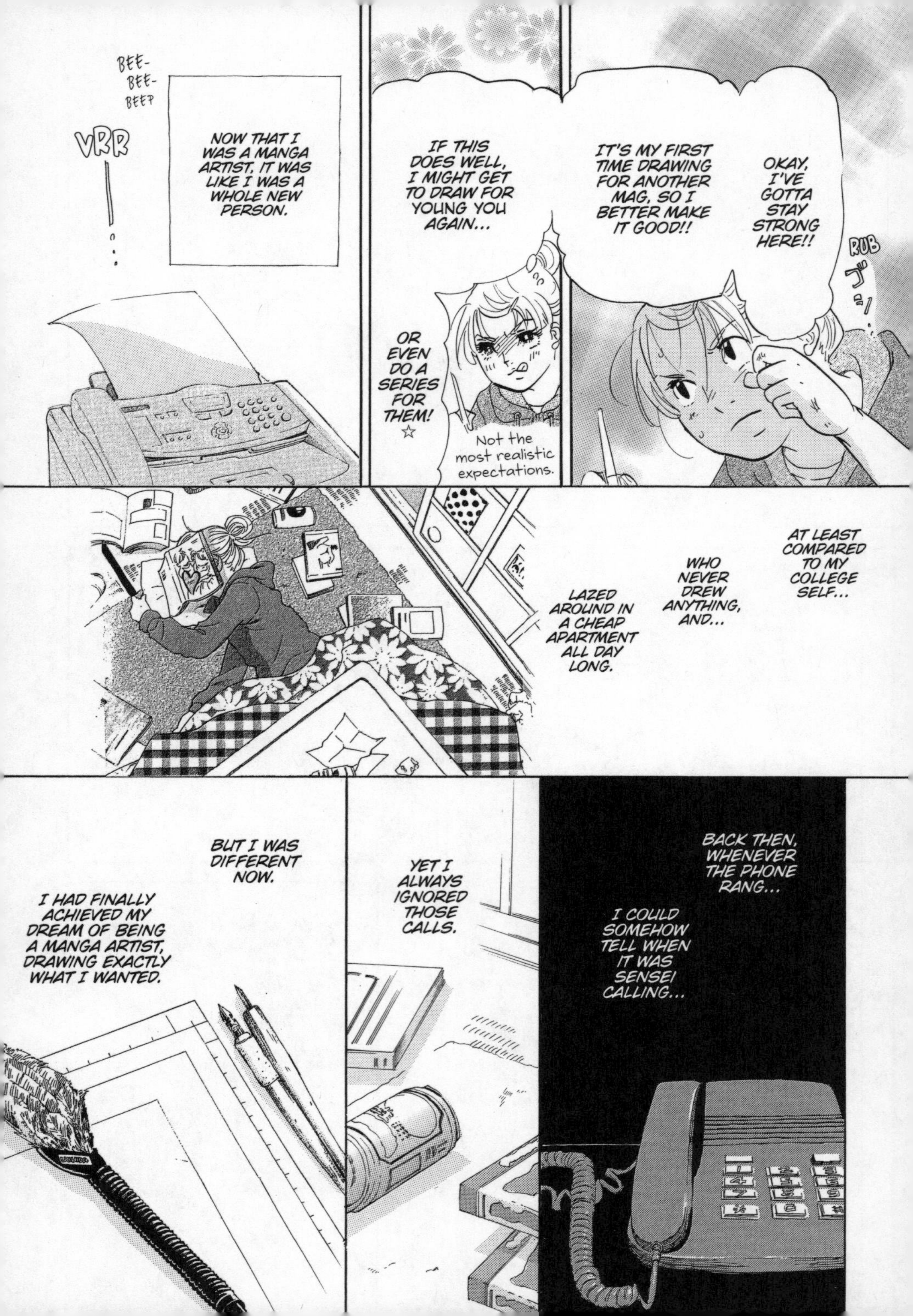
OKAY, I'VE GOTTA STAY STRONG HERE!!
IT'S MY FIRST TIME DRAWING FOR ANOTHER MAG, SO I BETTER MAKE IT GOOD!!
RUB
IF THIS DOES WELL, I MIGHT GET TO DRAW FOR YOUNG YOU AGAIN...
OR EVEN DO A SERIES FOR THEM! ☆
Not the most realistic expectations.
NOW THAT I WAS A MANGA ARTIST, IT WAS LIKE I WAS A WHOLE NEW PERSON.
BEE-BEE-BEEP
VRR
AT LEAST COMPARED TO MY COLLEGE SELF...
WHO NEVER DREW ANYTHING, AND...
LAZED AROUND IN A CHEAP APARTMENT ALL DAY LONG.
BACK THEN, WHENEVER THE PHONE RANG...
I COULD SOMEHOW TELL WHEN IT WAS SENSEI CALLING...
YET I ALWAYS IGNORED THOSE CALLS.
BUT I WAS DIFFERENT NOW.
I HAD FINALLY ACHIEVED MY DREAM OF BEING A MANGA ARTIST, DRAWING EXACTLY WHAT I WANTED.

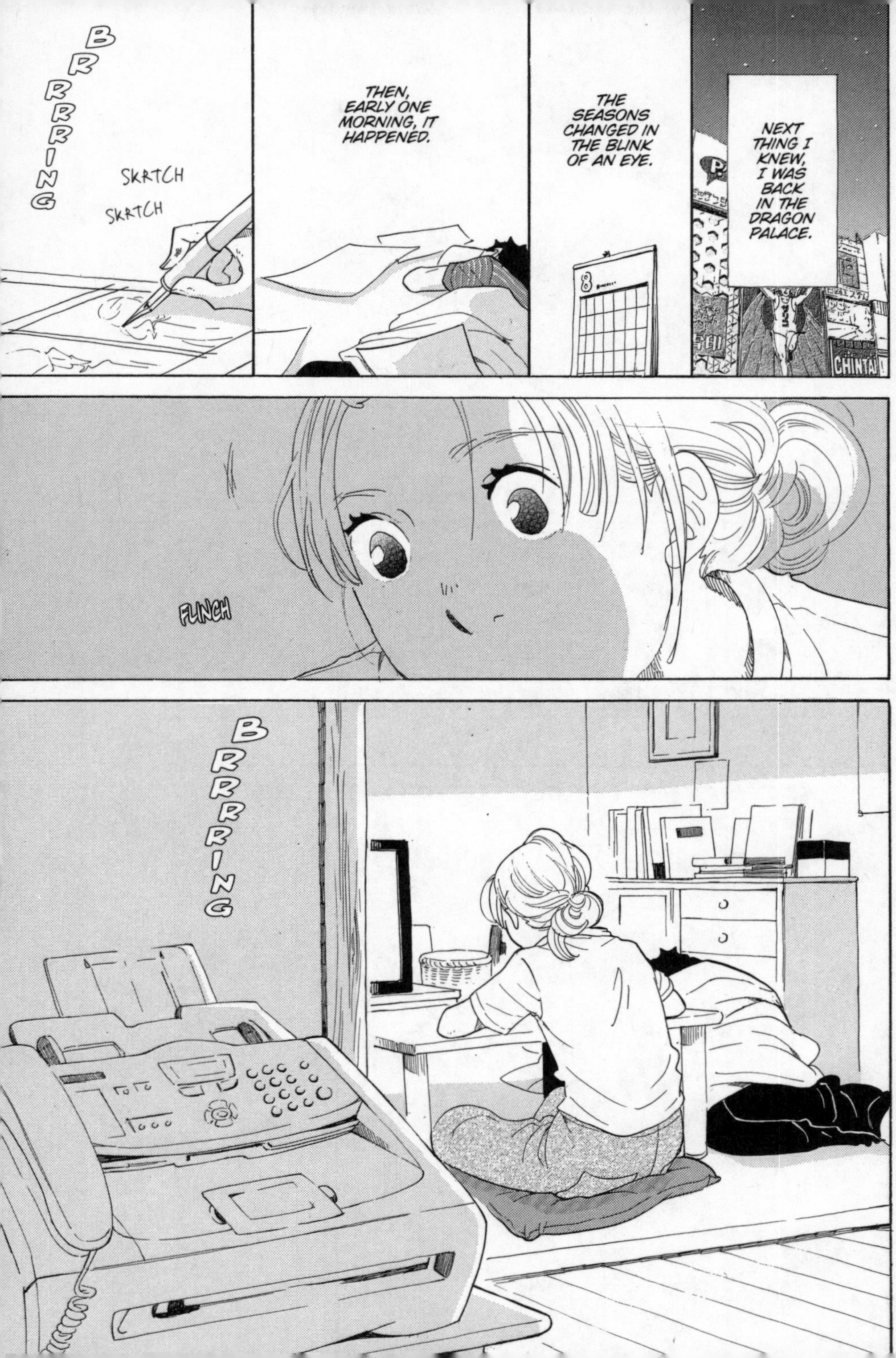
NEXT THING I KNEW, I WAS BACK IN THE DRAGON PALACE.
THE SEASONS CHANGED IN THE BLINK OF AN EYE.
THEN, EARLY ONE MORNING, IT HAPPENED.
BRRRRING
SKRTCH
SKRTCH
FLINCH
BRRRRING

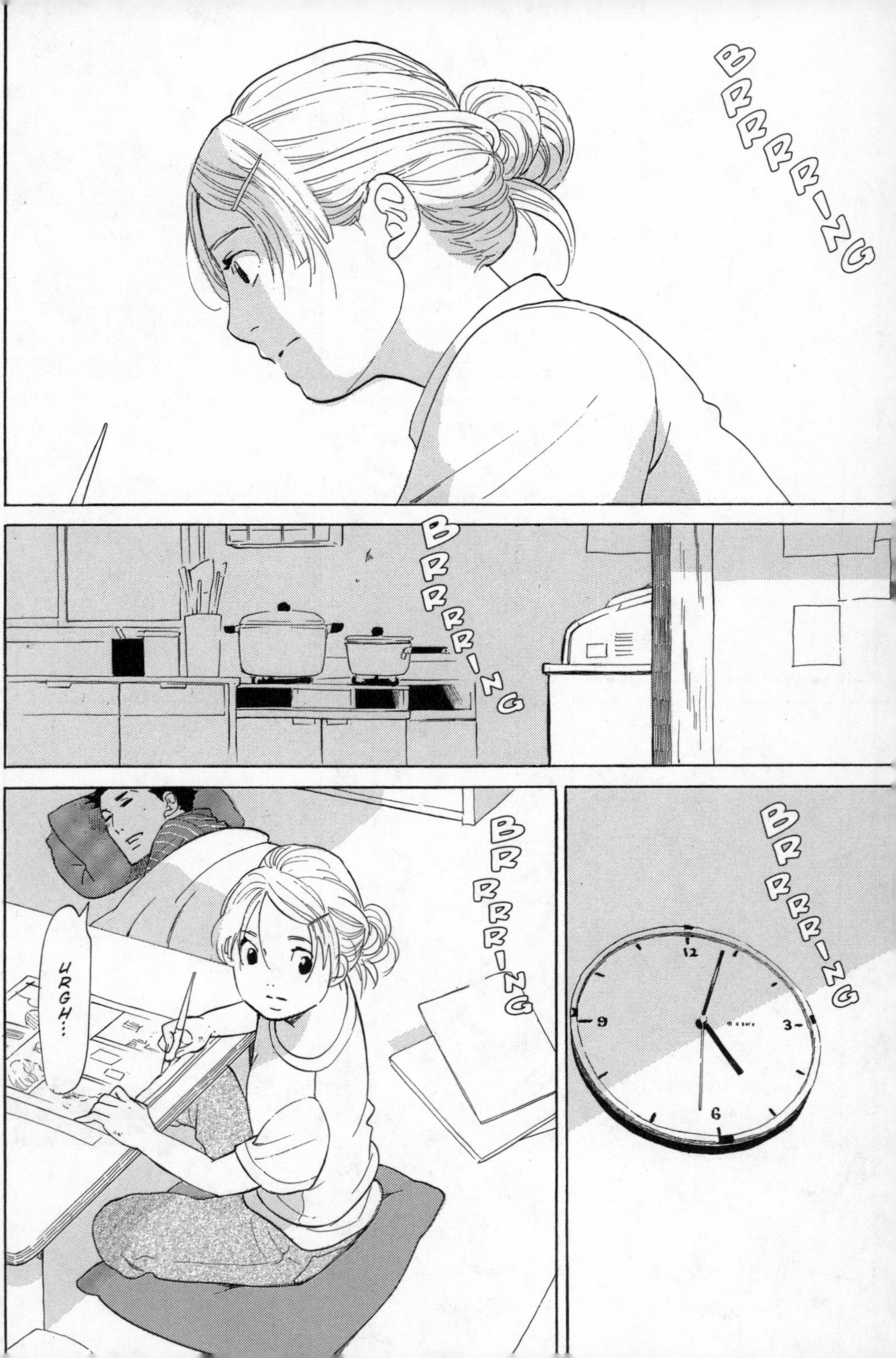
BRRRRR-RING
BRRRRRING
BRRRRR-RING
BRRRRRING
URGH...

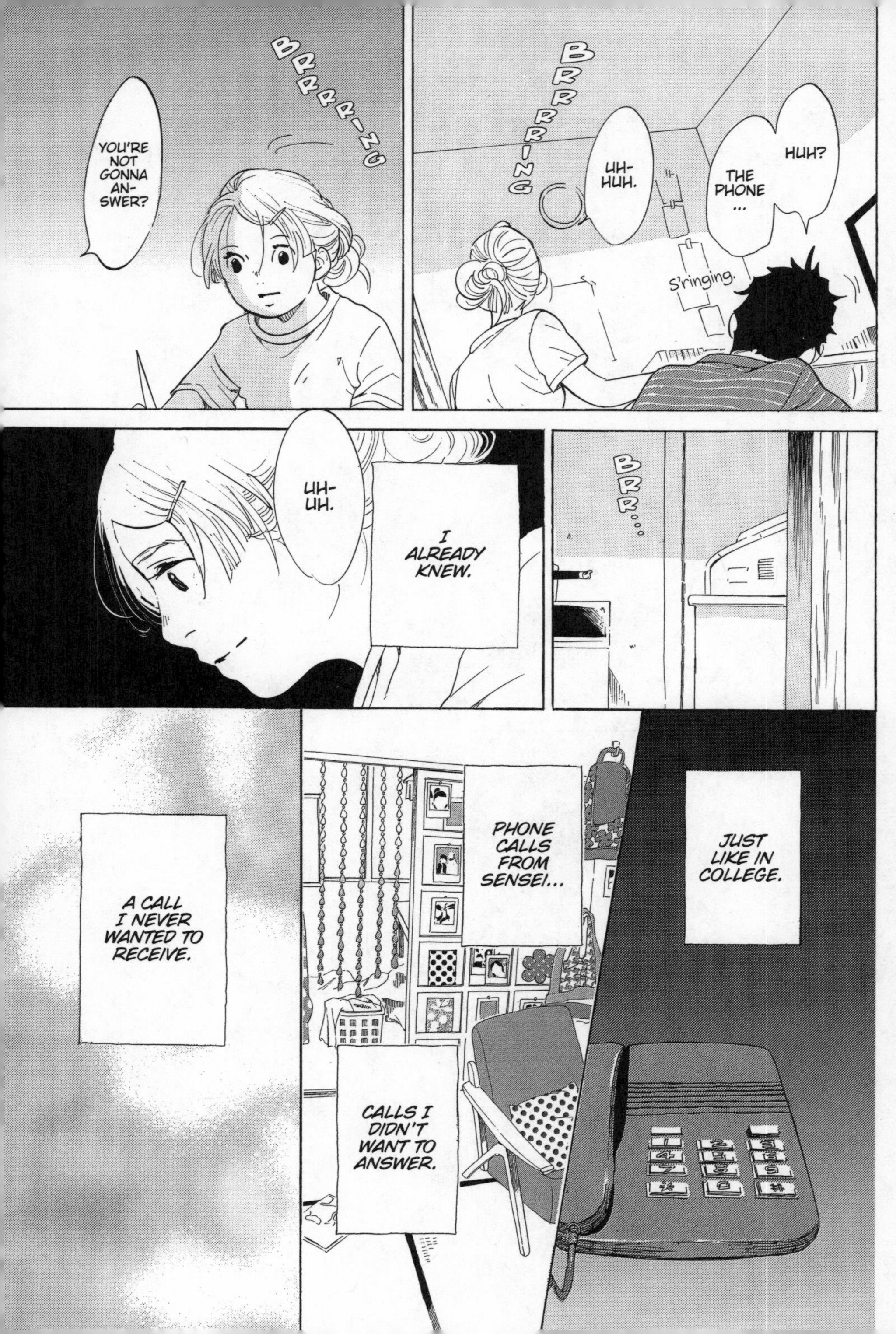
HUH?
THE PHONE ...
BRRRRING
UH-HUH.
S'ringing.
BRRRRRING
YOU'RE NOT GONNA AN-SWER?
BRRR...
I ALREADY KNEW.
UH-UH.
JUST LIKE IN COLLEGE.
PHONE CALLS FROM SENSEI...
CALLS I DIDN'T WANT TO ANSWER.
A CALL I NEVER WANTED TO RECEIVE.

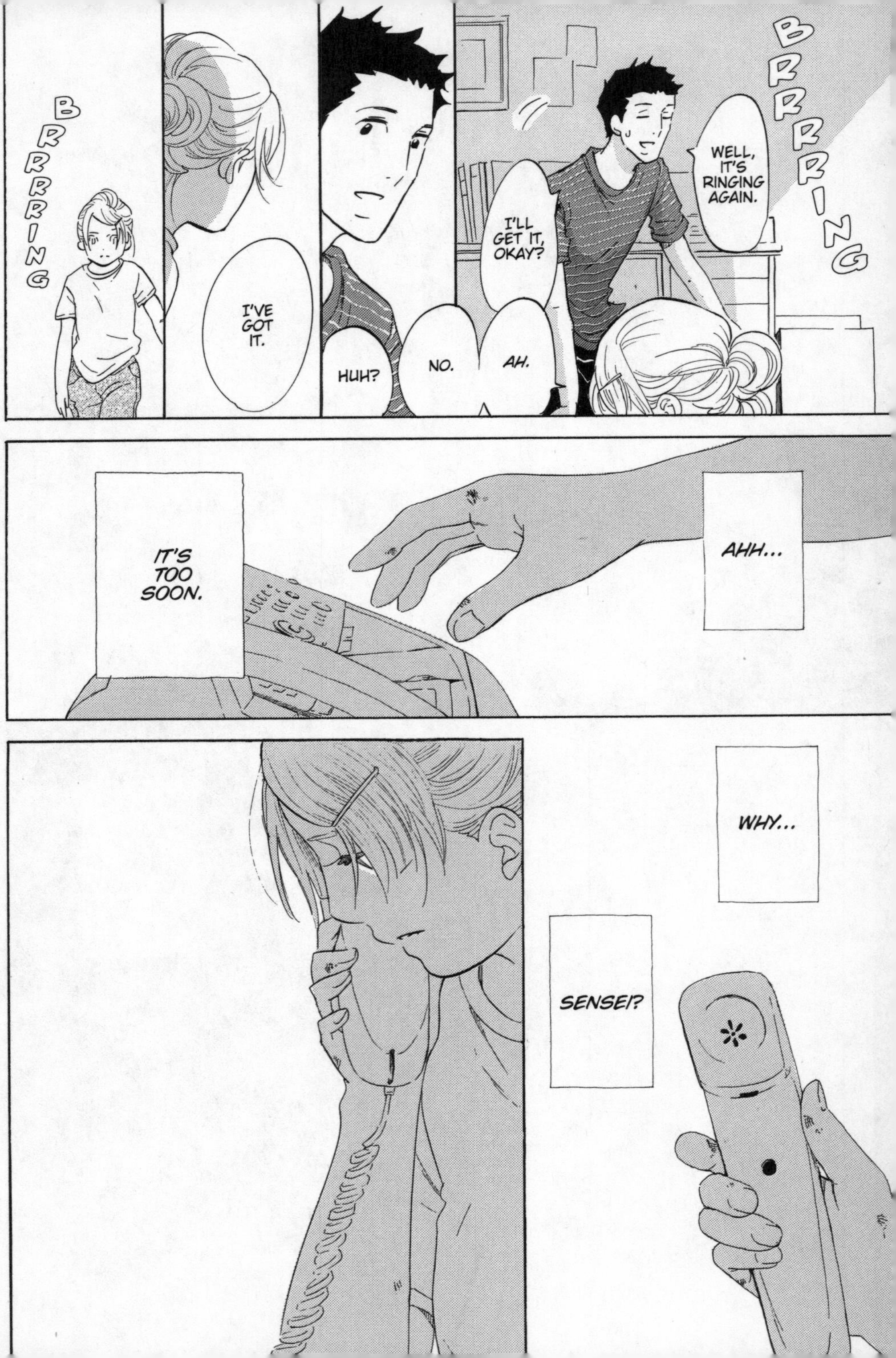
BRRRRING
WELL, IT'S RINGING AGAIN.
I'LL GET IT, OKAY?
AH.
NO.
HUH?
I'VE GOT IT.
BRRRRING
AHH...
IT'S TOO SOON.
WHY...
SENSEI?

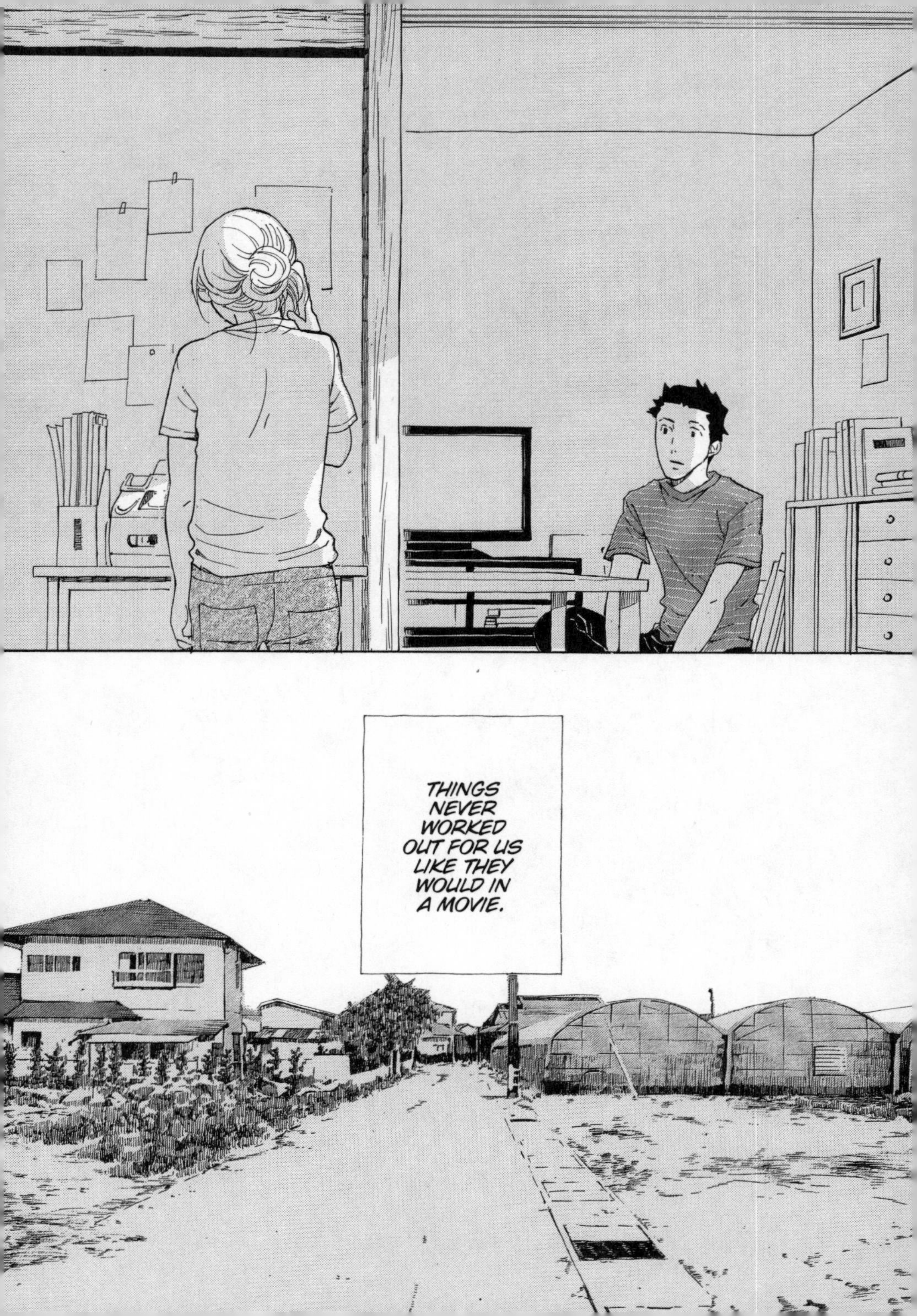
THINGS NEVER WORKED OUT FOR US LIKE THEY WOULD IN A MOVIE.

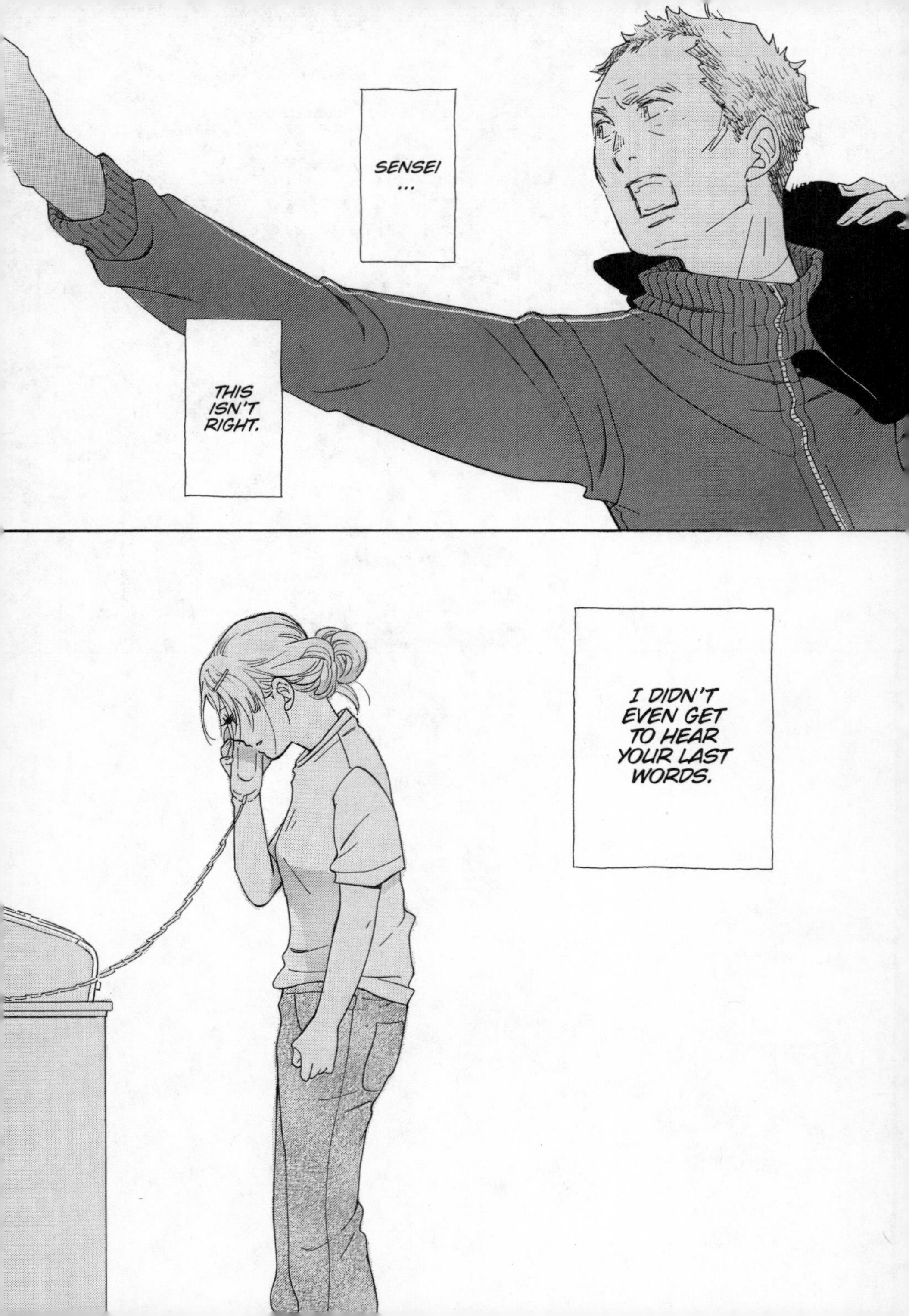
SENSEI ...
THIS ISN'T RIGHT.
I DIDN'T EVEN GET TO HEAR YOUR LAST WORDS.

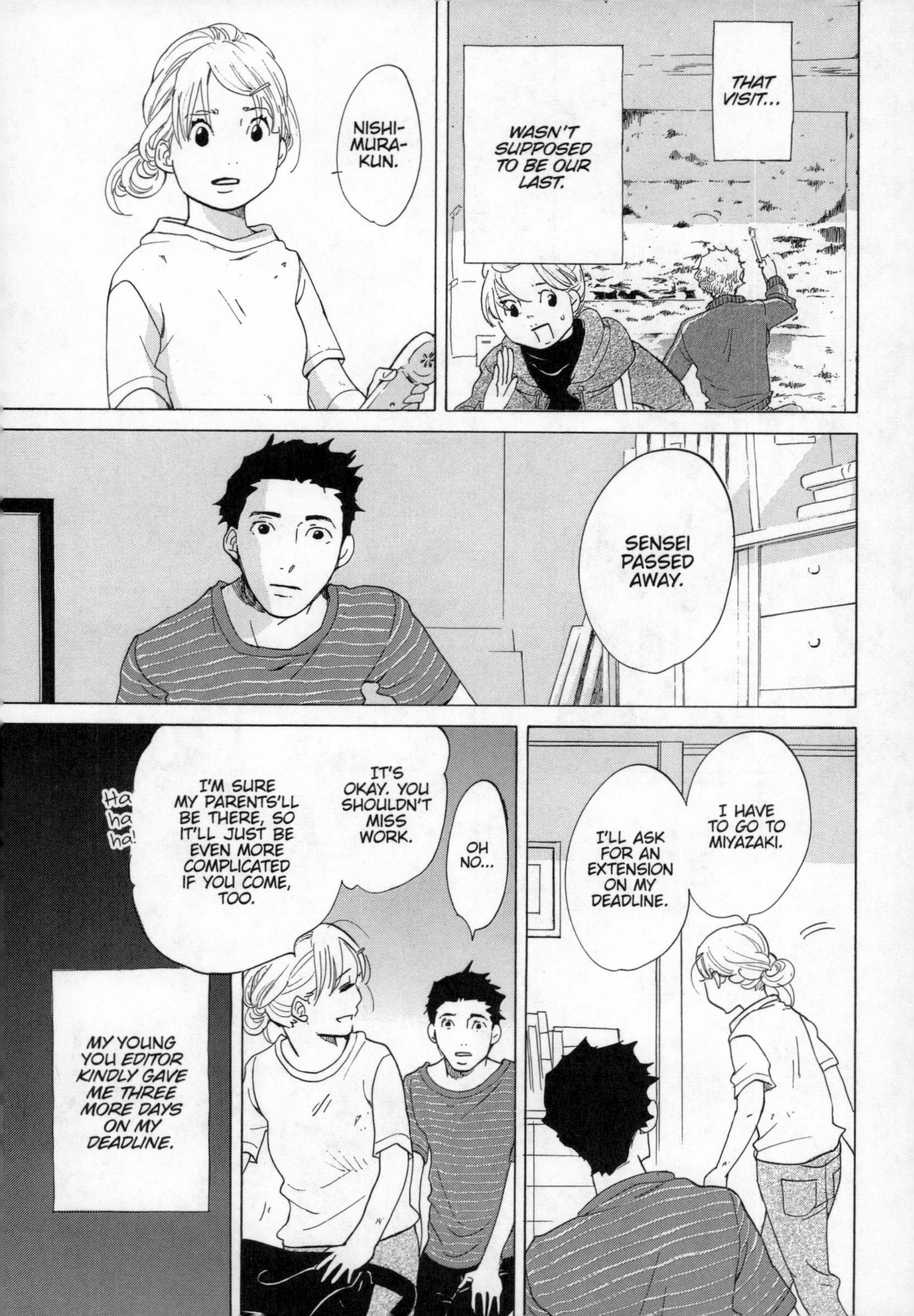
THAT VISIT...
WASN'T SUPPOSED TO BE OUR LAST.
NISHI-MURA-KUN.
SENSEI PASSED AWAY.
I HAVE TO GO TO MIYAZAKI.
I'LL ASK FOR AN EXTENSION ON MY DEADLINE.
OH NO...
IT'S OKAY. YOU SHOULDN'T MISS WORK.
I'M SURE MY PARENTS'LL BE THERE, SO IT'LL JUST BE EVEN MORE COMPLICATED IF YOU COME, TOO.
Ha ha ha!
MY YOUNG YOU EDITOR KINDLY GAVE ME THREE MORE DAYS ON MY DEADLINE.

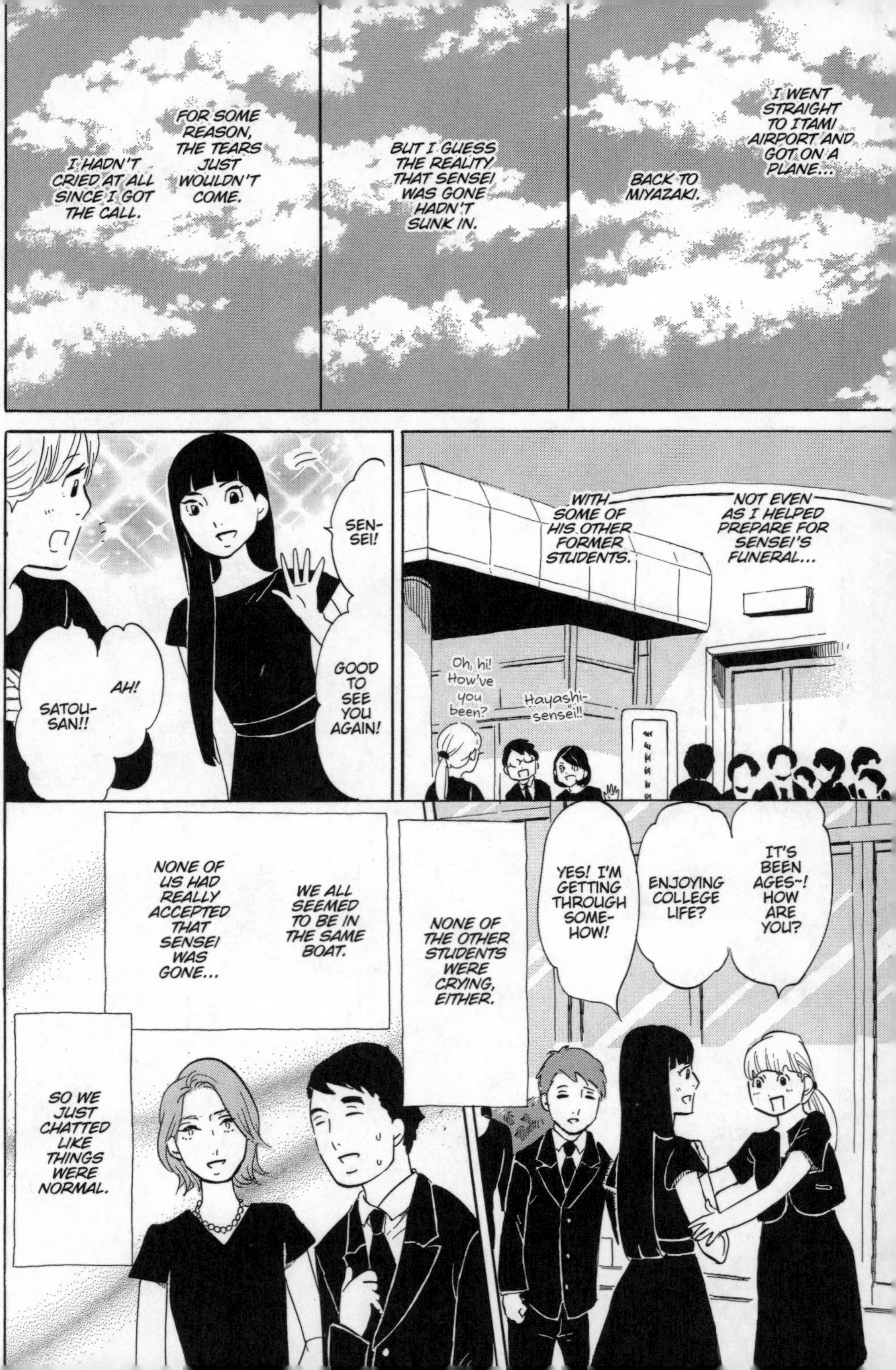
I WENT STRAIGHT TO ITAMI AIRPORT AND GOT ON A PLANE…
BACK TO MIYAZAKI.
BUT I GUESS THE REALITY THAT SENSEI WAS GONE HADN'T SUNK IN.
FOR SOME REASON, THE TEARS JUST WOULDN'T COME.
I HADN'T CRIED AT ALL SINCE I GOT THE CALL.
NOT EVEN AS I HELPED PREPARE FOR SENSEI'S FUNERAL…
WITH SOME OF HIS OTHER FORMER STUDENTS.
Hayashi-sensei!!
Oh, hi! How've you been?
SEN-SEI!
GOOD TO SEE YOU AGAIN!
AH!
SATOU-SAN!!
IT'S BEEN AGES~! HOW ARE YOU?
ENJOYING COLLEGE LIFE?
YES! I'M GETTING THROUGH SOME-HOW!
NONE OF THE OTHER STUDENTS WERE CRYING, EITHER.
WE ALL SEEMED TO BE IN THE SAME BOAT.
NONE OF US HAD REALLY ACCEPTED THAT SENSEI WAS GONE…
SO WE JUST CHATTED LIKE THINGS WERE NORMAL.

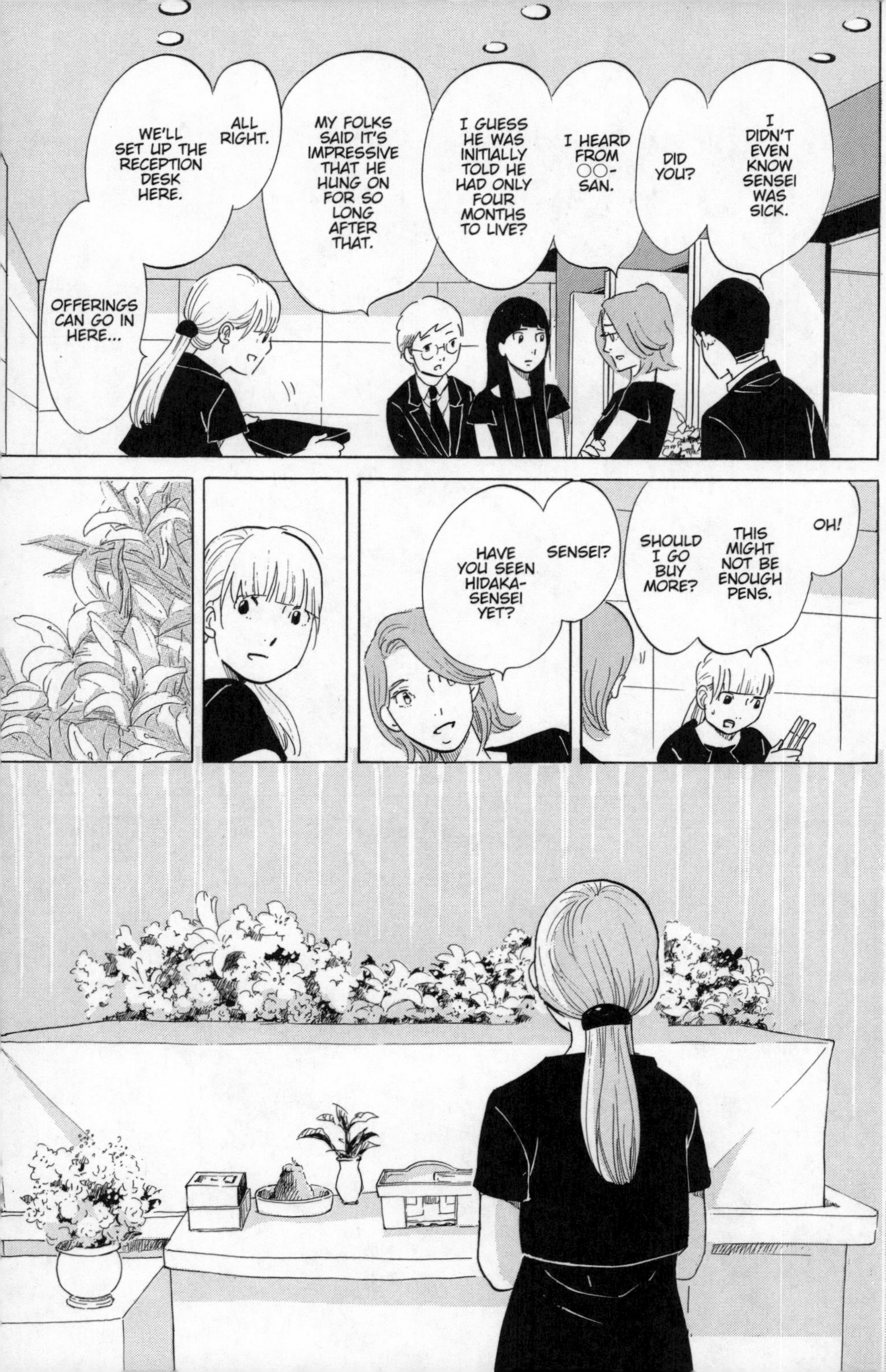
I DIDN'T EVEN KNOW SENSEI WAS SICK.
DID YOU?
I HEARD FROM ○○-SAN.
I GUESS HE WAS INITIALLY TOLD HE HAD ONLY FOUR MONTHS TO LIVE?
MY FOLKS SAID IT'S IMPRESSIVE THAT HE HUNG ON FOR SO LONG AFTER THAT.
ALL RIGHT.
WE'LL SET UP THE RECEPTION DESK HERE.
OFFERINGS CAN GO IN HERE...
OH!
THIS MIGHT NOT BE ENOUGH PENS.
SHOULD I GO BUY MORE?
SENSEI?
HAVE YOU SEEN HIDAKA-SENSEI YET?

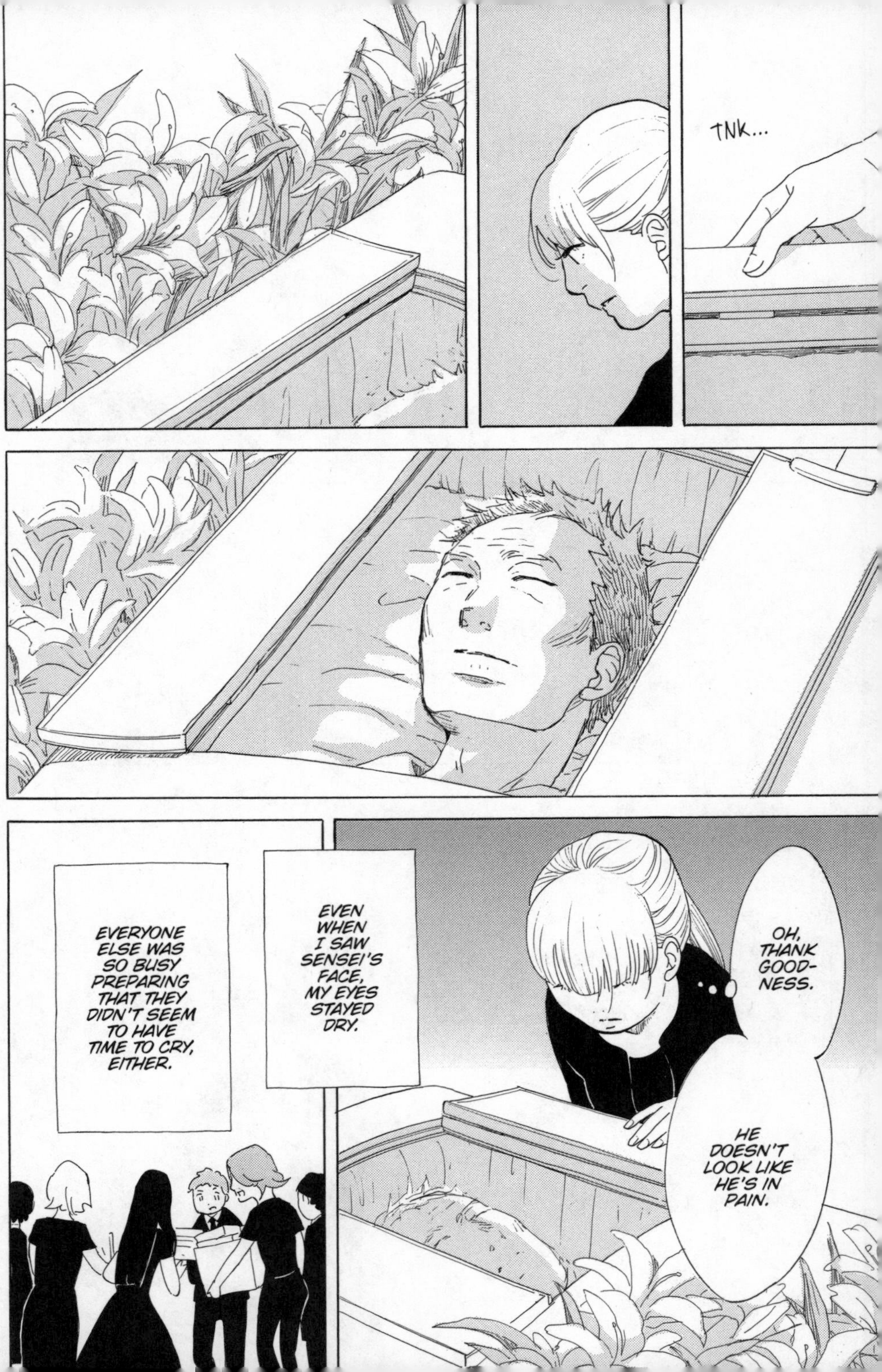
TNK...
OH, THANK GOODNESS.
HE DOESN'T LOOK LIKE HE'S IN PAIN.
EVEN WHEN I SAW SENSEI'S FACE, MY EYES STAYED DRY.
EVERYONE ELSE WAS SO BUSY PREPARING THAT THEY DIDN'T SEEM TO HAVE TIME TO CRY, EITHER.

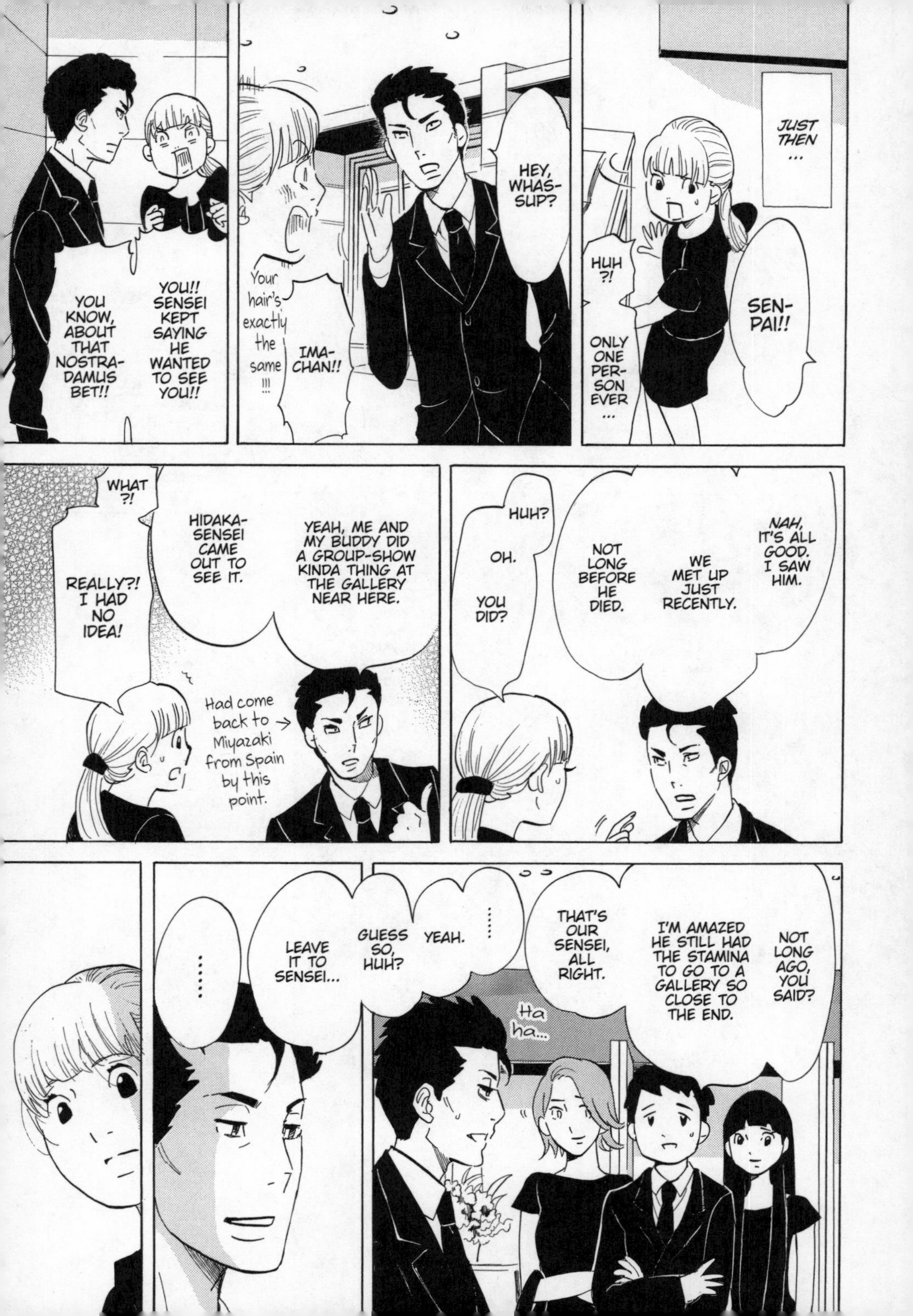
JUST THEN ...
SEN-PAI!!
HUH ?!
ONLY ONE PERSON EVER ...
HEY, WHASSUP?
IMA-CHAN!!
Your hair's exactly the same !!!
YOU!! SENSEI KEPT SAYING HE WANTED TO SEE YOU!!
YOU KNOW, ABOUT THAT NOSTRADAMUS BET!!
NAH, IT'S ALL GOOD. I SAW HIM.
WE MET UP JUST RECENTLY.
NOT LONG BEFORE HE DIED.
HUH?
OH.
YOU DID?
YEAH, ME AND MY BUDDY DID A GROUP-SHOW KINDA THING AT THE GALLERY NEAR HERE.
HIDAKA-SENSEI CAME OUT TO SEE IT.
WHAT ?!
REALLY?! I HAD NO IDEA!
Had come back to Miyazaki from Spain by this point.
NOT LONG AGO, YOU SAID?
I'M AMAZED HE STILL HAD THE STAMINA TO GO TO A GALLERY SO CLOSE TO THE END.
THAT'S OUR SENSEI, ALL RIGHT.
Ha ha...
......
YEAH.
GUESS SO, HUH?
LEAVE IT TO SENSEI...
......

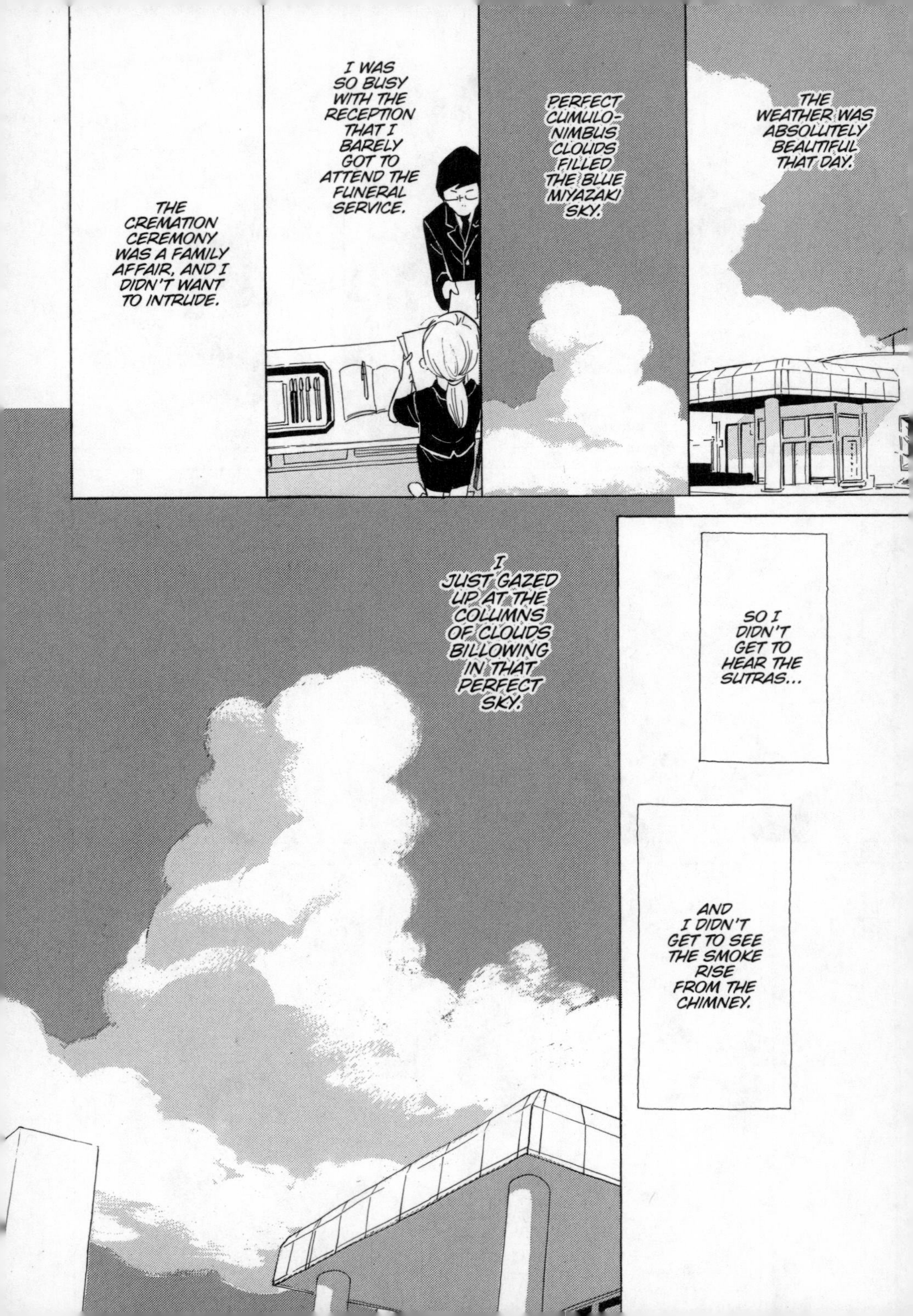
THE WEATHER WAS ABSOLUTELY BEAUTIFUL THAT DAY.
PERFECT CUMULO-NIMBUS CLOUDS FILLED THE BLUE MIYAZAKI SKY.
I WAS SO BUSY WITH THE RECEPTION THAT I BARELY GOT TO ATTEND THE FUNERAL SERVICE.
THE CREMATION CEREMONY WAS A FAMILY AFFAIR, AND I DIDN'T WANT TO INTRUDE.
SO I DIDN'T GET TO HEAR THE SUTRAS...
AND I DIDN'T GET TO SEE THE SMOKE RISE FROM THE CHIMNEY.
I JUST GAZED UP AT THE COLUMNS OF CLOUDS BILLOWING IN THAT PERFECT SKY.

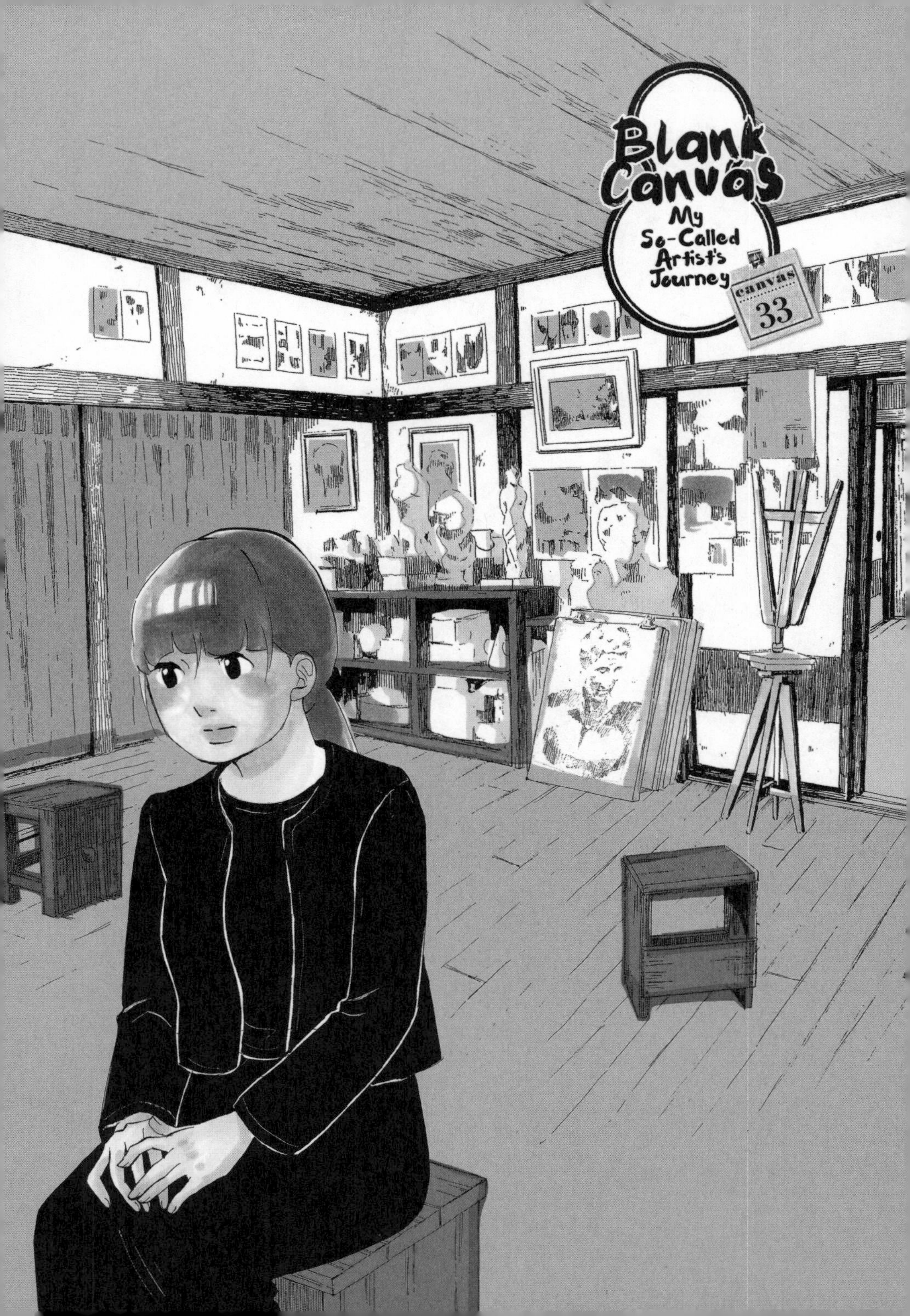
Blank Canvas
My So-Called Artist's Journey
canvas
33

Blank
Canvas
My So-Called
Artist's Journey

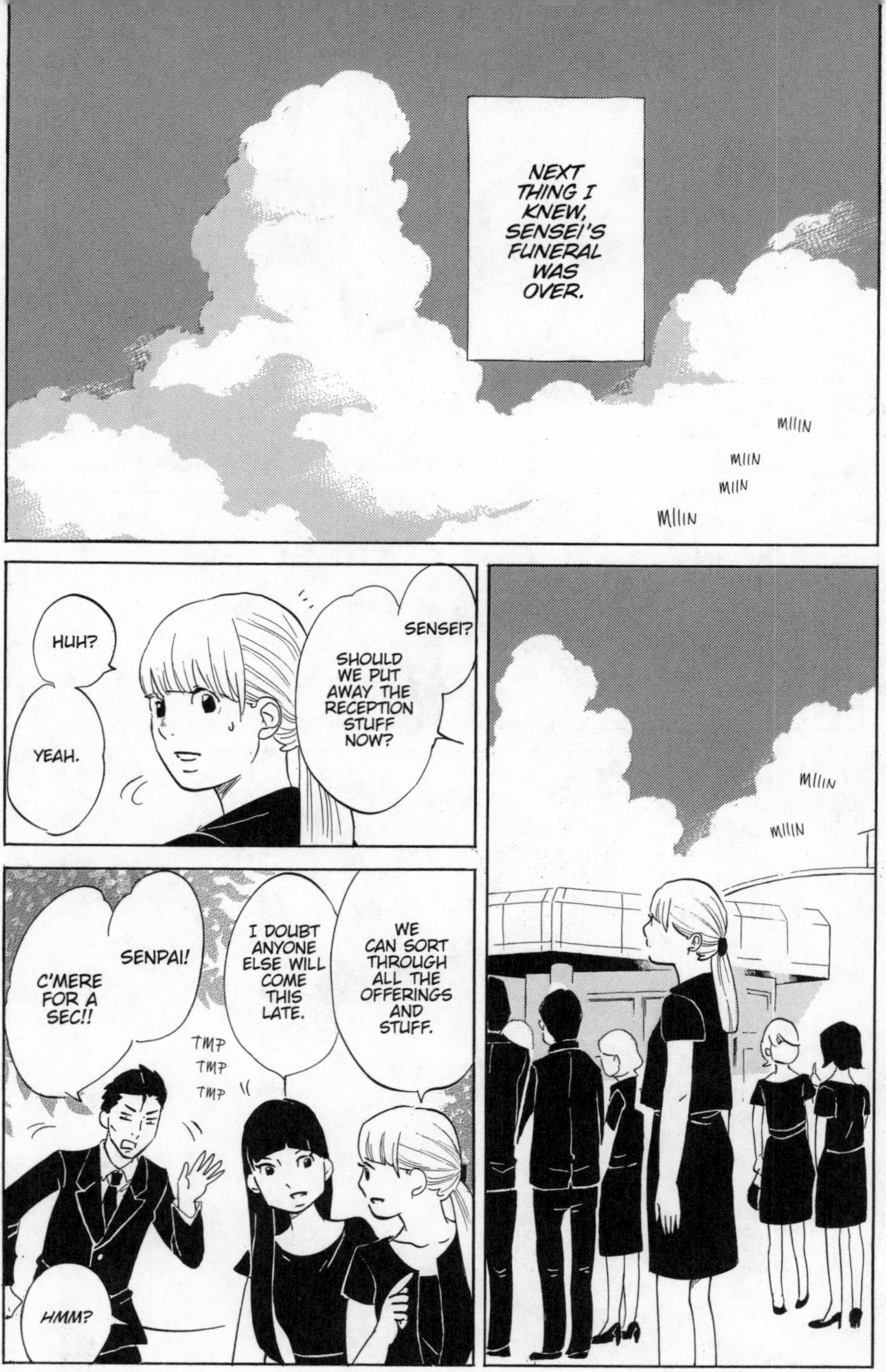
NEXT THING I KNEW, SENSEI'S FUNERAL WAS OVER.
MIIIN
MIIN
MIIN
MIIIN
MIIIN
MIIIN
SENSEI? SHOULD WE PUT AWAY THE RECEPTION STUFF NOW?
HUH?
YEAH.
WE CAN SORT THROUGH ALL THE OFFERINGS AND STUFF.
I DOUBT ANYONE ELSE WILL COME THIS LATE.
SENPAI! C'MERE FOR A SEC!!
TMP TMP TMP
HMM?

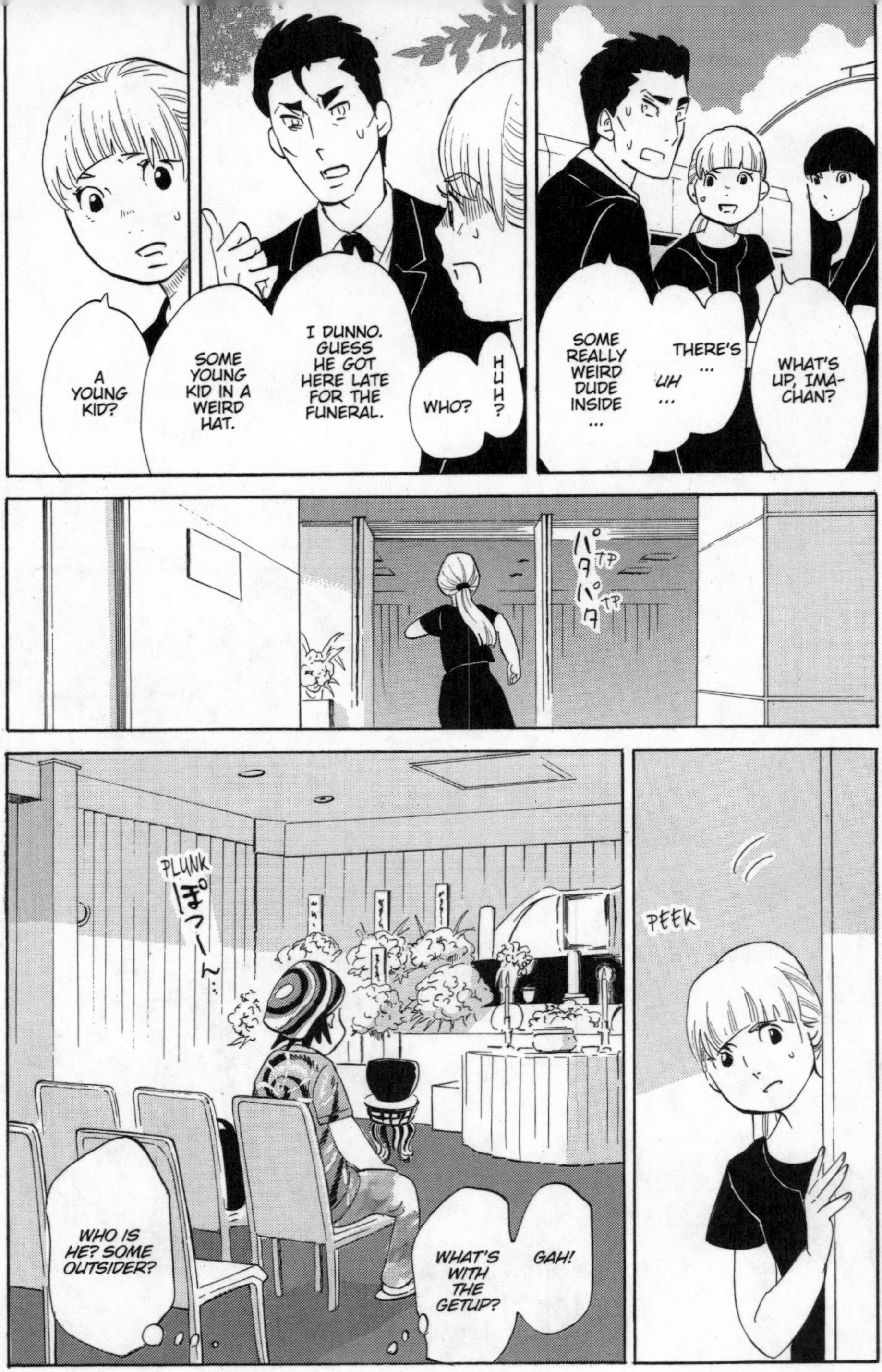
WHAT'S UP, IMA-CHAN?
THERE'S ... UH ... SOME REALLY WEIRD DUDE INSIDE ...
HUH?
WHO?
I DUNNO. GUESS HE GOT HERE LATE FOR THE FUNERAL.
SOME YOUNG KID IN A WEIRD HAT.
A YOUNG KID?
パタパタ TP TP
PEEK
GAH!
WHAT'S WITH THE GETUP?
WHO IS HE? SOME OUTSIDER?
PLUNK
ぽつーん…

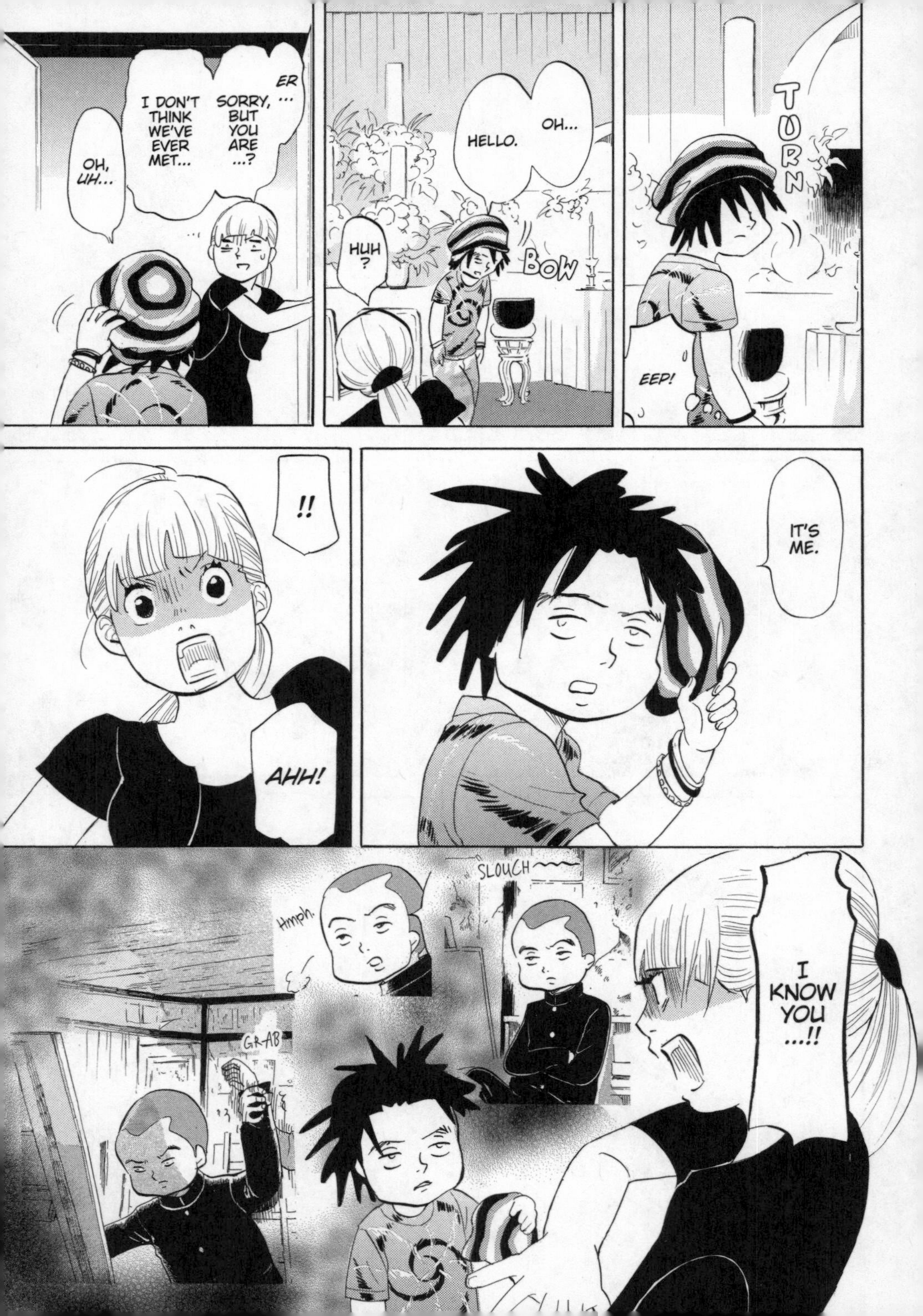
TURN
EEP!
OH...
HELLO.
BOW
HUH?
ER...
SORRY, BUT YOU ARE ...?
I DON'T THINK WE'VE EVER MET...
OH, UH...
...
IT'S ME.
!!
AHH!
I KNOW YOU ...!!
SLOUCH
Hmph.
GRAB

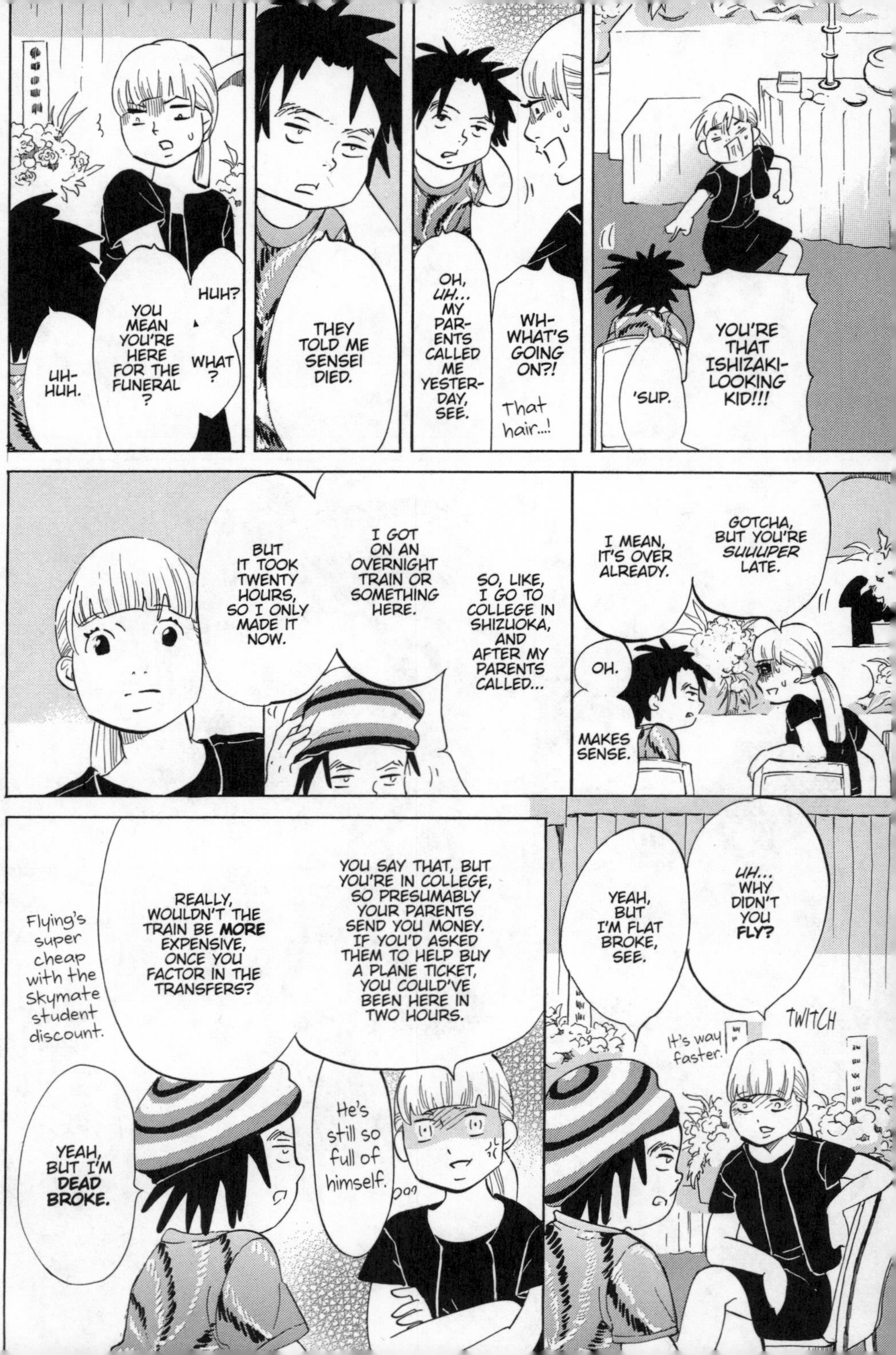
YOU'RE THAT ISHIZAKI-LOOKING KID!!!
'SUP.
WH-WHAT'S GOING ON?!
That hair...!
OH, UH... MY PARENTS CALLED ME YESTERDAY, SEE.
THEY TOLD ME SENSEI DIED.
HUH? WHAT?
YOU MEAN YOU'RE HERE FOR THE FUNERAL?
UH-HUH.
GOTCHA, BUT YOU'RE SUUUPER LATE.
I MEAN, IT'S OVER ALREADY.
OH.
MAKES SENSE.
SO, LIKE, I GO TO COLLEGE IN SHIZUOKA, AND AFTER MY PARENTS CALLED...
I GOT ON AN OVERNIGHT TRAIN OR SOMETHING HERE.
BUT IT TOOK TWENTY HOURS, SO I ONLY MADE IT NOW.
UH... WHY DIDN'T YOU FLY?
YEAH, BUT I'M FLAT BROKE, SEE.
TWITCH
It's way faster.
YOU SAY THAT, BUT YOU'RE IN COLLEGE, SO PRESUMABLY YOUR PARENTS SEND YOU MONEY. IF YOU'D ASKED THEM TO HELP BUY A PLANE TICKET, YOU COULD'VE BEEN HERE IN TWO HOURS.
REALLY, WOULDN'T THE TRAIN BE MORE EXPENSIVE, ONCE YOU FACTOR IN THE TRANSFERS?
Flying's super cheap with the Skymate student discount.
He's still so full of himself.
YEAH, BUT I'M DEAD BROKE.

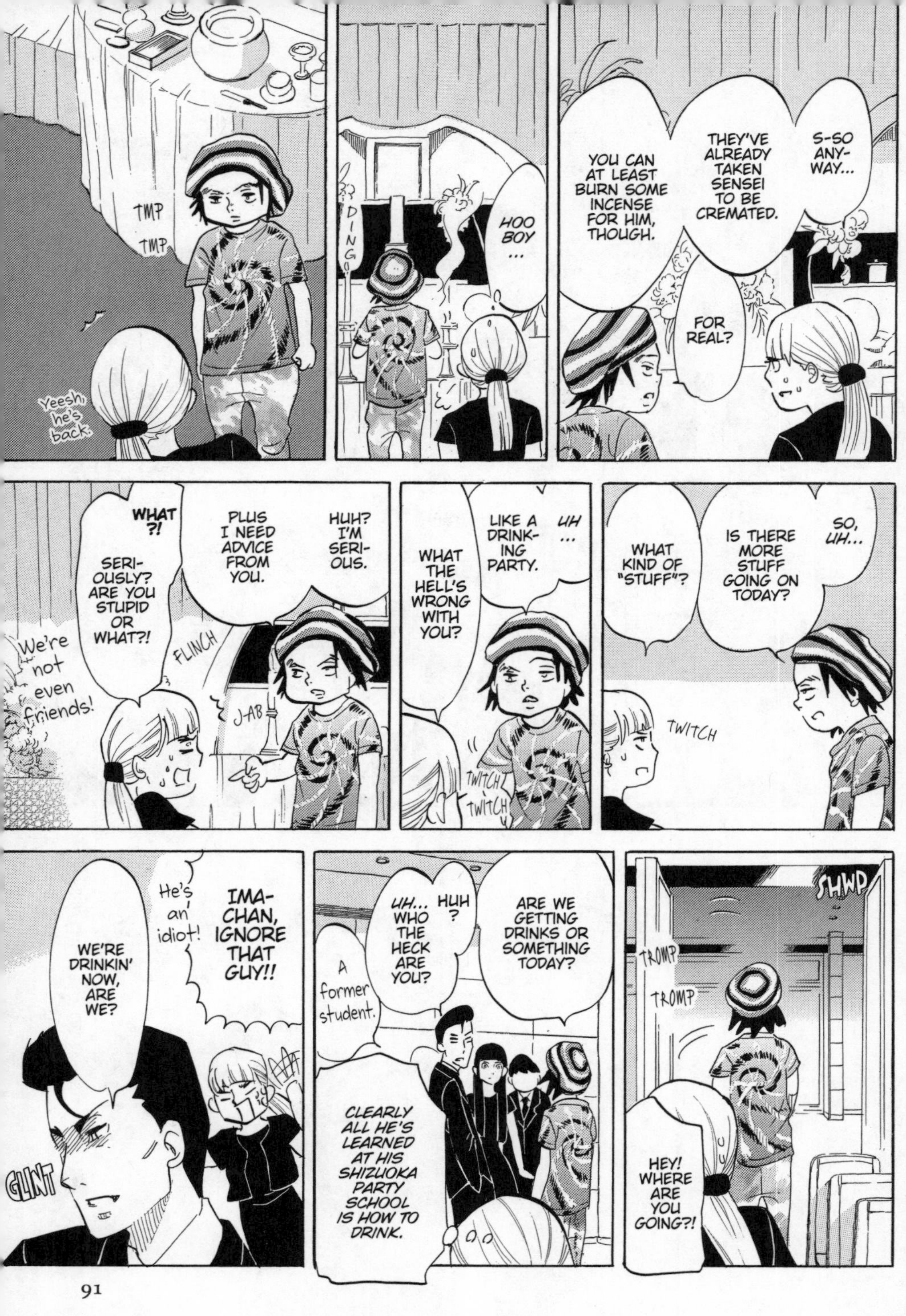
S-SO ANYWAY...
THEY'VE ALREADY TAKEN SENSEI TO BE CREMATED.
YOU CAN AT LEAST BURN SOME INCENSE FOR HIM, THOUGH.
FOR REAL?
DING
HOO BOY ...
TMP
TMP
Yeesh, he's back.
SO, UH...
IS THERE MORE STUFF GOING ON TODAY?
WHAT KIND OF "STUFF"?
TWITCH
UH ...
LIKE A DRINKING PARTY.
WHAT THE HELL'S WRONG WITH YOU?
TWITCH
TWITCH
HUH? I'M SERIOUS.
PLUS I NEED ADVICE FROM YOU.
WHAT?!
SERIOUSLY? ARE YOU STUPID OR WHAT?!
FLINCH
JAB
We're not even friends!
SHWP
TROMP
TROMP
HEY! WHERE ARE YOU GOING?!
ARE WE GETTING DRINKS OR SOMETHING TODAY?
HUH ?
UH... WHO THE HECK ARE YOU?
A former student.
CLEARLY ALL HE'S LEARNED AT HIS SHIZUOKA PARTY SCHOOL IS HOW TO DRINK.
IMA-CHAN, IGNORE THAT GUY!!
He's an' idiot!
WE'RE DRINKIN' NOW, ARE WE?
GLINT

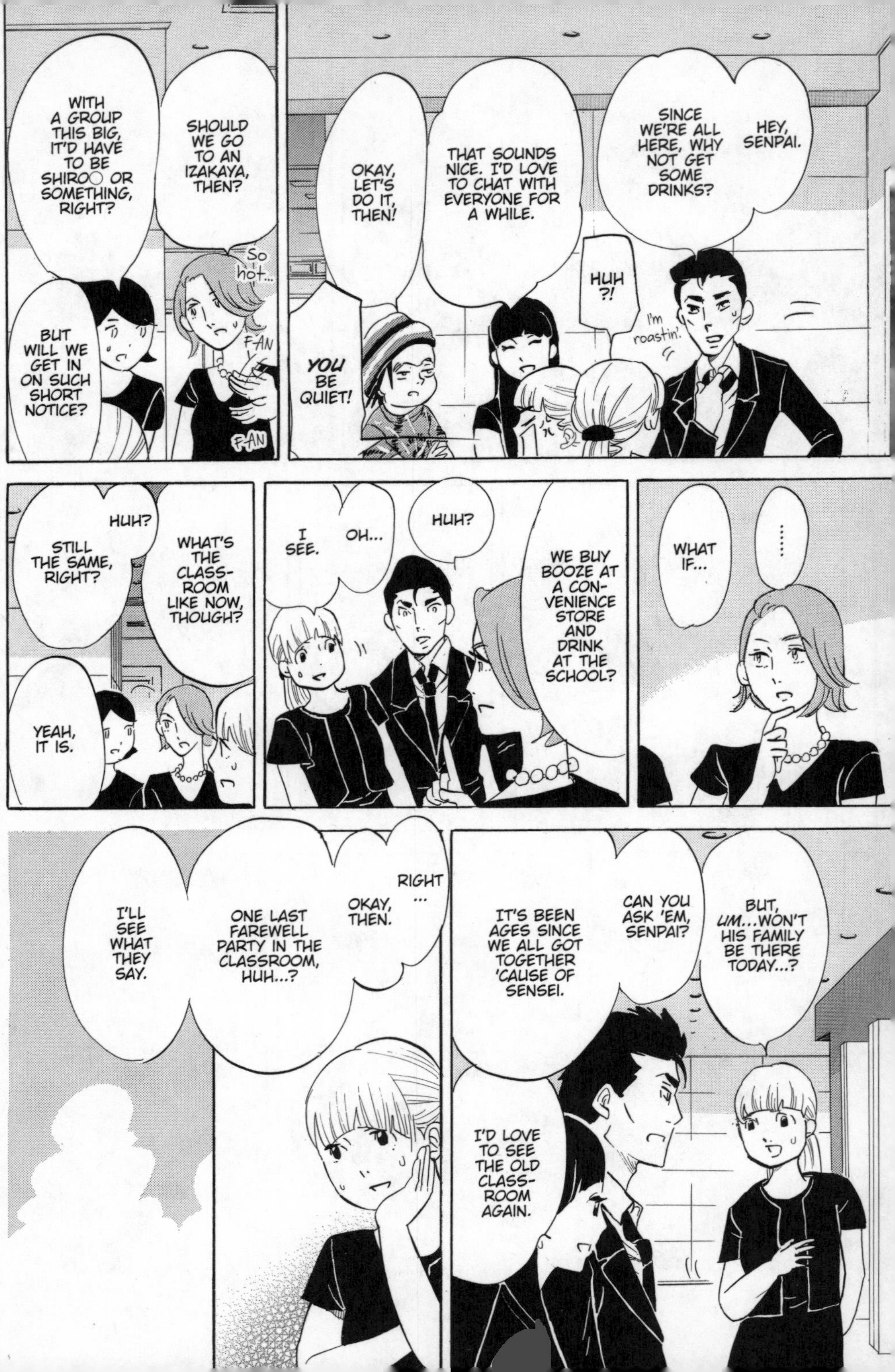
HEY, SENPAI.
SINCE WE'RE ALL HERE, WHY NOT GET SOME DRINKS?
I'm roastin'.
HUH?!
THAT SOUNDS NICE. I'D LOVE TO CHAT WITH EVERYONE FOR A WHILE.
OKAY, LET'S DO IT, THEN!
YOU BE QUIET!
SHOULD WE GO TO AN IZAKAYA, THEN?
WITH A GROUP THIS BIG, IT'D HAVE TO BE SHIRO○ OR SOMETHING, RIGHT?
So hot...
FAN
BUT WILL WE GET IN ON SUCH SHORT NOTICE?
FAN
......
WHAT IF...
WE BUY BOOZE AT A CONVENIENCE STORE AND DRINK AT THE SCHOOL?
HUH?
OH...
I SEE.
WHAT'S THE CLASSROOM LIKE NOW, THOUGH?
HUH?
STILL THE SAME, RIGHT?
YEAH, IT IS.
BUT, *UM*...WON'T HIS FAMILY BE THERE TODAY...?
CAN YOU ASK 'EM, SENPAI?
IT'S BEEN AGES SINCE WE ALL GOT TOGETHER 'CAUSE OF SENSEI.
I'D LOVE TO SEE THE OLD CLASSROOM AGAIN.
RIGHT...
OKAY, THEN.
ONE LAST FAREWELL PARTY IN THE CLASSROOM, HUH...?
I'LL SEE WHAT THEY SAY.

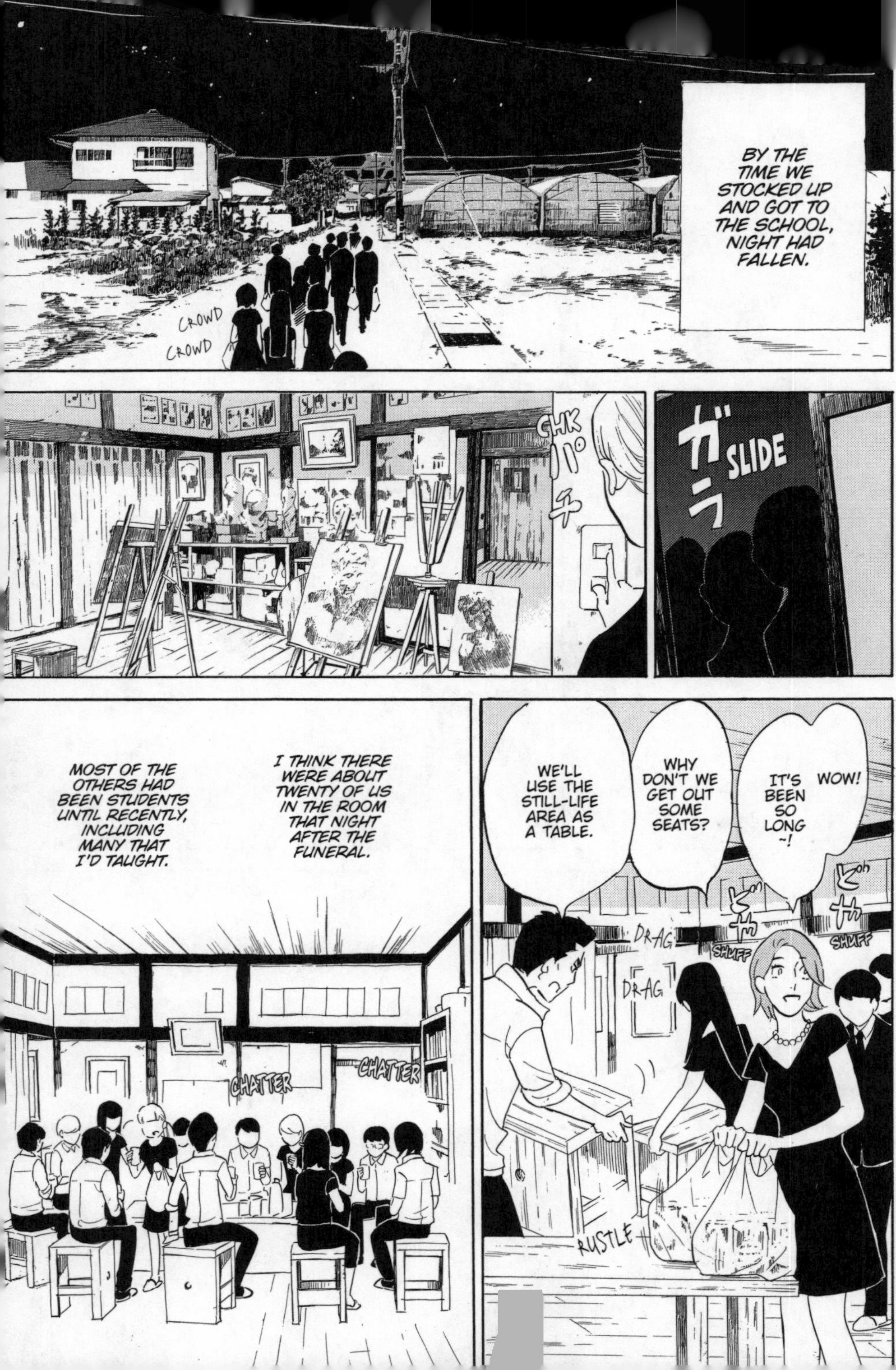
BY THE TIME WE STOCKED UP AND GOT TO THE SCHOOL, NIGHT HAD FALLEN.
CROWD
CROWD
ガラ
SLIDE
パチ
CHK
WOW!
IT'S BEEN SO LONG~!
WHY DON'T WE GET OUT SOME SEATS?
WE'LL USE THE STILL-LIFE AREA AS A TABLE.
どか
SHUFF
どか
SHUFF
DRAG
DRAG
RUSTLE
I THINK THERE WERE ABOUT TWENTY OF US IN THE ROOM THAT NIGHT AFTER THE FUNERAL.
MOST OF THE OTHERS HAD BEEN STUDENTS UNTIL RECENTLY, INCLUDING MANY THAT I'D TAUGHT.
CHATTER
CHATTER

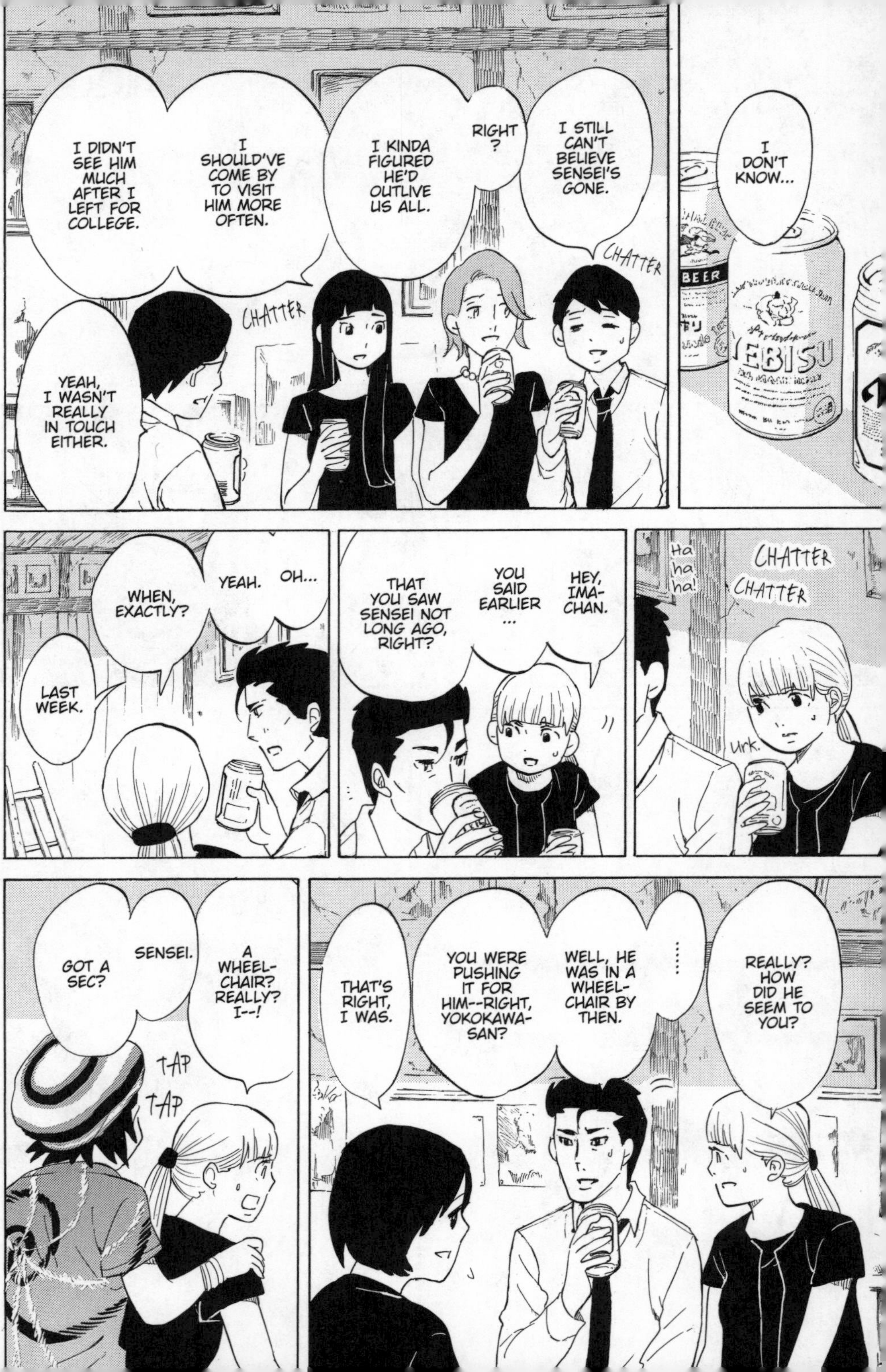
I DON'T KNOW...
I STILL CAN'T BELIEVE SENSEI'S GONE.
CHATTER
RIGHT?
I KINDA FIGURED HE'D OUTLIVE US ALL.
I SHOULD'VE COME BY TO VISIT HIM MORE OFTEN.
I DIDN'T SEE HIM MUCH AFTER I LEFT FOR COLLEGE.
CHATTER
YEAH, I WASN'T REALLY IN TOUCH EITHER.
CHATTER
CHATTER
Ha ha ha!
urk.
HEY, IMA-CHAN.
YOU SAID EARLIER...
THAT YOU SAW SENSEI NOT LONG AGO, RIGHT?
OH...
YEAH.
WHEN, EXACTLY?
LAST WEEK.
REALLY? HOW DID HE SEEM TO YOU?
......
WELL, HE WAS IN A WHEEL-CHAIR BY THEN.
YOU WERE PUSHING IT FOR HIM--RIGHT, YOKOKAWA-SAN?
THAT'S RIGHT, I WAS.
A WHEEL-CHAIR? REALLY? I--!
SENSEI.
GOT A SEC?
TAP
TAP

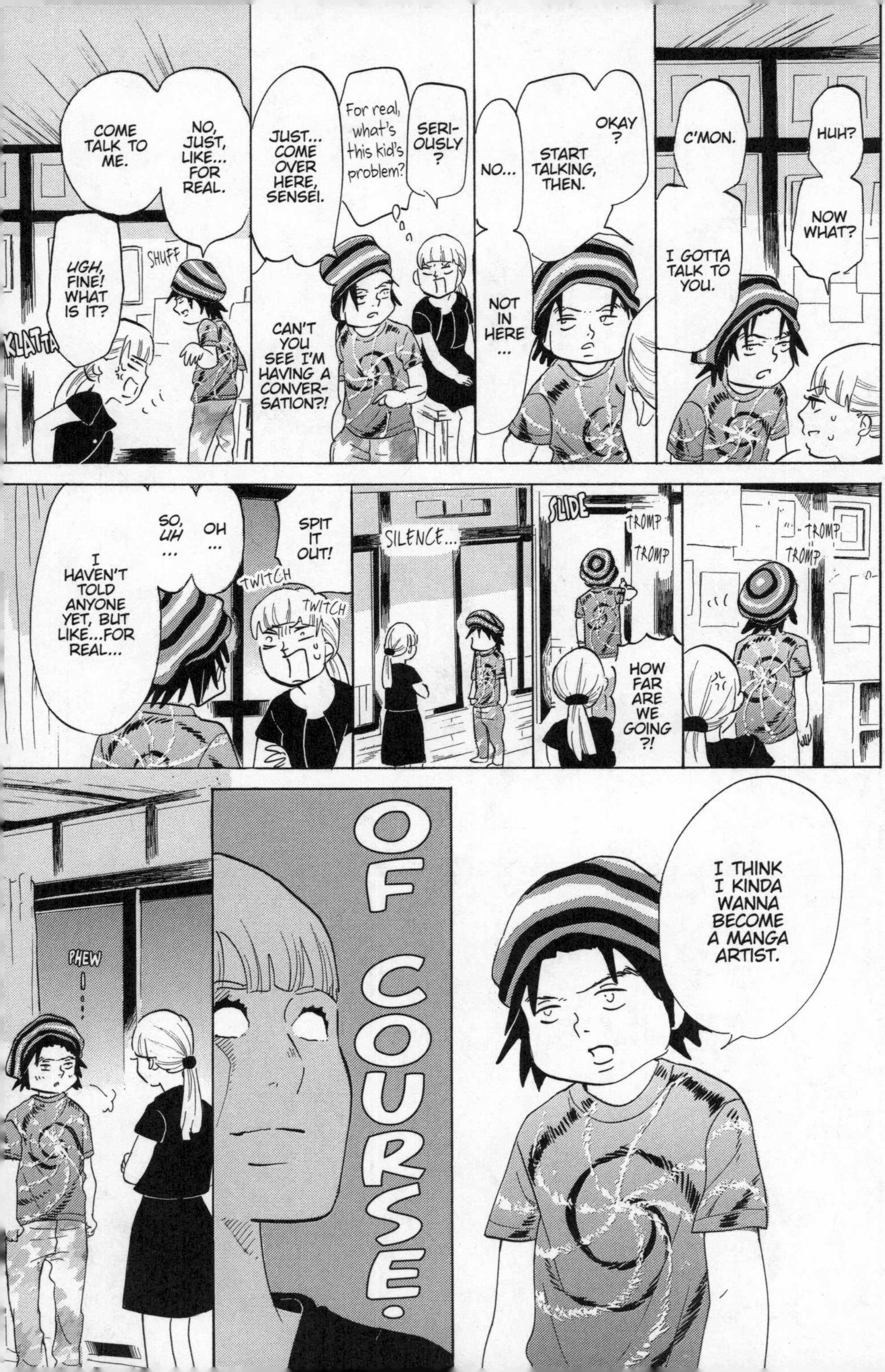
HUH?
C'MON.
NOW WHAT?
I GOTTA TALK TO YOU.
OKAY?
START TALKING, THEN.
NO...
NOT IN HERE...
SERIOUSLY?
For real, what's this kid's problem?
JUST... COME OVER HERE, SENSEI.
CAN'T YOU SEE I'M HAVING A CONVERSATION?!
NO, JUST, LIKE... FOR REAL.
COME TALK TO ME.
SHUFF
UGH, FINE! WHAT IS IT?
KLATTA
TROMP
TROMP
HOW FAR ARE WE GOING?!
SLIDE
TROMP
TROMP
SILENCE...
SPIT IT OUT!
TWITCH
TWITCH
OH...
SO, UH...
I HAVEN'T TOLD ANYONE YET, BUT LIKE...FOR REAL...
I THINK I KINDA WANNA BECOME A MANGA ARTIST.
OF COURSE.
PHEW

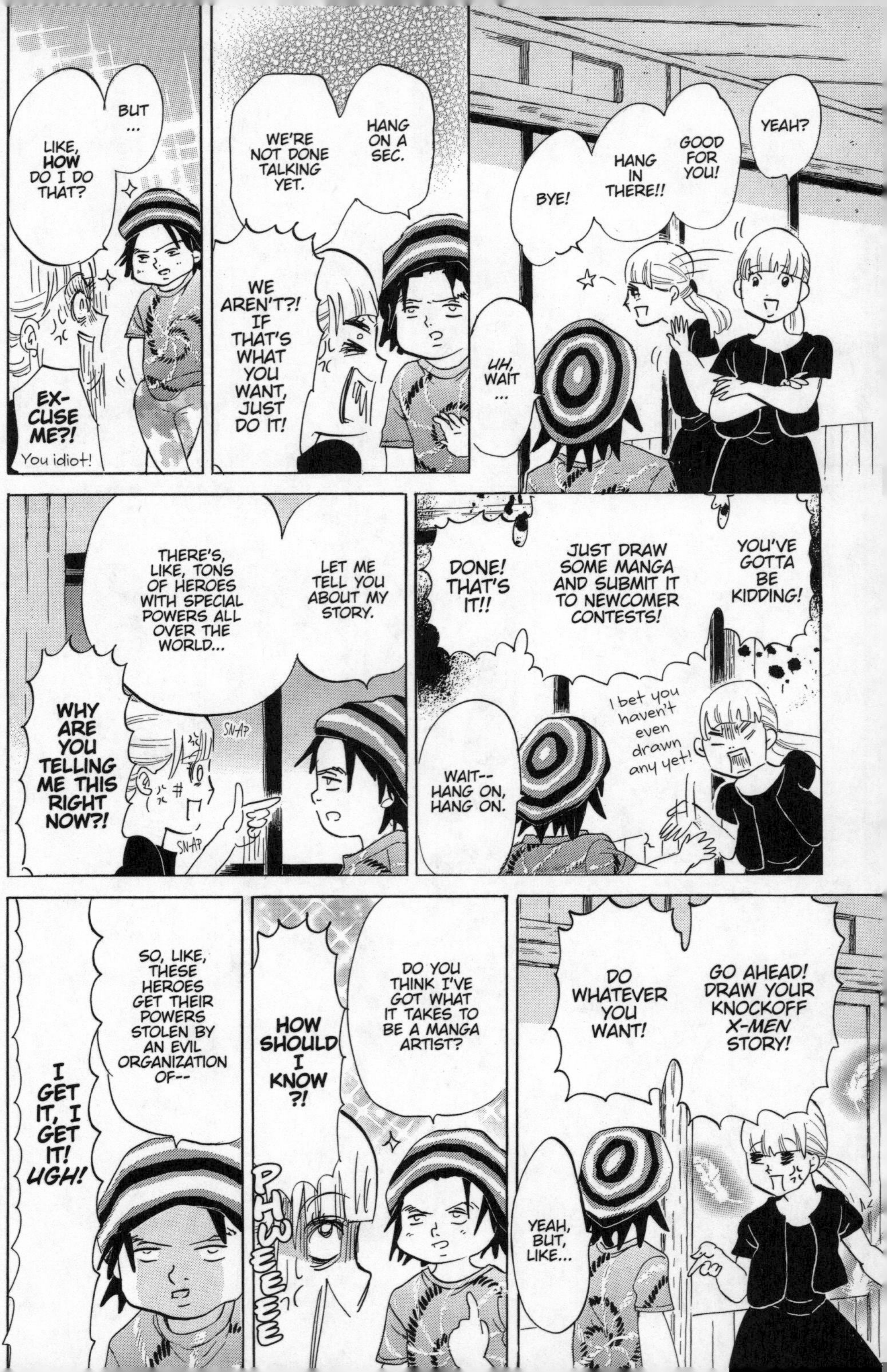
YEAH?
GOOD FOR YOU!
HANG IN THERE!!
BYE!
UH, WAIT ...
HANG ON A SEC.
WE'RE NOT DONE TALKING YET.
WE AREN'T?! IF THAT'S WHAT YOU WANT, JUST DO IT!
BUT ...
LIKE, HOW DO I DO THAT?
EX-CUSE ME?!
You idiot!
YOU'VE GOTTA BE KIDDING!
JUST DRAW SOME MANGA AND SUBMIT IT TO NEWCOMER CONTESTS!
DONE! THAT'S IT!!
I bet you haven't even drawn any yet!
WAIT-- HANG ON, HANG ON.
LET ME TELL YOU ABOUT MY STORY.
THERE'S, LIKE, TONS OF HEROES WITH SPECIAL POWERS ALL OVER THE WORLD...
WHY ARE YOU TELLING ME THIS RIGHT NOW?!
SNAP
SNAP
GO AHEAD! DRAW YOUR KNOCKOFF X-MEN STORY!
DO WHATEVER YOU WANT!
YEAH, BUT, LIKE...
DO YOU THINK I'VE GOT WHAT IT TAKES TO BE A MANGA ARTIST?
HOW SHOULD I KNOW?!
SO, LIKE, THESE HEROES GET THEIR POWERS STOLEN BY AN EVIL ORGANIZATION OF--
I GET IT, I GET IT! UGH!

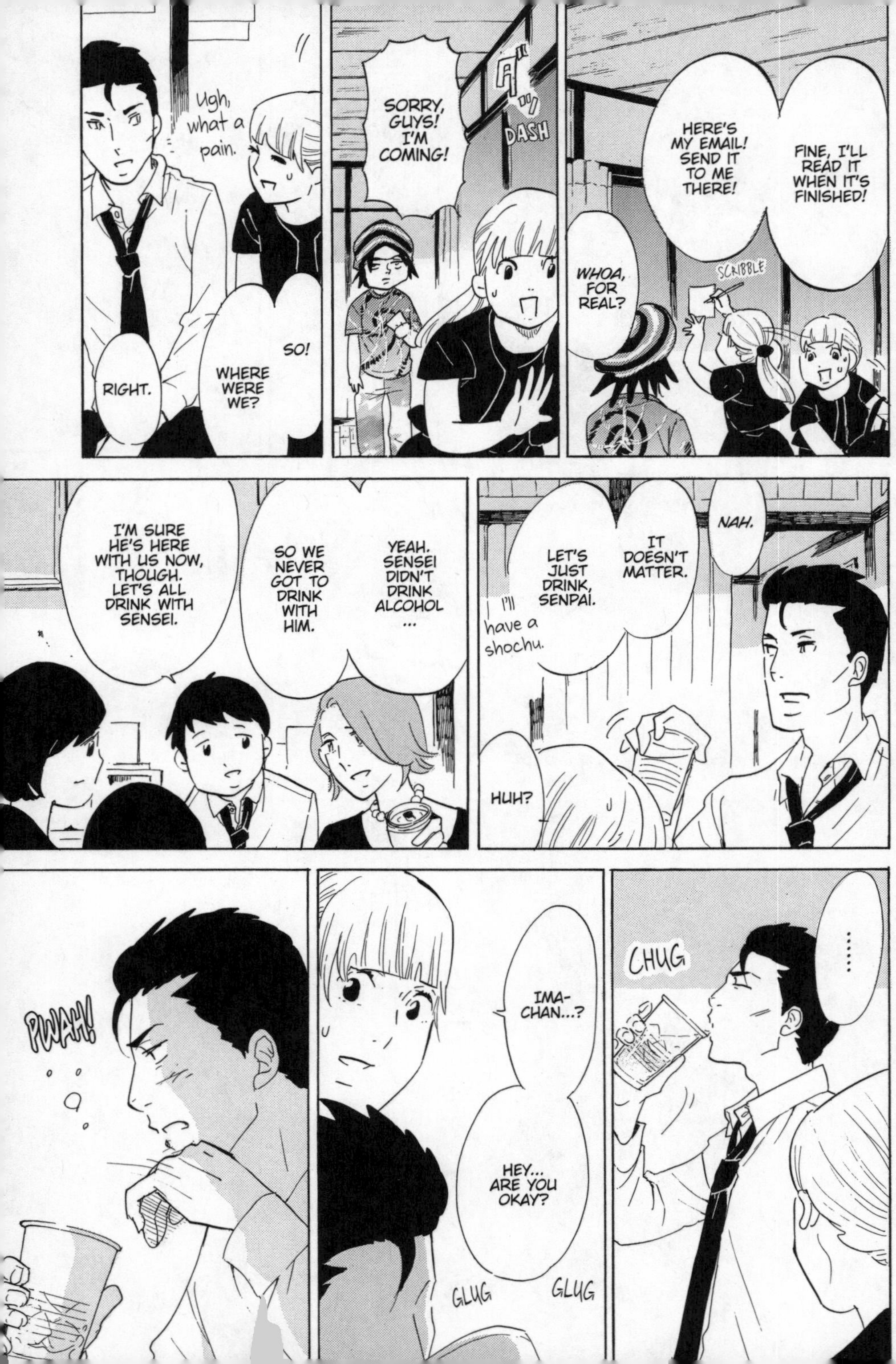
FINE, I'LL READ IT WHEN IT'S FINISHED!
HERE'S MY EMAIL! SEND IT TO ME THERE!
SCRIBBLE
WHOA, FOR REAL?
DASH
SORRY, GUYS! I'M COMING!
Ugh, what a pain.
SO!
WHERE WERE WE?
RIGHT.
NAH.
IT DOESN'T MATTER.
LET'S JUST DRINK, SENPAI.
I'll have a shochu.
HUH?
YEAH. SENSEI DIDN'T DRINK ALCOHOL...
SO WE NEVER GOT TO DRINK WITH HIM.
I'M SURE HE'S HERE WITH US NOW, THOUGH. LET'S ALL DRINK WITH SENSEI.
......
CHUG
IMA-CHAN...?
HEY... ARE YOU OKAY?
GLUG
GLUG
PWAH!

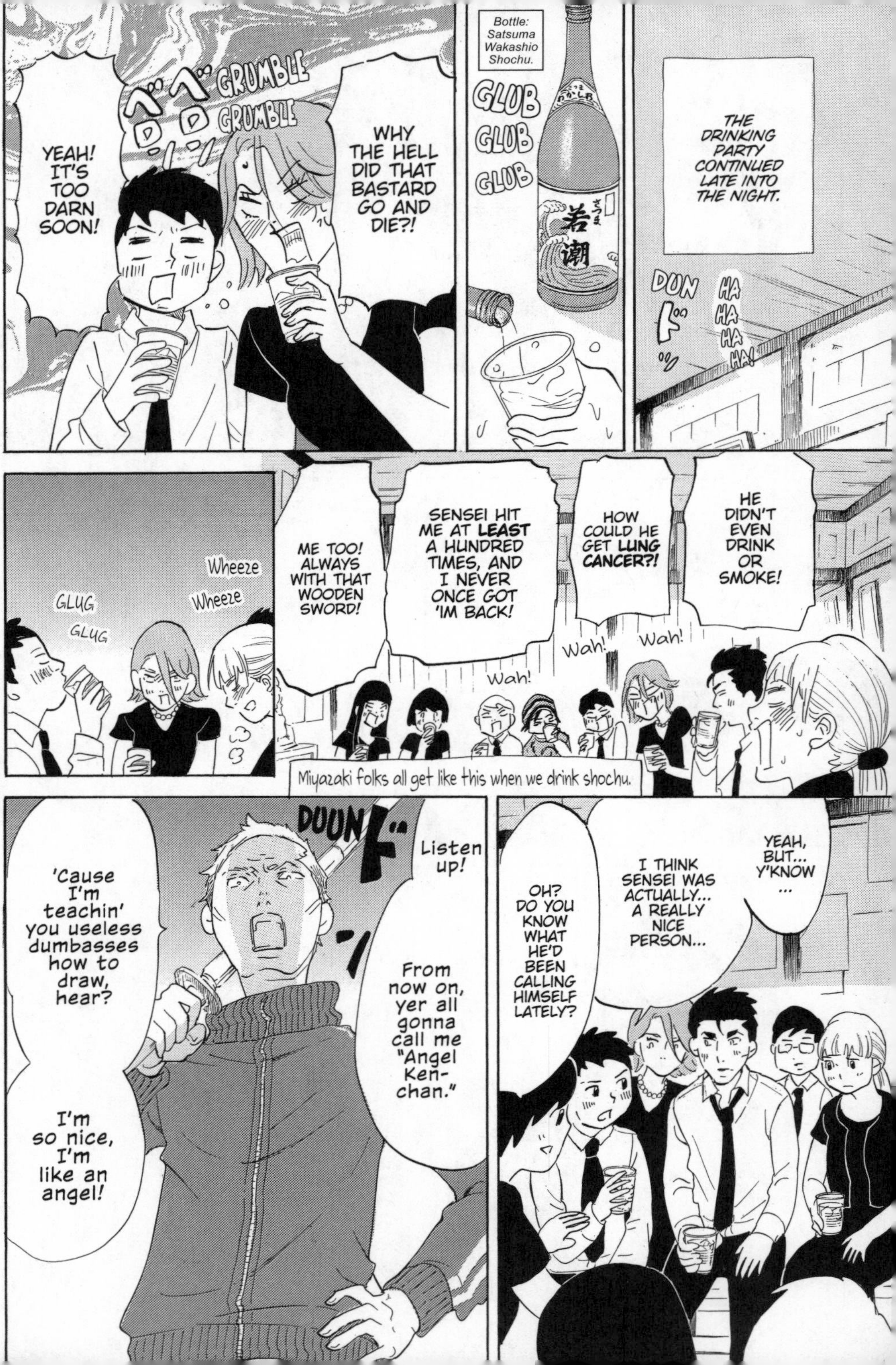
THE DRINKING PARTY CONTINUED LATE INTO THE NIGHT.
DUN
HA HA HA HA HA!
Bottle: Satsuma Wakashio Shochu.
GLUB GLUB GLUB
若潮
WHY THE HELL DID THAT BASTARD GO AND DIE?!
GRUMBLE GRUMBLE
YEAH! IT'S TOO DARN SOON!
HE DIDN'T EVEN DRINK OR SMOKE!
HOW COULD HE GET **LUNG CANCER?!**
SENSEI HIT ME AT **LEAST** A HUNDRED TIMES, AND I NEVER ONCE GOT 'IM BACK!
ME TOO! ALWAYS WITH THAT WOODEN SWORD!
Wah! Wah!
Wah!
Miyazaki folks all get like this when we drink shochu.
Wheeze Wheeze
GLUG GLUG
YEAH, BUT... Y'KNOW ...
I THINK SENSEI WAS ACTUALLY... A REALLY NICE PERSON...
OH? DO YOU KNOW WHAT HE'D BEEN CALLING HIMSELF LATELY?
DUUN
Listen up!
From now on, yer all gonna call me "Angel Ken-chan."
'Cause I'm teachin' you useless dumbasses how to draw, hear?
I'm so nice, I'm like an angel!

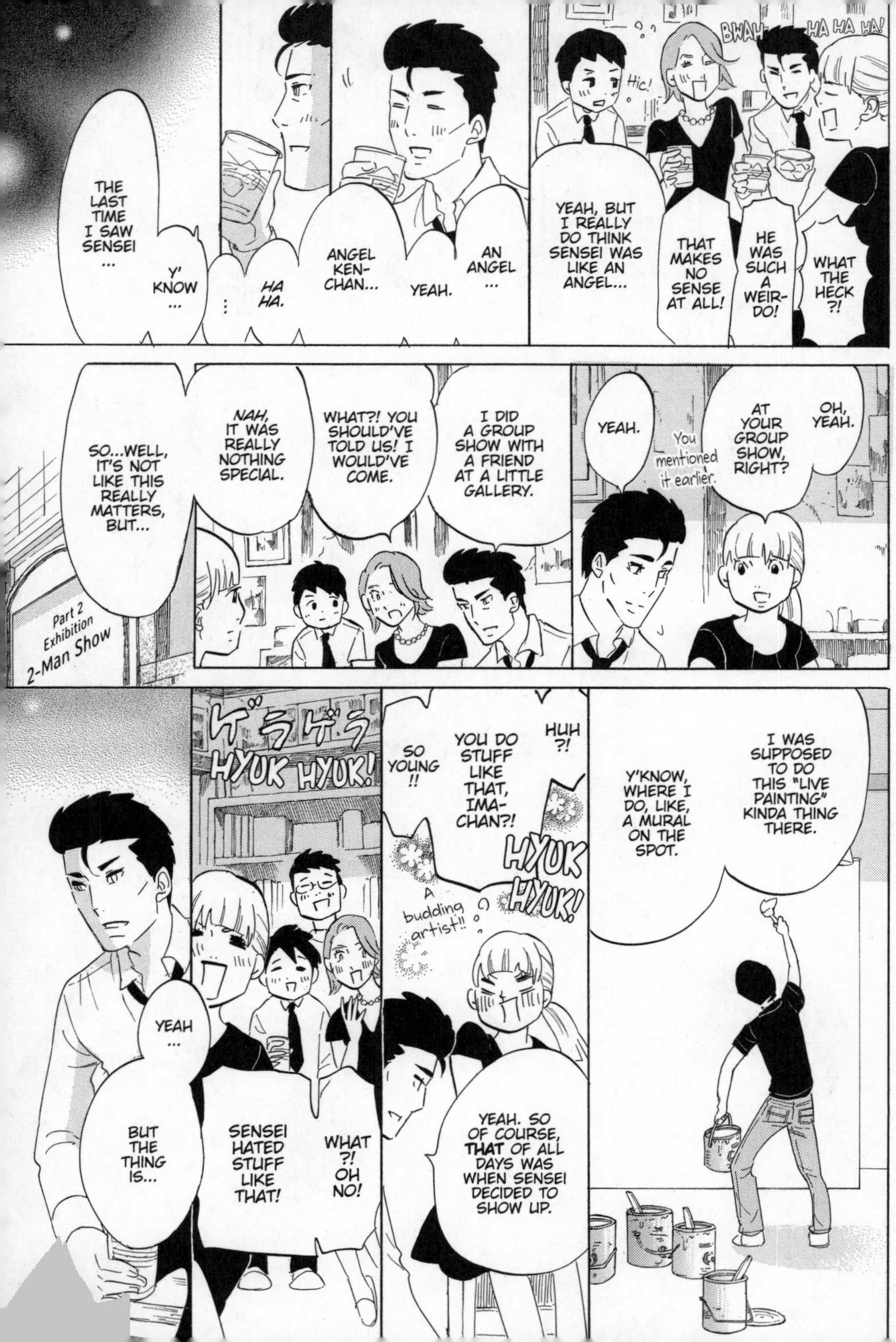

BWAH HA HA HA!
??
Hic!
WHAT THE HECK?!
HE WAS SUCH A WEIR-DO!
THAT MAKES NO SENSE AT ALL!
YEAH, BUT I REALLY DO THINK SENSEI WAS LIKE AN ANGEL...
AN ANGEL...
YEAH.
ANGEL KEN-CHAN...
HA HA.
...
Y' KNOW...
THE LAST TIME I SAW SENSEI...
OH, YEAH.
AT YOUR GROUP SHOW, RIGHT?
You mentioned it earlier.
YEAH.
I DID A GROUP SHOW WITH A FRIEND AT A LITTLE GALLERY.
WHAT?! YOU SHOULD'VE TOLD US! I WOULD'VE COME.
NAH, IT WAS REALLY NOTHING SPECIAL.
SO...WELL, IT'S NOT LIKE THIS REALLY MATTERS, BUT...
Part 2 Exhibition 2-Man Show
I WAS SUPPOSED TO DO THIS "LIVE PAINTING" KINDA THING THERE.
Y'KNOW, WHERE I DO, LIKE, A MURAL ON THE SPOT.
HUH?!
YOU DO STUFF LIKE THAT, IMA-CHAN?!
SO YOUNG!!
HYUK HYUK!
A budding artist!!
YEAH. SO OF COURSE, **THAT** OF ALL DAYS WAS WHEN SENSEI DECIDED TO SHOW UP.
ゲラゲラ
HYUK HYUK!
WHAT?! OH NO!
SENSEI HATED STUFF LIKE THAT!
YEAH...
BUT THE THING IS...

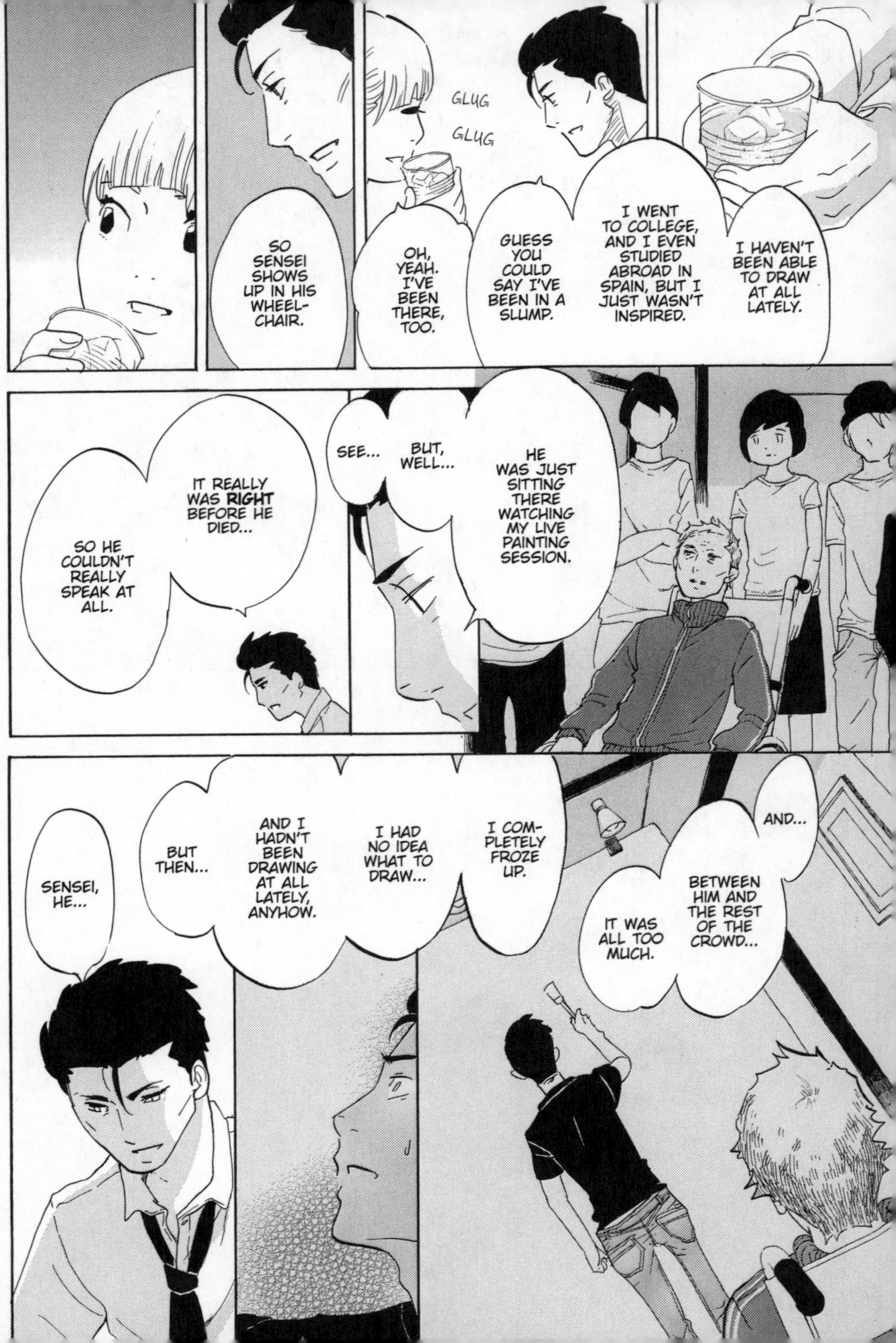
I HAVEN'T BEEN ABLE TO DRAW AT ALL LATELY.
I WENT TO COLLEGE, AND I EVEN STUDIED ABROAD IN SPAIN, BUT I JUST WASN'T INSPIRED.
GUESS YOU COULD SAY I'VE BEEN IN A SLUMP.
GLUG
GLUG
OH, YEAH. I'VE BEEN THERE, TOO.
SO SENSEI SHOWS UP IN HIS WHEEL-CHAIR.
HE WAS JUST SITTING THERE WATCHING MY LIVE PAINTING SESSION.
BUT, WELL...
SEE...
IT REALLY WAS **RIGHT** BEFORE HE DIED...
SO HE COULDN'T REALLY SPEAK AT ALL.
AND...
BETWEEN HIM AND THE REST OF THE CROWD...
IT WAS ALL TOO MUCH.
I COM-PLETELY FROZE UP.
I HAD NO IDEA WHAT TO DRAW...
AND I HADN'T BEEN DRAWING AT ALL LATELY, ANYHOW.
BUT THEN...
SENSEI, HE...

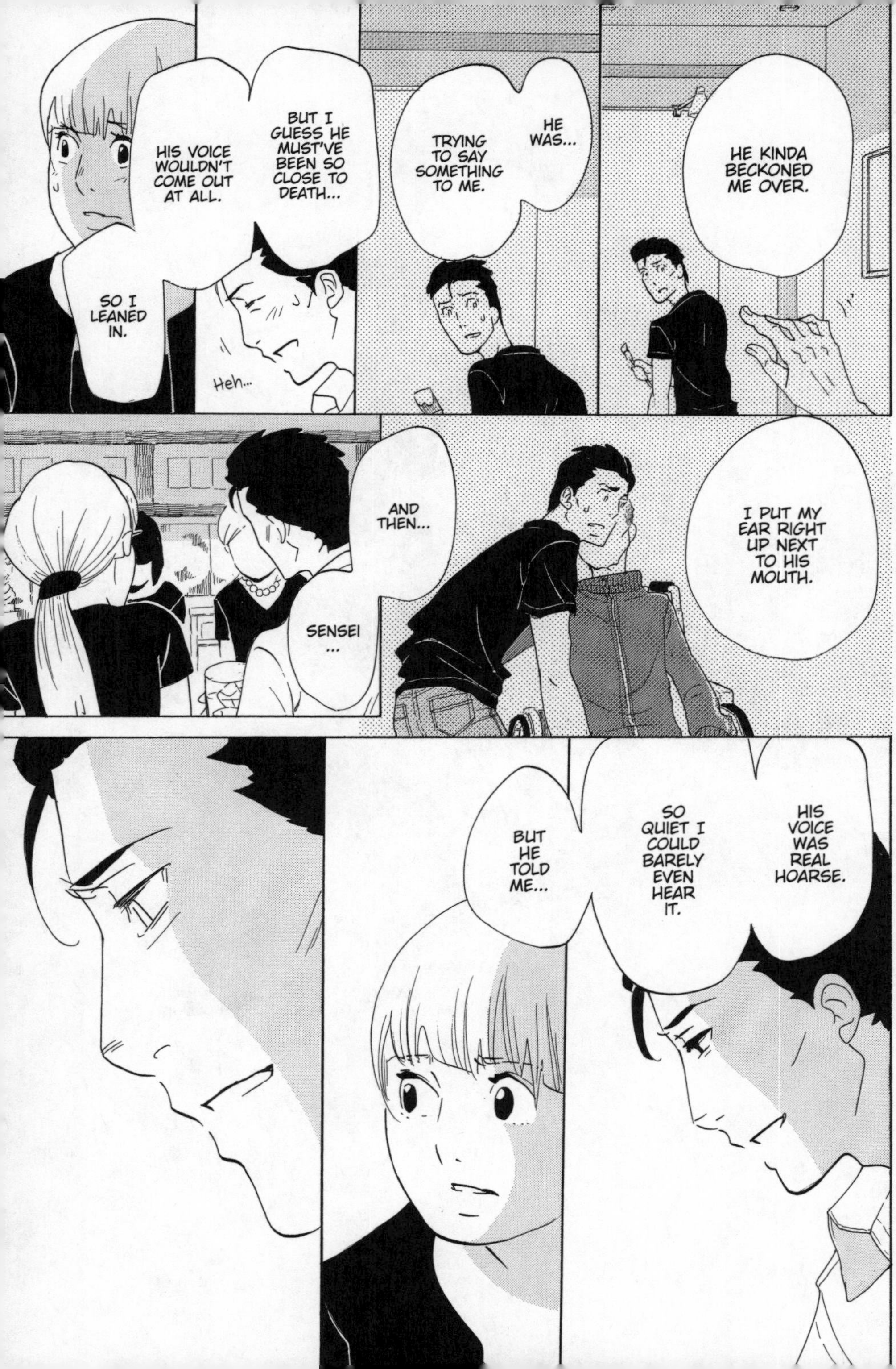
HE KINDA BECKONED ME OVER.
HE WAS...
TRYING TO SAY SOMETHING TO ME.
BUT I GUESS HE MUST'VE BEEN SO CLOSE TO DEATH...
HIS VOICE WOULDN'T COME OUT AT ALL.
SO I LEANED IN.
Heh...
I PUT MY EAR RIGHT UP NEXT TO HIS MOUTH.
AND THEN...
SENSEI ...
HIS VOICE WAS REAL HOARSE.
SO QUIET I COULD BARELY EVEN HEAR IT.
BUT HE TOLD ME...

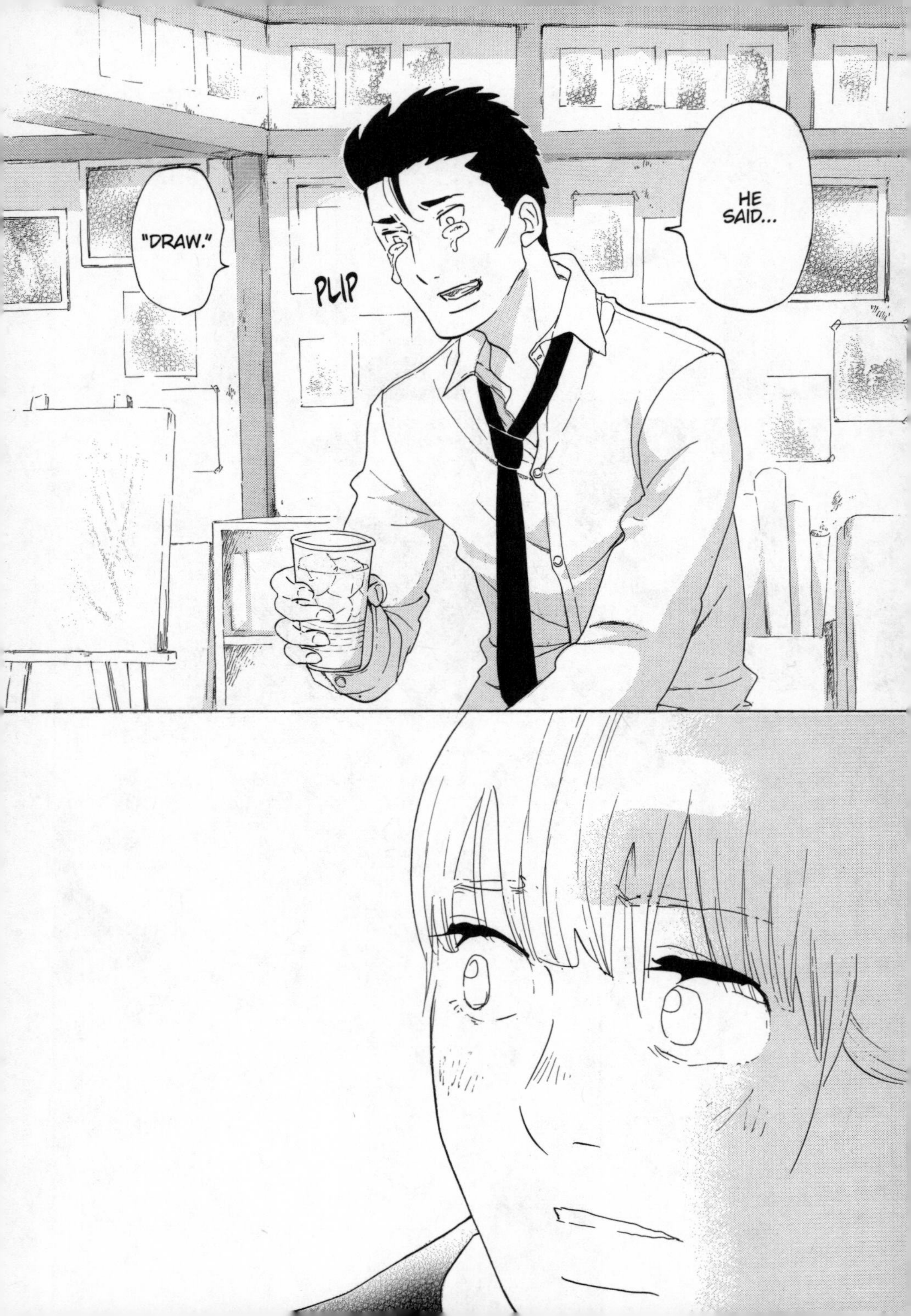
HE SAID...
"DRAW."
PLIP

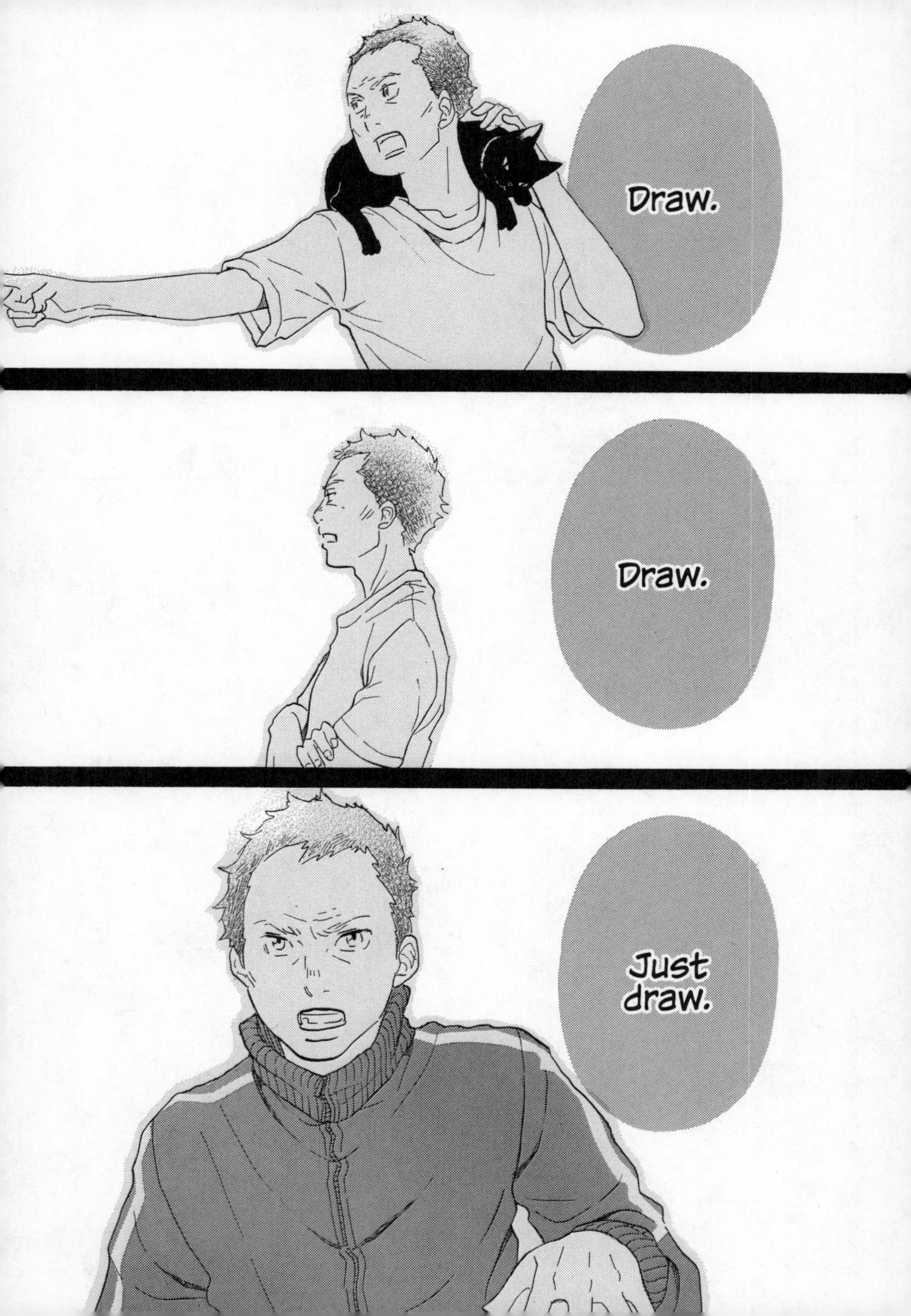
Draw.
Draw.
Just draw.

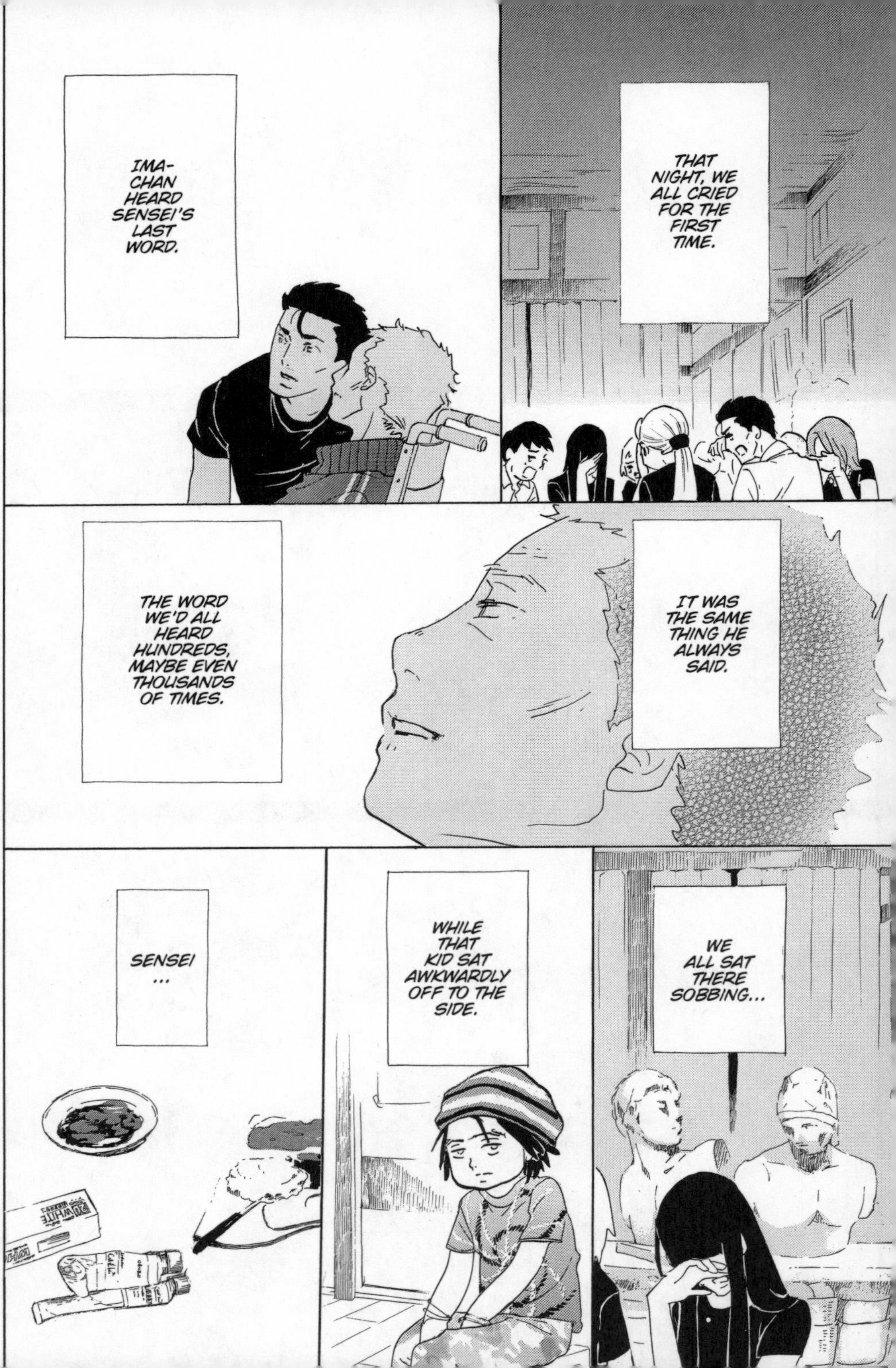
THAT NIGHT, WE ALL CRIED FOR THE FIRST TIME.
IMA-CHAN HEARD SENSEI'S LAST WORD.
IT WAS THE SAME THING HE ALWAYS SAID.
THE WORD WE'D ALL HEARD HUNDREDS, MAYBE EVEN THOUSANDS OF TIMES.
WE ALL SAT THERE SOBBING...
WHILE THAT KID SAT AWKWARDLY OFF TO THE SIDE.
SENSEI ...

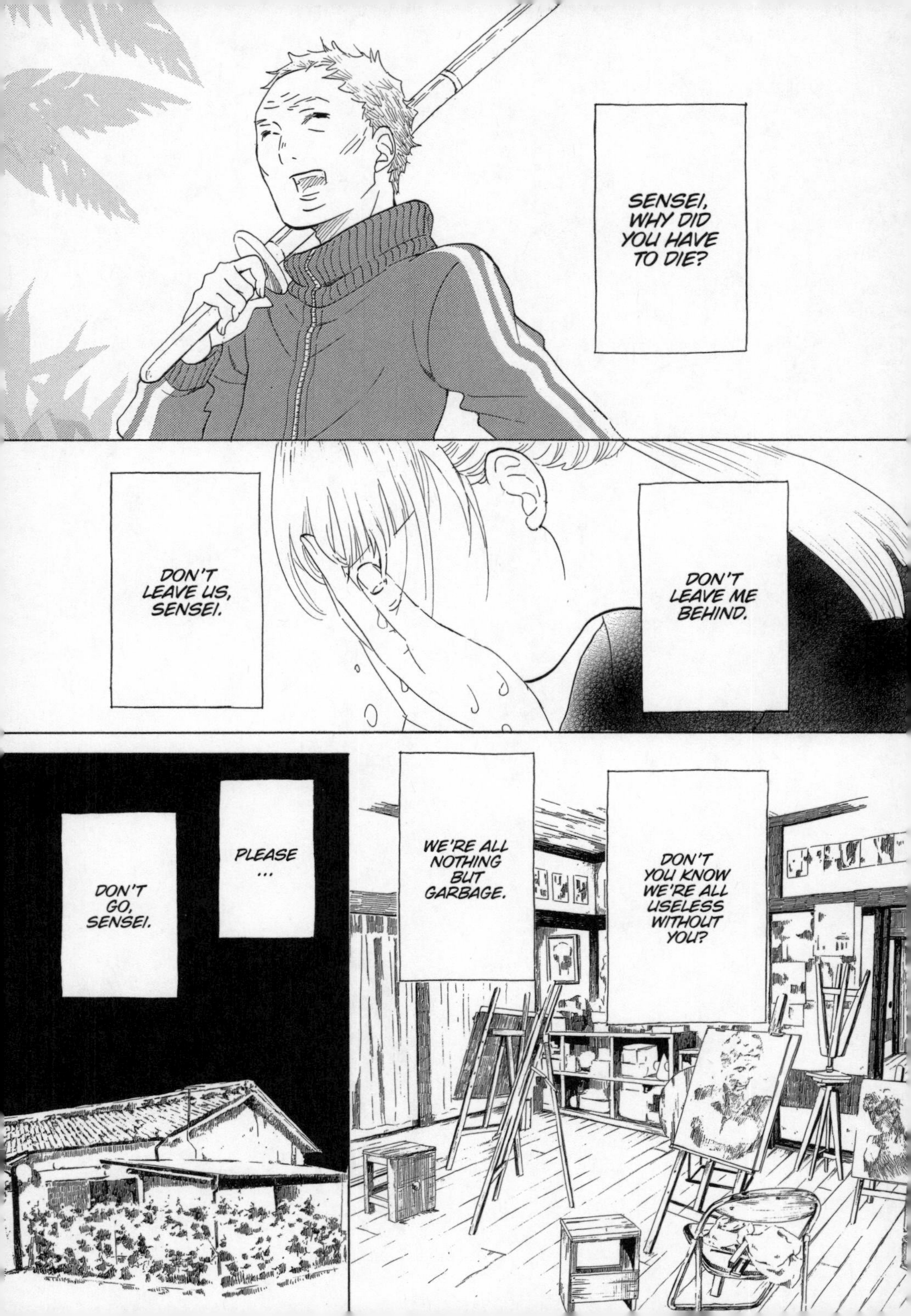
SENSEI, WHY DID YOU HAVE TO DIE?
DON'T LEAVE ME BEHIND.
DON'T LEAVE US, SENSEI.
DON'T YOU KNOW WE'RE ALL USELESS WITHOUT YOU?
WE'RE ALL NOTHING BUT GARBAGE.
PLEASE ...
DON'T GO, SENSEI.

Blank
Canvas
My So-Called
Artist's Journey

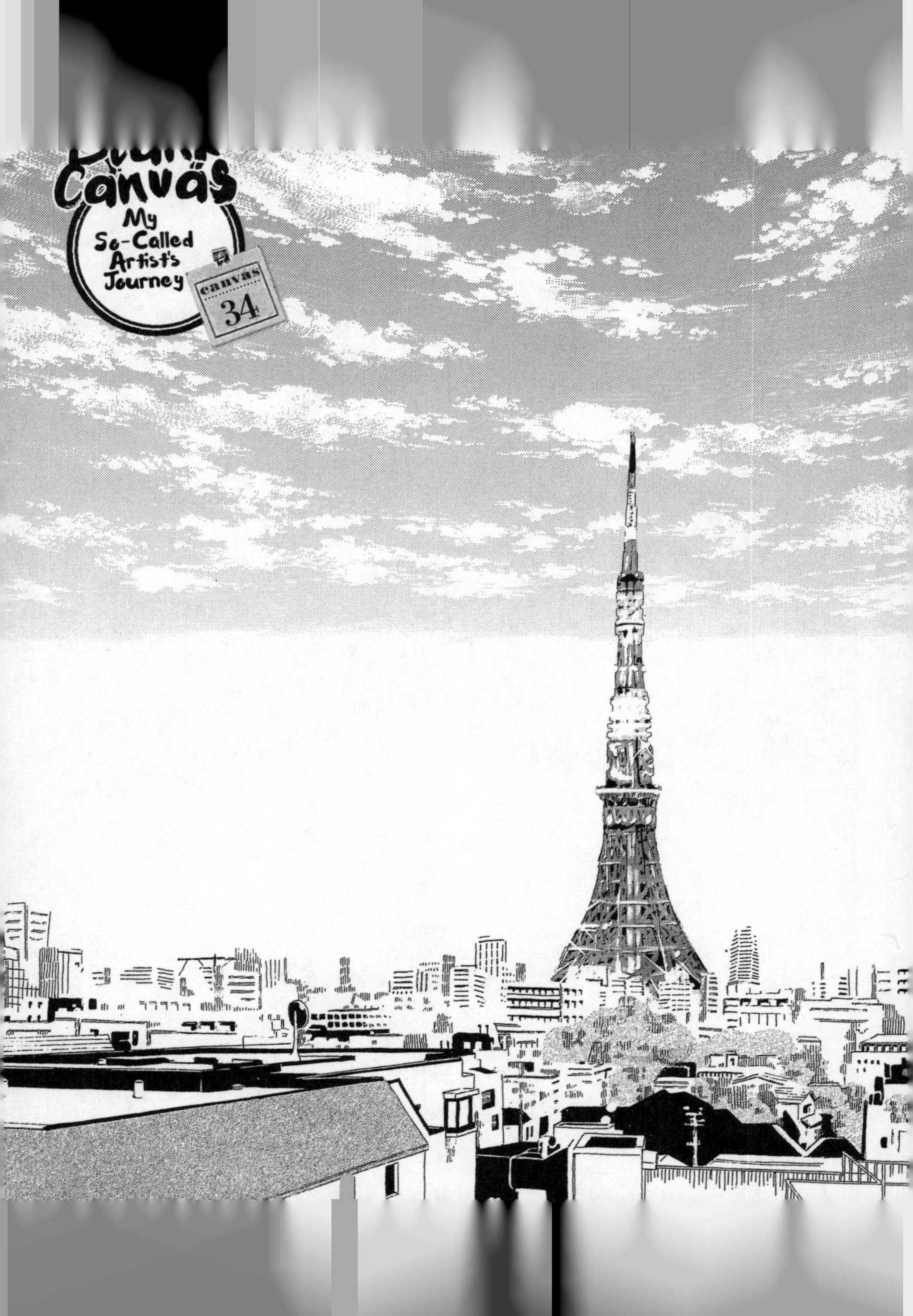
Canvas
My So-Called Artist's Journey
canvas
34

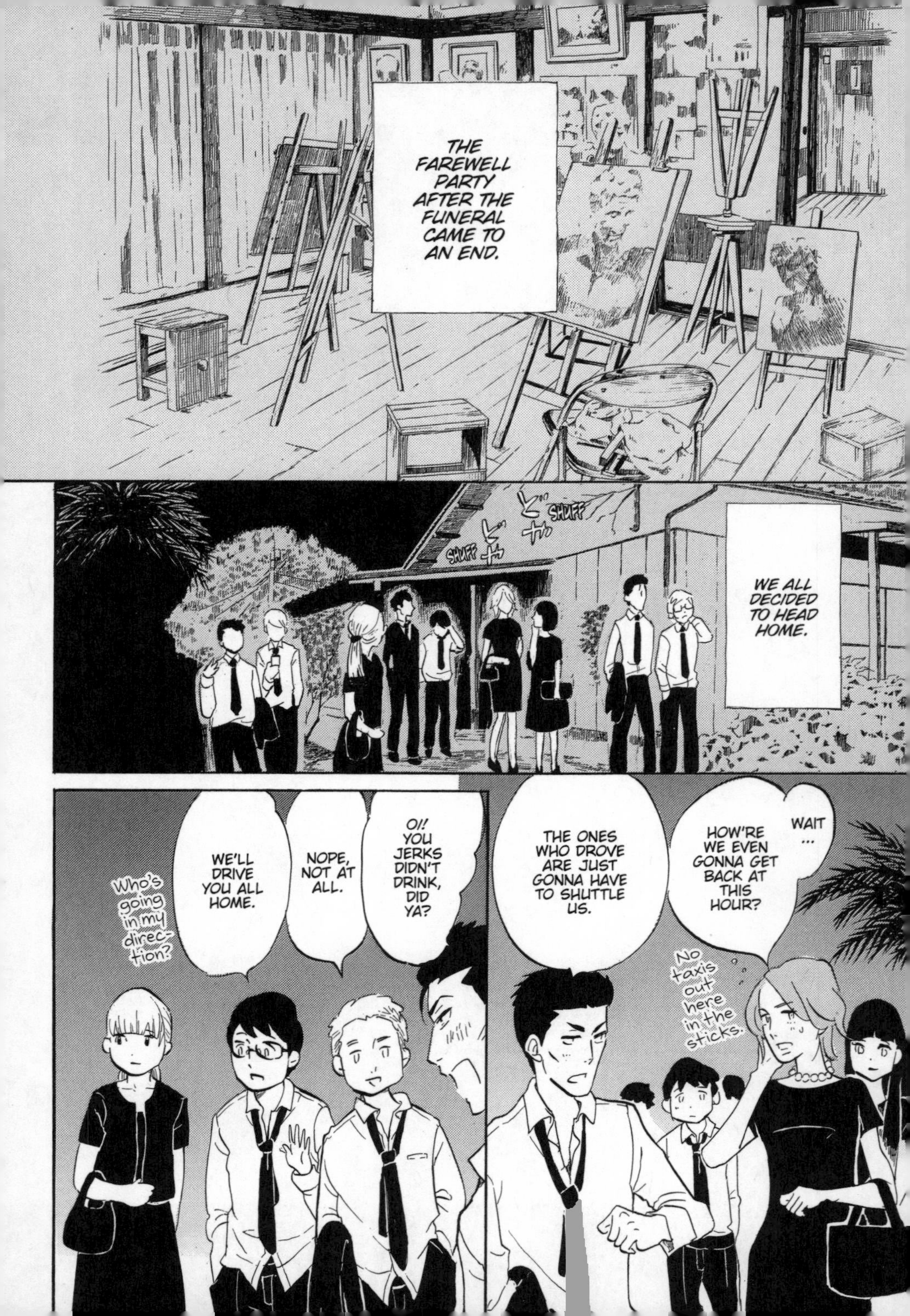
THE FAREWELL PARTY AFTER THE FUNERAL CAME TO AN END.
SHUFF
SHUFF
WE ALL DECIDED TO HEAD HOME.
WAIT ...
HOW'RE WE EVEN GONNA GET BACK AT THIS HOUR?
No taxis out here in the sticks.
THE ONES WHO DROVE ARE JUST GONNA HAVE TO SHUTTLE US.
OI! YOU JERKS DIDN'T DRINK, DID YA?
NOPE, NOT AT ALL.
WE'LL DRIVE YOU ALL HOME.
Who's going in my direction?

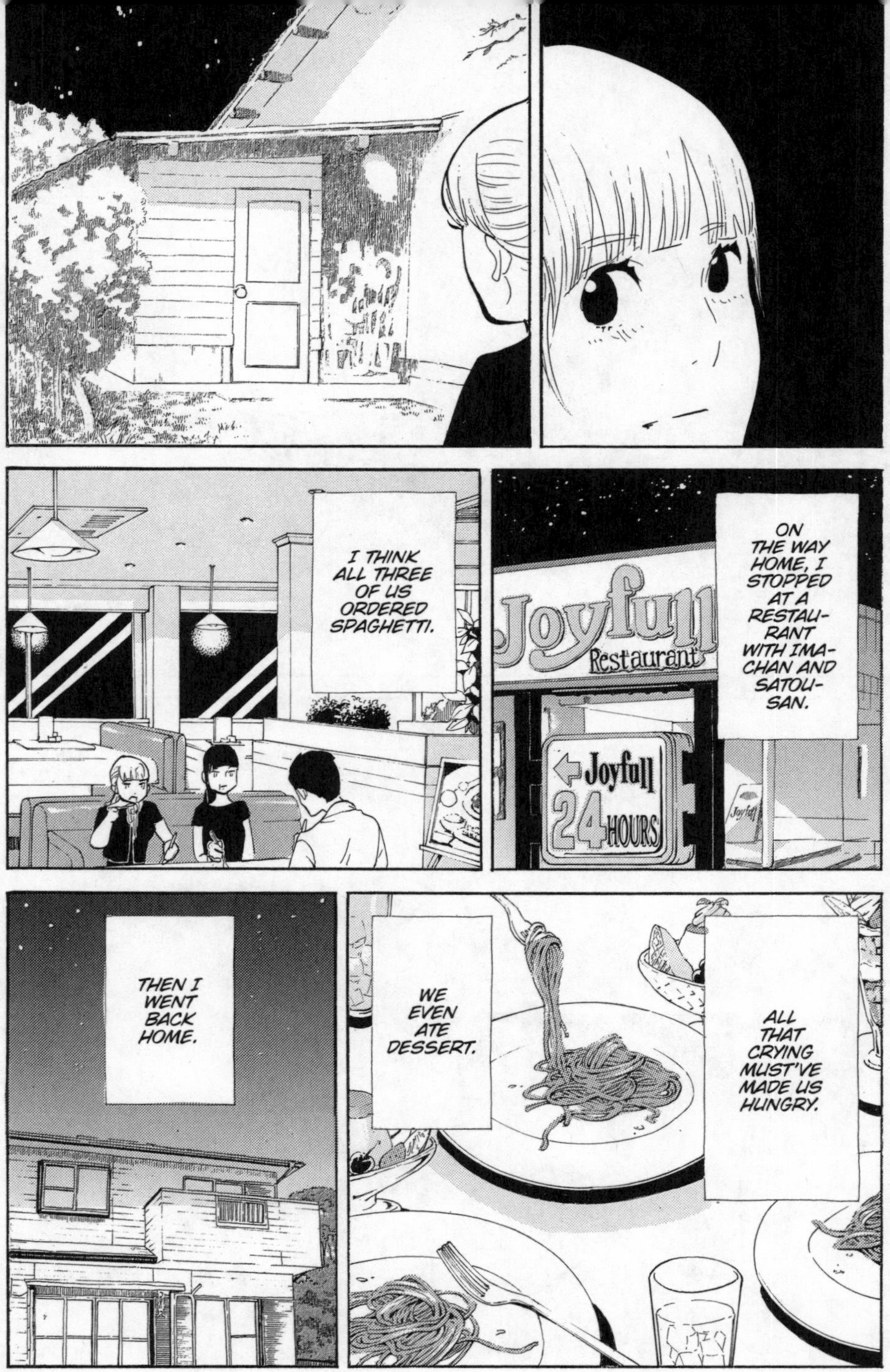
ON THE WAY HOME, I STOPPED AT A RESTAU-RANT WITH IMA-CHAN AND SATOU-SAN.
Joyfull
Restaurant
Joyfull
24 HOURS
I THINK ALL THREE OF US ORDERED SPAGHETTI.
ALL THAT CRYING MUST'VE MADE US HUNGRY.
WE EVEN ATE DESSERT.
THEN I WENT BACK HOME.

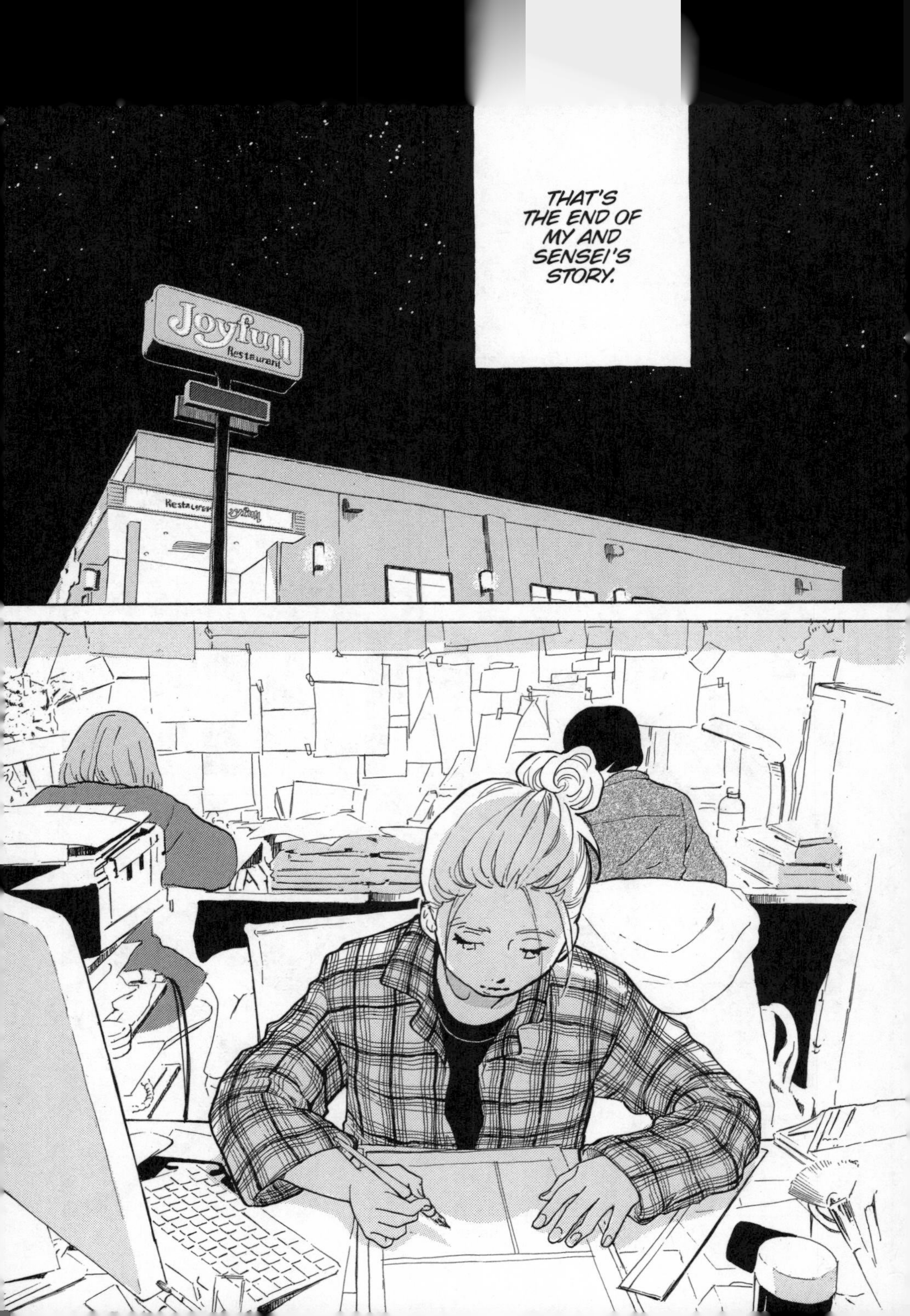
THAT'S THE END OF MY AND SENSEI'S STORY.
Joyfull
Restaurant

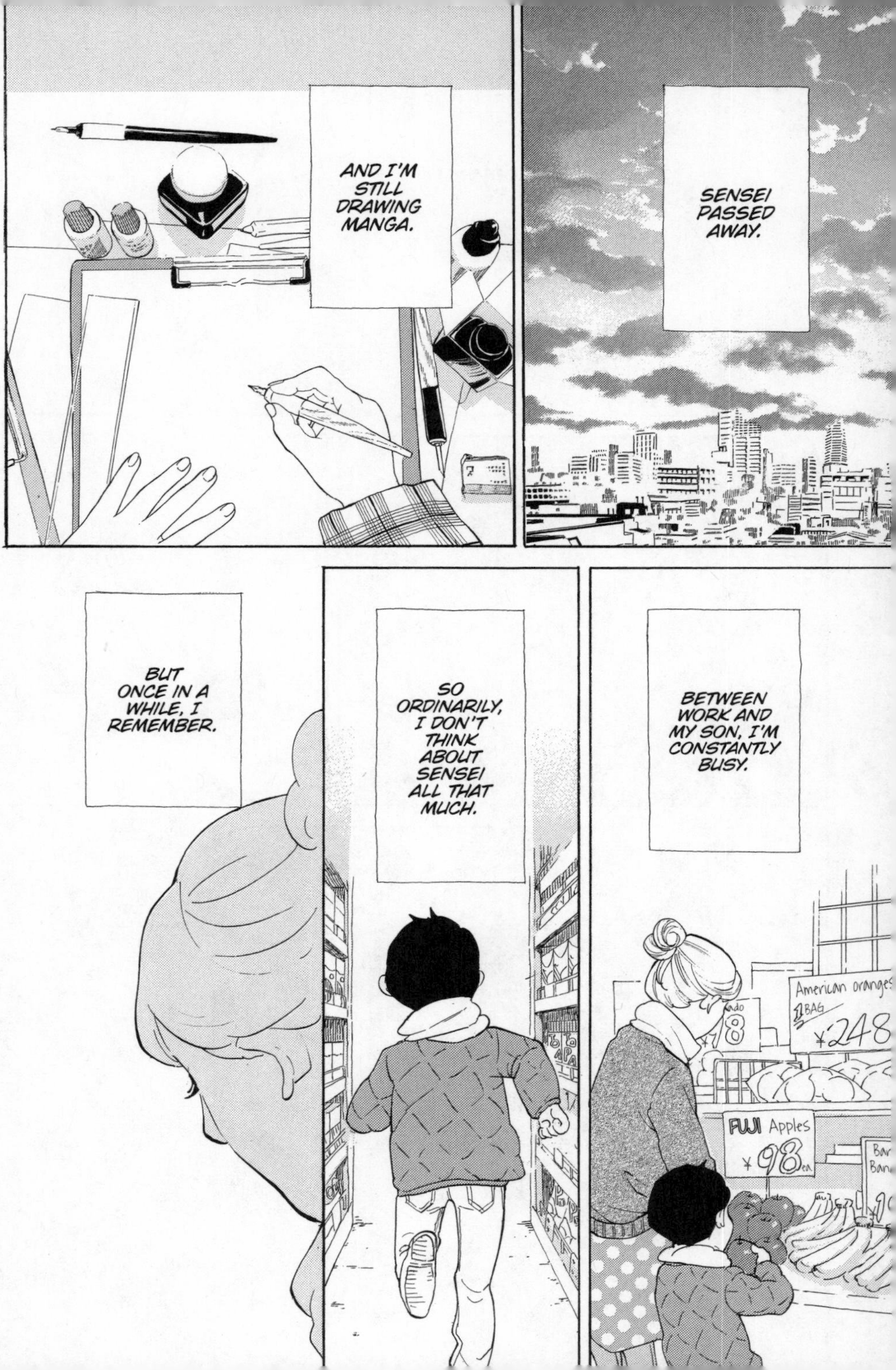
SENSEI PASSED AWAY.
AND I'M STILL DRAWING MANGA.
BETWEEN WORK AND MY SON, I'M CONSTANTLY BUSY.
American oranges
1 BAG
¥248
FUJI Apples
¥98 ea
SO ORDINARILY, I DON'T THINK ABOUT SENSEI ALL THAT MUCH.
BUT ONCE IN A WHILE, I REMEMBER.

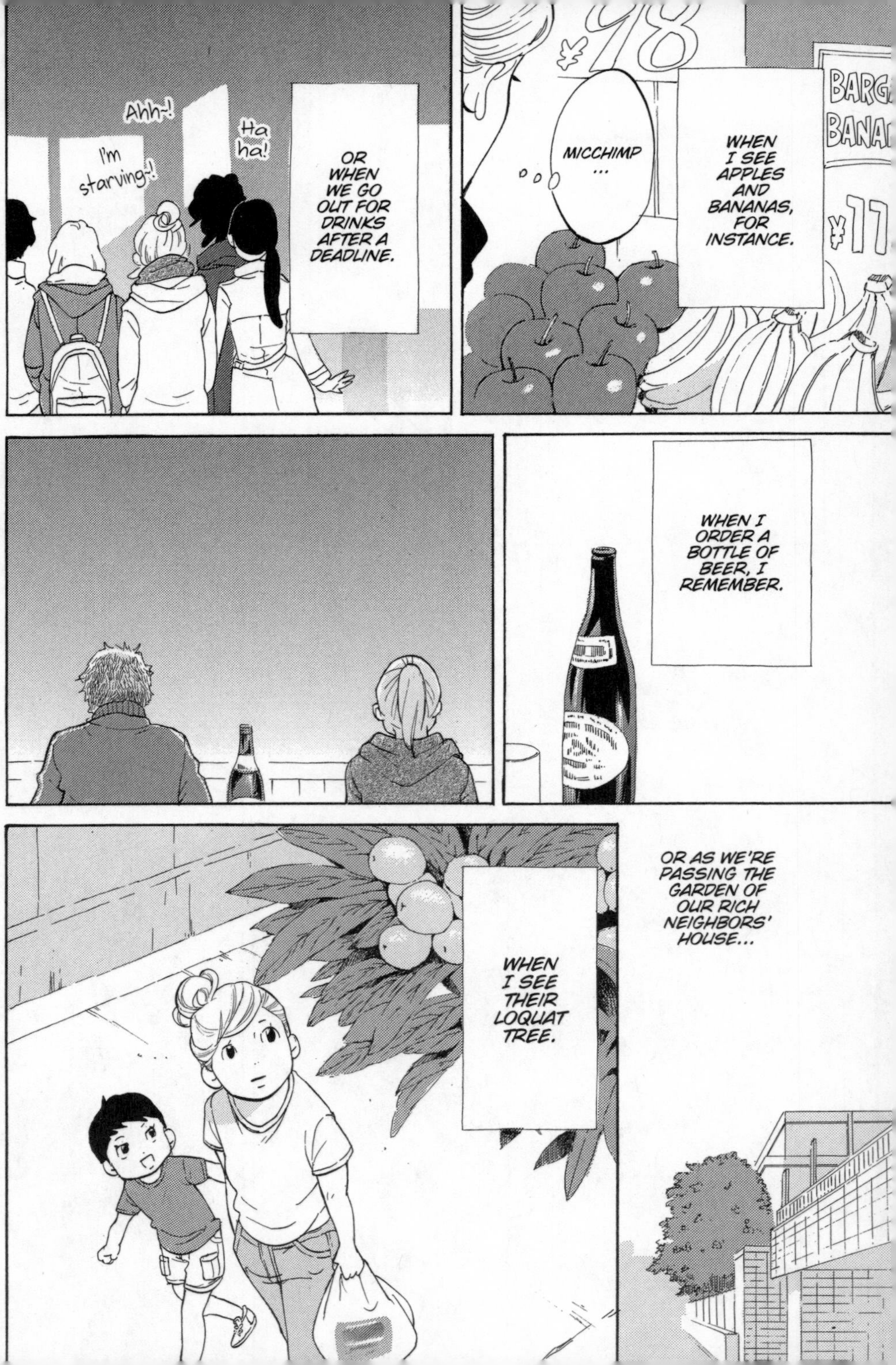
¥98
WHEN I SEE APPLES AND BANANAS, FOR INSTANCE.
MICCHIMP…
OR WHEN WE GO OUT FOR DRINKS AFTER A DEADLINE.
Ha ha!
Ahh~!
I'm starving~!
WHEN I ORDER A BOTTLE OF BEER, I REMEMBER.
OR AS WE'RE PASSING THE GARDEN OF OUR RICH NEIGHBORS' HOUSE…
WHEN I SEE THEIR LOQUAT TREE.

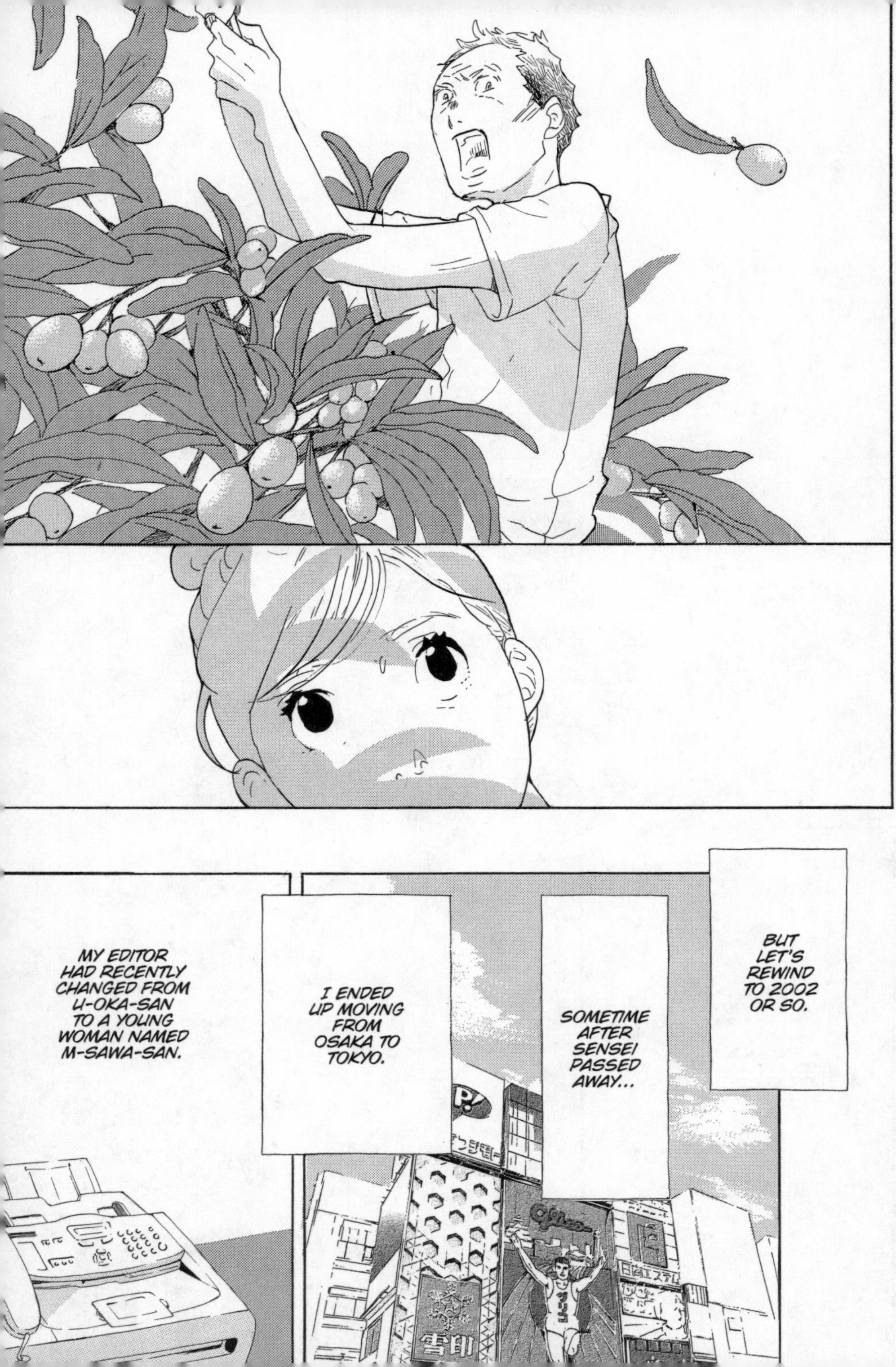
BUT LET'S REWIND TO 2002 OR SO.
SOMETIME AFTER SENSEI PASSED AWAY...
I ENDED UP MOVING FROM OSAKA TO TOKYO.
MY EDITOR HAD RECENTLY CHANGED FROM U-OKA-SAN TO A YOUNG WOMAN NAMED M-SAWA-SAN.

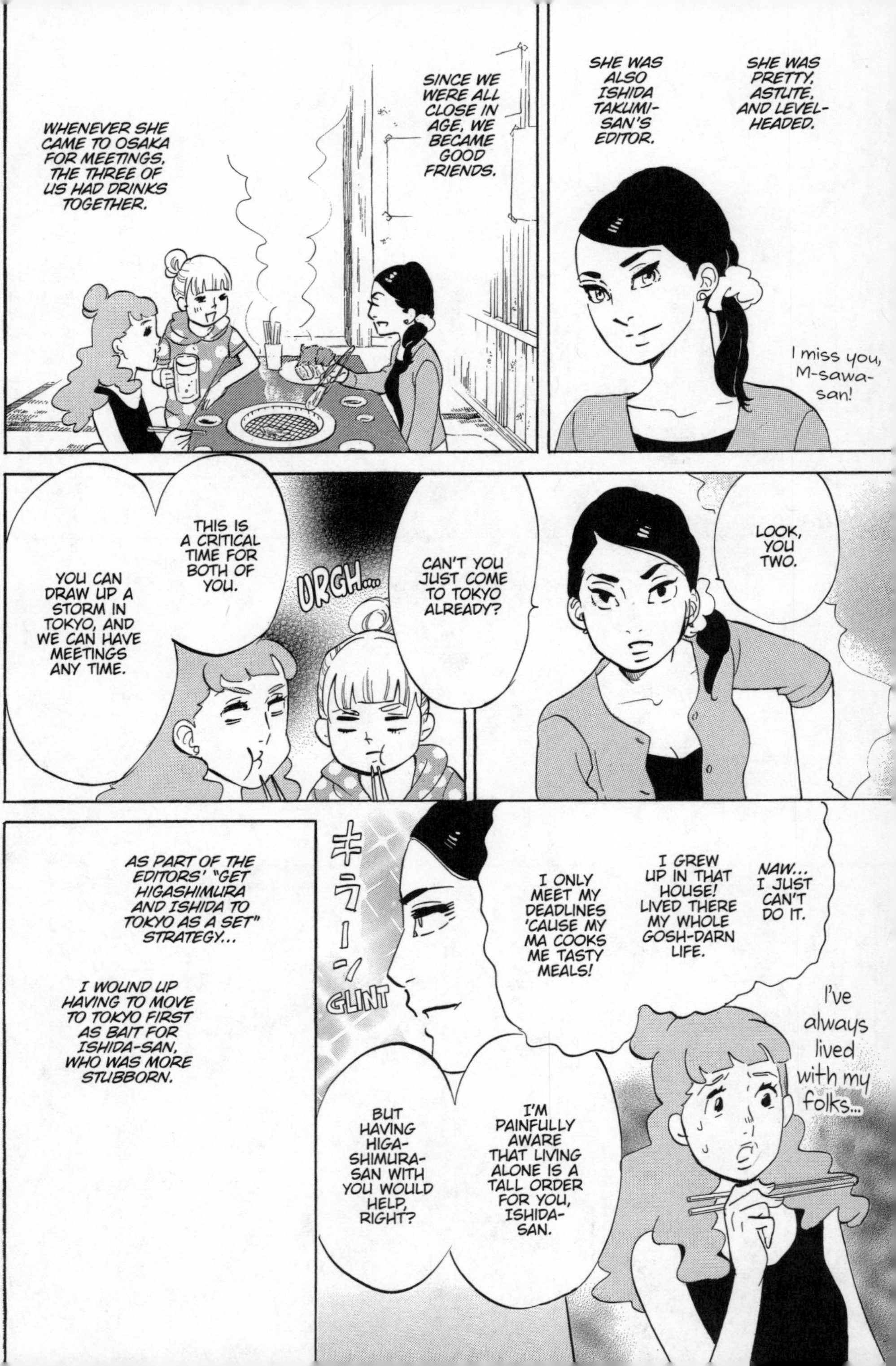
SHE WAS PRETTY, ASTUTE, AND LEVEL-HEADED.
SHE WAS ALSO ISHIDA TAKUMI-SAN'S EDITOR.
I miss you, M-sawa-san!
SINCE WE WERE ALL CLOSE IN AGE, WE BECAME GOOD FRIENDS.
WHENEVER SHE CAME TO OSAKA FOR MEETINGS, THE THREE OF US HAD DRINKS TOGETHER.
LOOK, YOU TWO.
CAN'T YOU JUST COME TO TOKYO ALREADY?
URGH...
THIS IS A CRITICAL TIME FOR BOTH OF YOU.
YOU CAN DRAW UP A STORM IN TOKYO, AND WE CAN HAVE MEETINGS ANY TIME.
NAW... I JUST CAN'T DO IT.
I GREW UP IN THAT HOUSE! LIVED THERE MY WHOLE GOSH-DARN LIFE.
I ONLY MEET MY DEADLINES 'CAUSE MY MA COOKS ME TASTY MEALS!
キラーン
GLINT
I've always lived with my folks...
I'M PAINFULLY AWARE THAT LIVING ALONE IS A TALL ORDER FOR YOU, ISHIDA-SAN.
BUT HAVING HIGA-SHIMURA-SAN WITH YOU WOULD HELP, RIGHT?
AS PART OF THE EDITORS' "GET HIGASHIMURA AND ISHIDA TO TOKYO AS A SET" STRATEGY...
I WOUND UP HAVING TO MOVE TO TOKYO FIRST AS BAIT FOR ISHIDA-SAN, WHO WAS MORE STUBBORN.

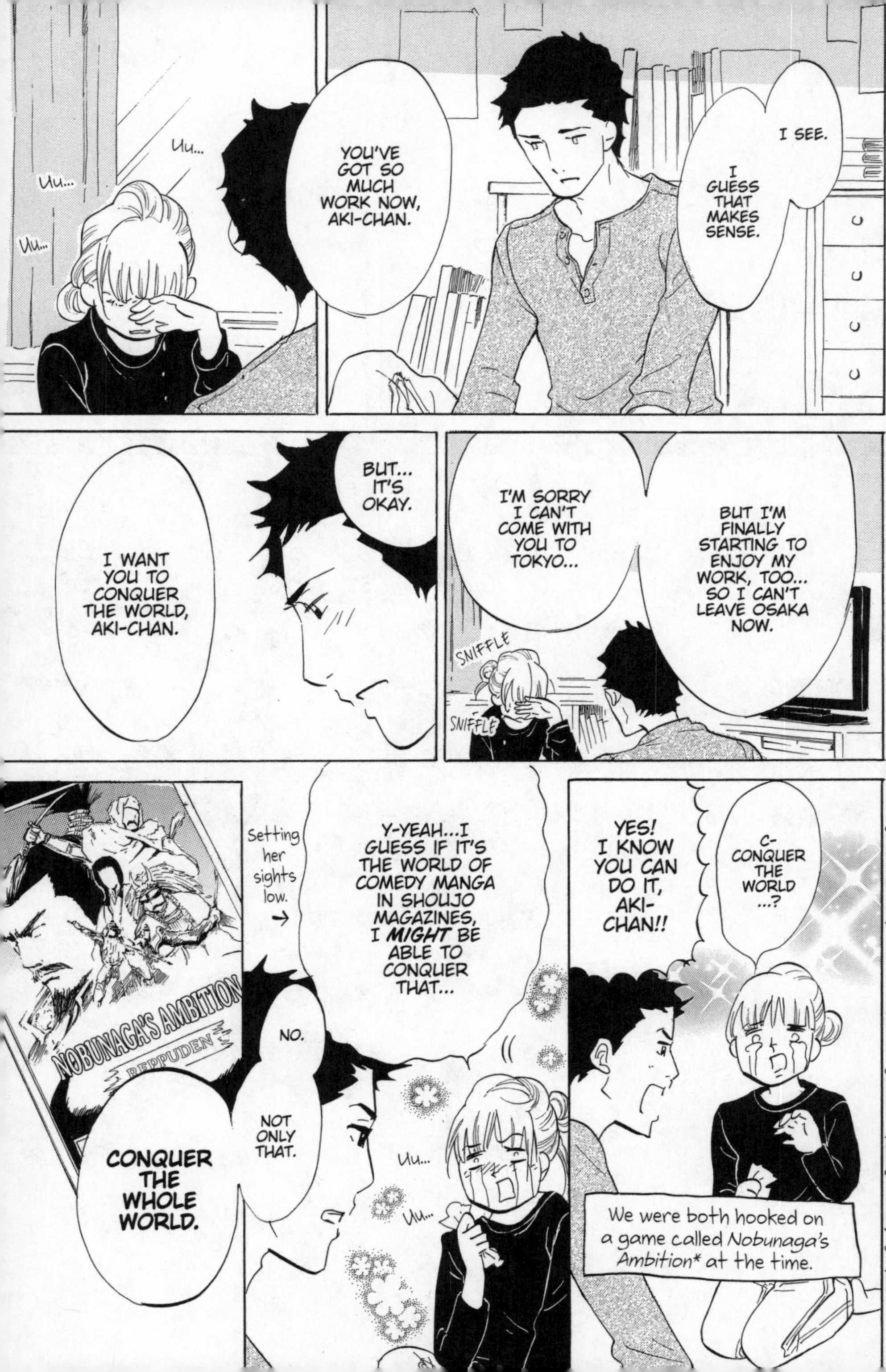
I SEE.
I GUESS THAT MAKES SENSE.
YOU'VE GOT SO MUCH WORK NOW, AKI-CHAN.
Uu...
Uu...
Uu...
I'M SORRY I CAN'T COME WITH YOU TO TOKYO...
BUT I'M FINALLY STARTING TO ENJOY MY WORK, TOO... SO I CAN'T LEAVE OSAKA NOW.
SNIFFLE
SNIFFLE
BUT... IT'S OKAY.
I WANT YOU TO CONQUER THE WORLD, AKI-CHAN.
C-CONQUER THE WORLD ...?
YES! I KNOW YOU CAN DO IT, AKI-CHAN!!
We were both hooked on a game called Nobunaga's Ambition* at the time.
Y-YEAH...I GUESS IF IT'S THE WORLD OF COMEDY MANGA IN SHOUJO MAGAZINES, I MIGHT BE ABLE TO CONQUER THAT...
Setting her sights low. →
NO.
NOT ONLY THAT.
CONQUER THE WHOLE WORLD.
Uu...
Uu...
NOBUNAGA'S AMBITION
REPPUDEN

*Nobunaga's Ambition: Reppuden: A strategy RPG series in which the player controls Nobunaga or another Japanese warlord, with the goal of conquering and unifying Japan.

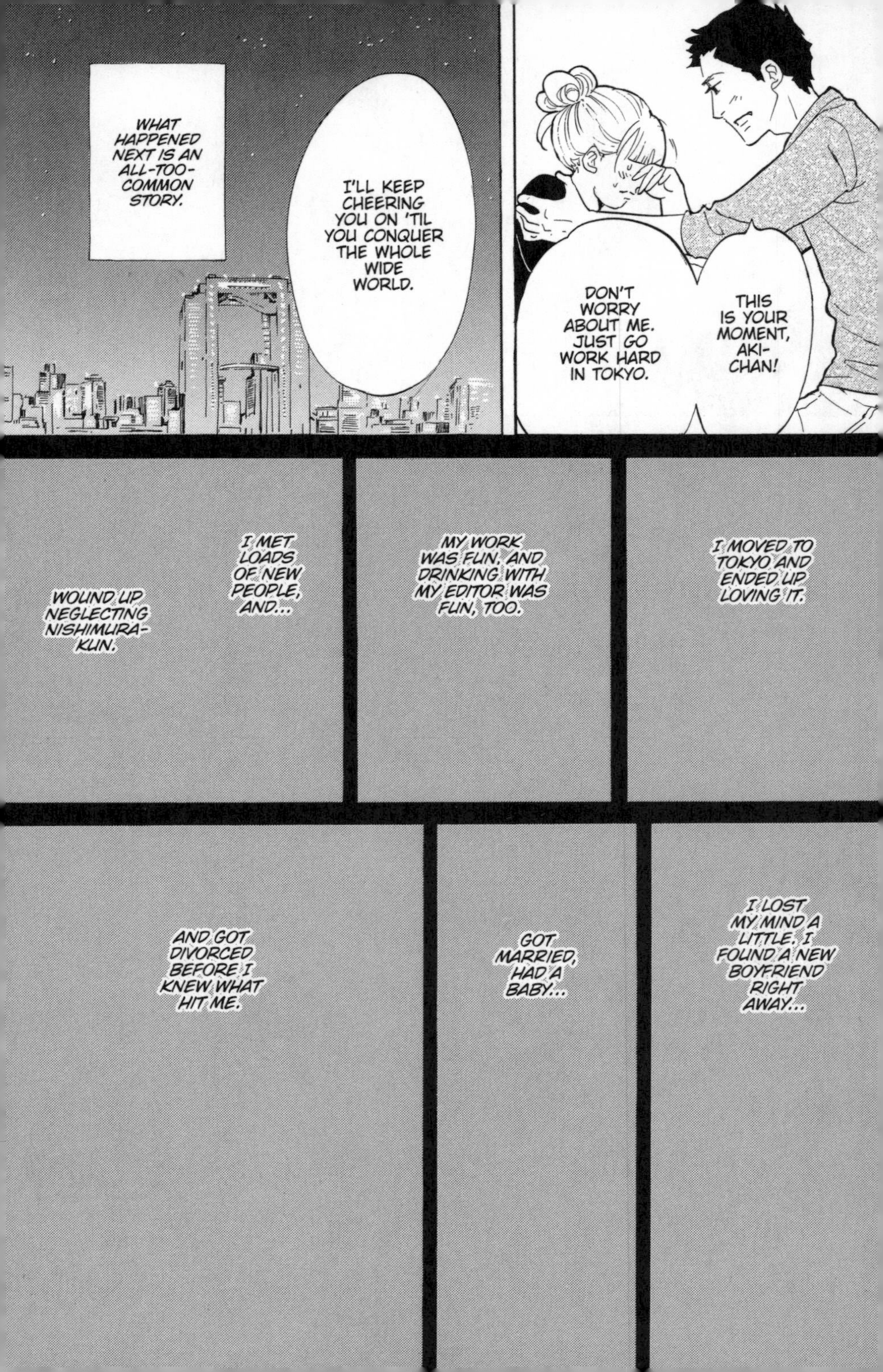
THIS IS YOUR MOMENT, AKI-CHAN!
DON'T WORRY ABOUT ME. JUST GO WORK HARD IN TOKYO.
I'LL KEEP CHEERING YOU ON 'TIL YOU CONQUER THE WHOLE WIDE WORLD.
WHAT HAPPENED NEXT IS AN ALL-TOO-COMMON STORY.
I MOVED TO TOKYO AND ENDED UP LOVING IT.
MY WORK WAS FUN, AND DRINKING WITH MY EDITOR WAS FUN, TOO.
I MET LOADS OF NEW PEOPLE, AND...
WOUND UP NEGLECTING NISHIMURA-KUN.
I LOST MY MIND A LITTLE. I FOUND A NEW BOYFRIEND RIGHT AWAY...
GOT MARRIED, HAD A BABY...
AND GOT DIVORCED BEFORE I KNEW WHAT HIT ME.

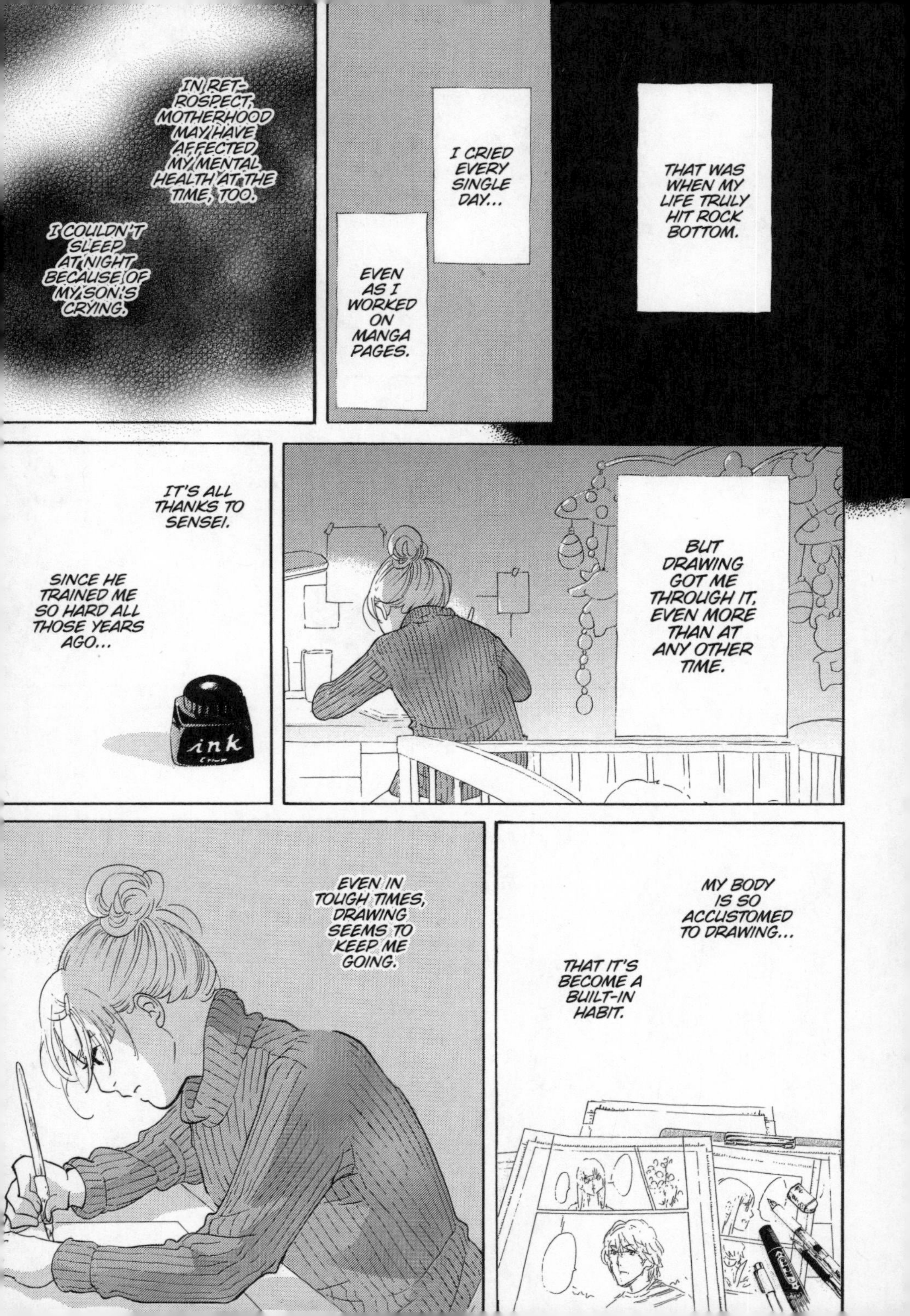
THAT WAS WHEN MY LIFE TRULY HIT ROCK BOTTOM.
I CRIED EVERY SINGLE DAY...
EVEN AS I WORKED ON MANGA PAGES.
IN RETROSPECT, MOTHERHOOD MAY HAVE AFFECTED MY MENTAL HEALTH AT THE TIME, TOO.
I COULDN'T SLEEP AT NIGHT BECAUSE OF MY SON'S CRYING.
BUT DRAWING GOT ME THROUGH IT, EVEN MORE THAN AT ANY OTHER TIME.
IT'S ALL THANKS TO SENSEI.
SINCE HE TRAINED ME SO HARD ALL THOSE YEARS AGO...
ink
MY BODY IS SO ACCUSTOMED TO DRAWING...
THAT IT'S BECOME A BUILT-IN HABIT.
EVEN IN TOUGH TIMES, DRAWING SEEMS TO KEEP ME GOING.

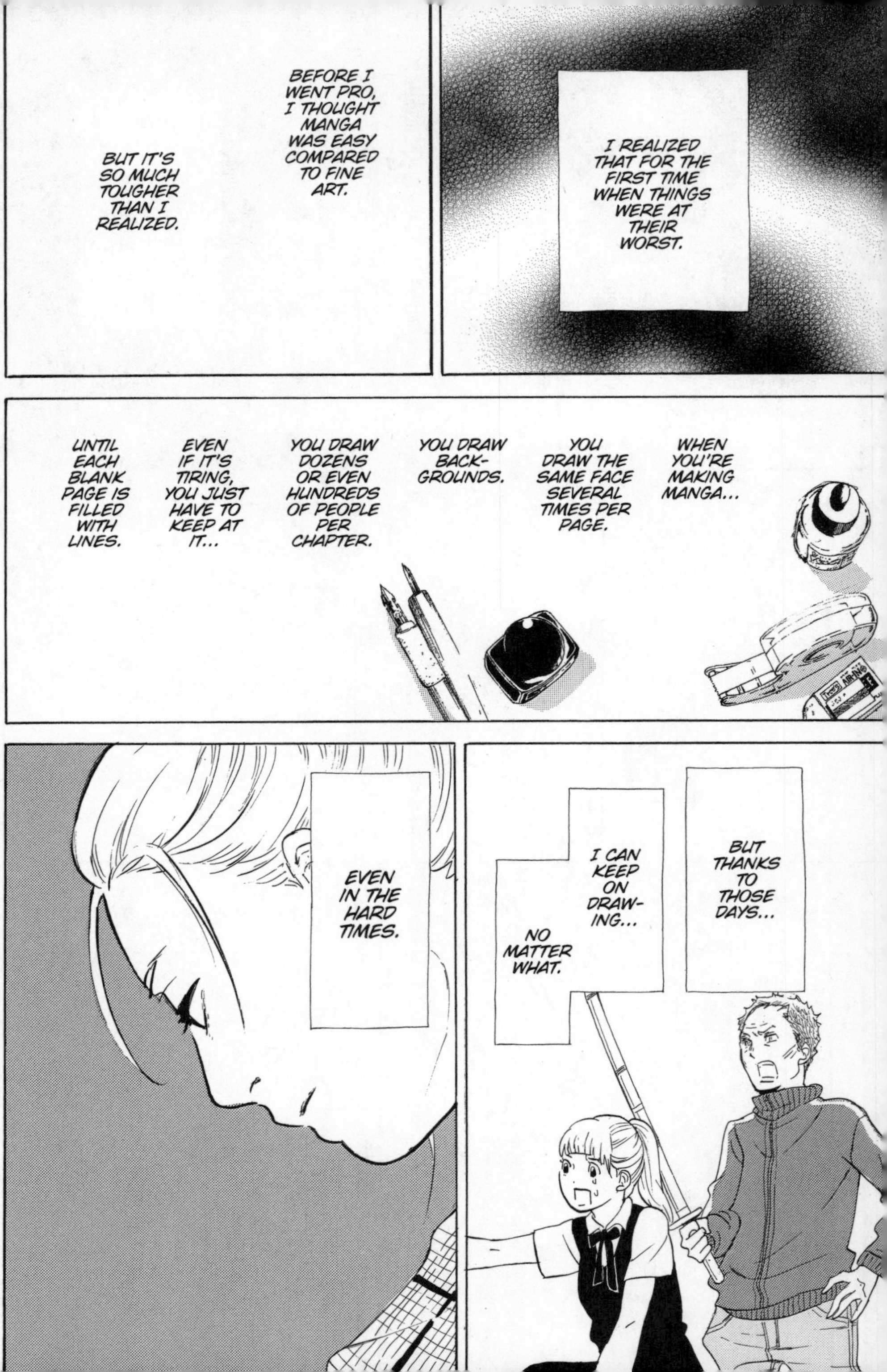
I REALIZED THAT FOR THE FIRST TIME WHEN THINGS WERE AT THEIR WORST.
BEFORE I WENT PRO, I THOUGHT MANGA WAS EASY COMPARED TO FINE ART.
BUT IT'S SO MUCH TOUGHER THAN I REALIZED.
WHEN YOU'RE MAKING MANGA...
YOU DRAW THE SAME FACE SEVERAL TIMES PER PAGE.
YOU DRAW BACK-GROUNDS.
YOU DRAW DOZENS OR EVEN HUNDREDS OF PEOPLE PER CHAPTER.
EVEN IF IT'S TIRING, YOU JUST HAVE TO KEEP AT IT...
UNTIL EACH BLANK PAGE IS FILLED WITH LINES.
BUT THANKS TO THOSE DAYS...
I CAN KEEP ON DRAW-ING...
NO MATTER WHAT.
EVEN IN THE HARD TIMES.

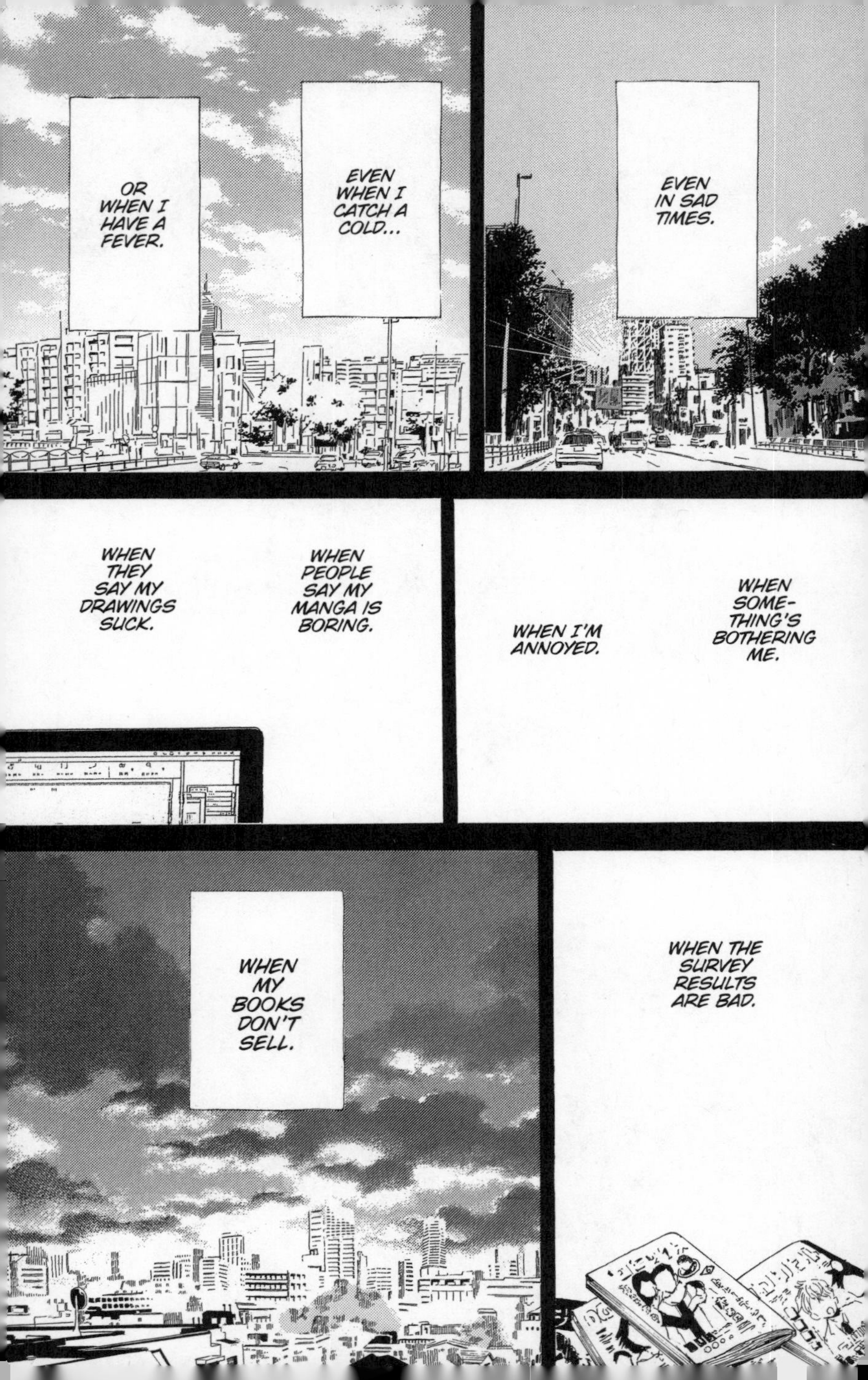
EVEN IN SAD TIMES.
EVEN WHEN I CATCH A COLD...
OR WHEN I HAVE A FEVER.
WHEN SOME-THING'S BOTHERING ME.
WHEN I'M ANNOYED.
WHEN PEOPLE SAY MY MANGA IS BORING.
WHEN THEY SAY MY DRAWINGS SUCK.
WHEN THE SURVEY RESULTS ARE BAD.
WHEN MY BOOKS DON'T SELL.

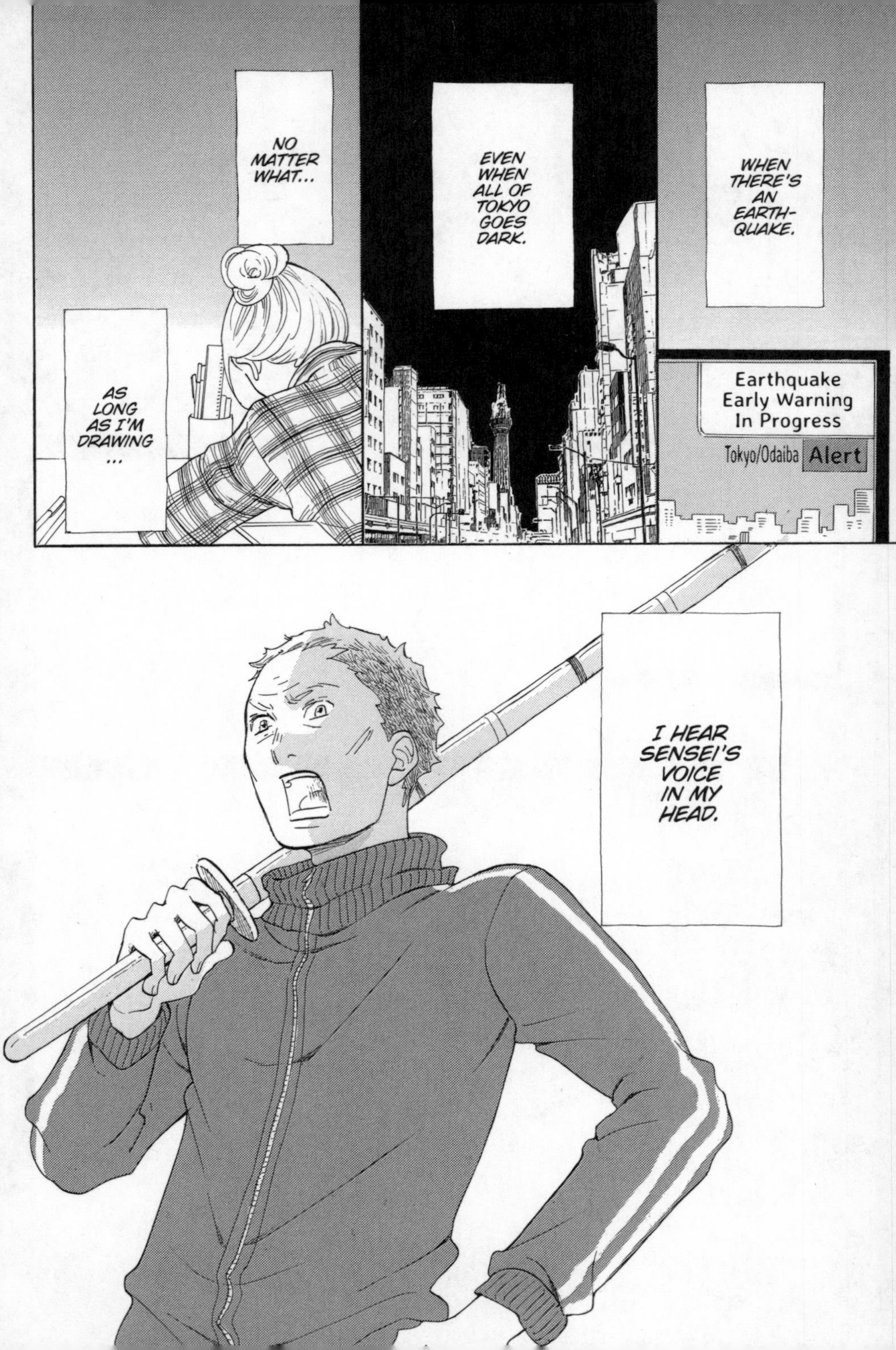
WHEN THERE'S AN EARTH-QUAKE.
Earthquake Early Warning In Progress
Tokyo/Odaiba
Alert
EVEN WHEN ALL OF TOKYO GOES DARK.
NO MATTER WHAT...
AS LONG AS I'M DRAWING...
I HEAR SENSEI'S VOICE IN MY HEAD.

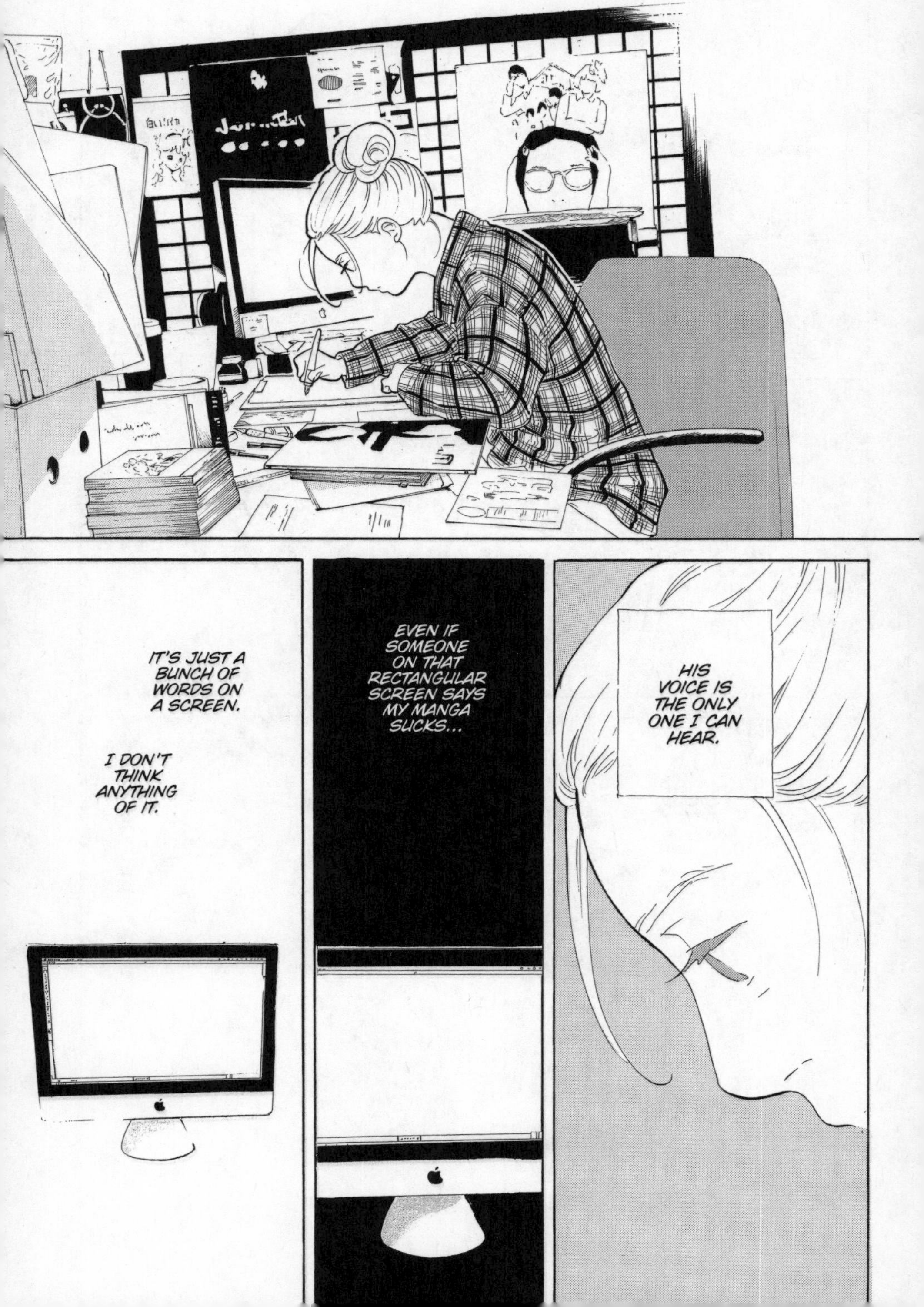
HIS VOICE IS THE ONLY ONE I CAN HEAR.
EVEN IF SOMEONE ON THAT RECTANGULAR SCREEN SAYS MY MANGA SUCKS...
IT'S JUST A BUNCH OF WORDS ON A SCREEN.
I DON'T THINK ANYTHING OF IT.

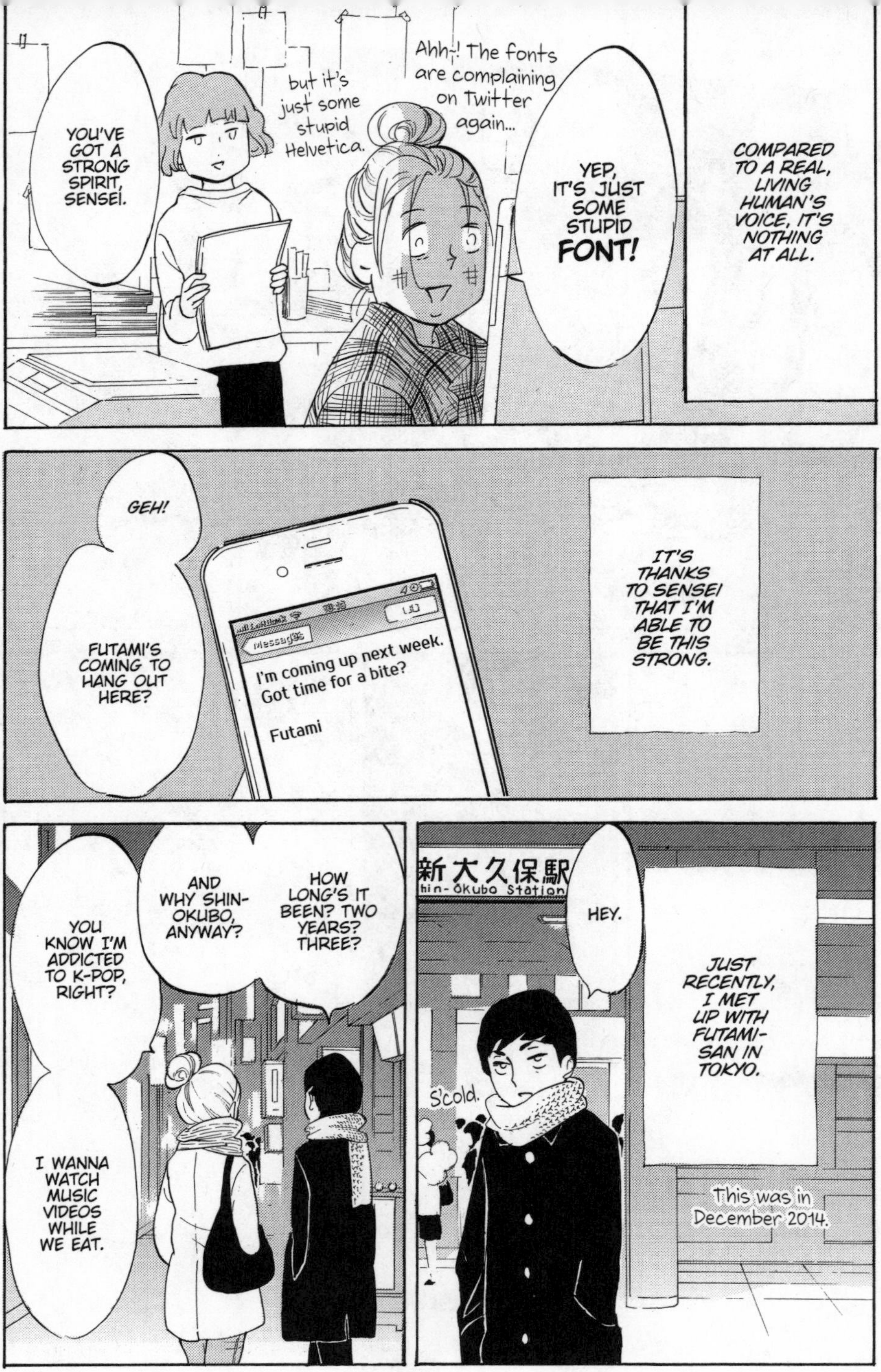
COMPARED TO A REAL, LIVING HUMAN'S VOICE, IT'S NOTHING AT ALL.
YEP, IT'S JUST SOME STUPID FONT!
Ahh~! The fonts are complaining on Twitter again...
but it's just some stupid Helvetica.
YOU'VE GOT A STRONG SPIRIT, SENSEI.
IT'S THANKS TO SENSEI THAT I'M ABLE TO BE THIS STRONG.
Messages
I'm coming up next week. Got time for a bite?
Futami
GEH!
FUTAMI'S COMING TO HANG OUT HERE?
JUST RECENTLY, I MET UP WITH FUTAMI-SAN IN TOKYO.
新大久保駅
hin-Okubo Station
HEY.
S'cold.
This was in December 2014.
HOW LONG'S IT BEEN? TWO YEARS? THREE?
AND WHY SHIN-OKUBO, ANYWAY?
YOU KNOW I'M ADDICTED TO K-POP, RIGHT?
I WANNA WATCH MUSIC VIDEOS WHILE WE EAT.

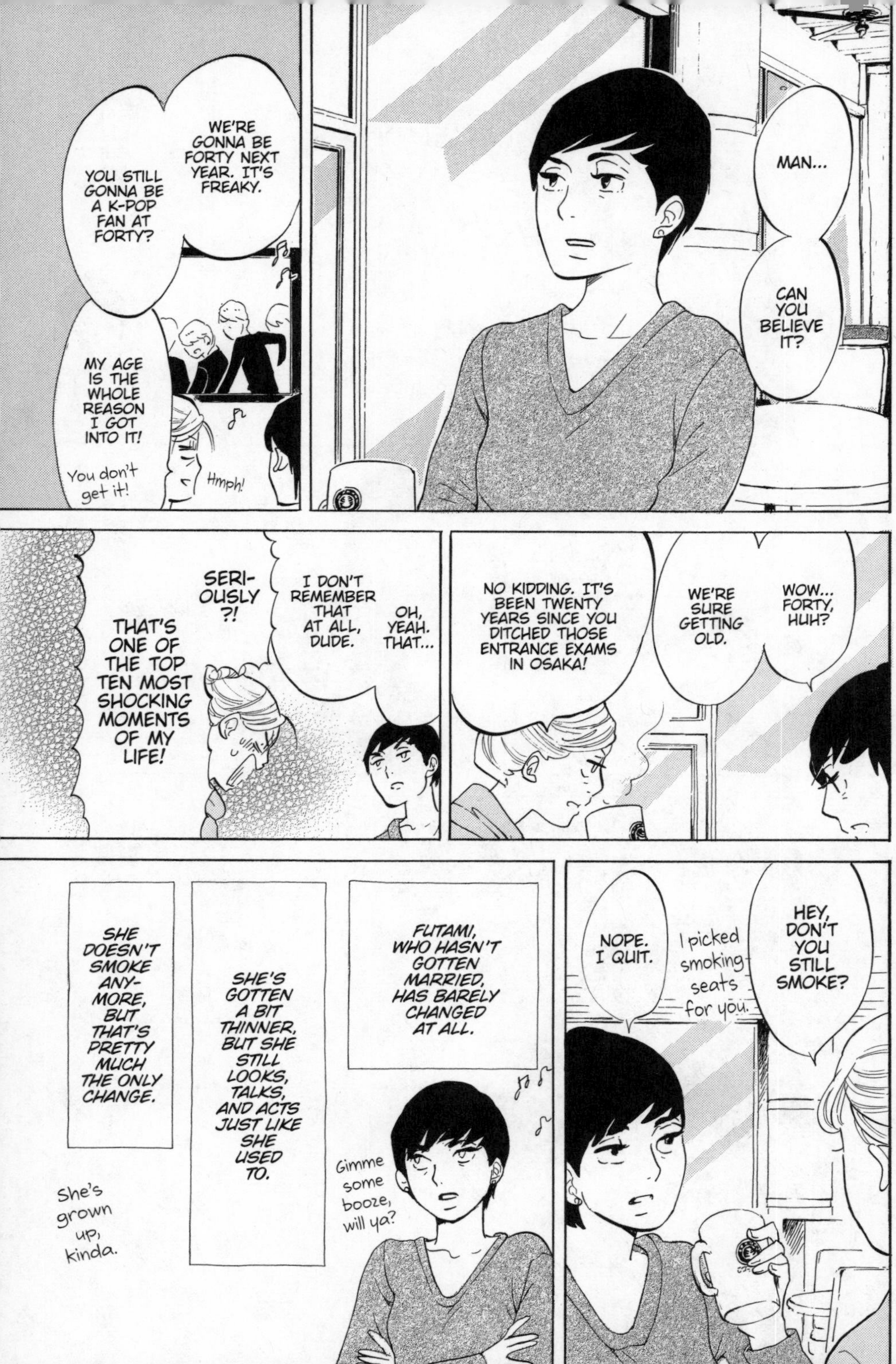
MAN...
CAN YOU BELIEVE IT?
WE'RE GONNA BE FORTY NEXT YEAR. IT'S FREAKY.
YOU STILL GONNA BE A K-POP FAN AT FORTY?
MY AGE IS THE WHOLE REASON I GOT INTO IT!
Hmph!
You don't get it!
WOW... FORTY, HUH?
WE'RE SURE GETTING OLD.
NO KIDDING. IT'S BEEN TWENTY YEARS SINCE YOU DITCHED THOSE ENTRANCE EXAMS IN OSAKA!
OH, YEAH. THAT...
I DON'T REMEMBER THAT AT ALL, DUDE.
SERI-OUSLY?!
THAT'S ONE OF THE TOP TEN MOST SHOCKING MOMENTS OF MY LIFE!
HEY, DON'T YOU STILL SMOKE?
I picked smoking-seats for you.
NOPE. I QUIT.
FUTAMI, WHO HASN'T GOTTEN MARRIED, HAS BARELY CHANGED AT ALL.
SHE'S GOTTEN A BIT THINNER, BUT SHE STILL LOOKS, TALKS, AND ACTS JUST LIKE SHE USED TO.
SHE DOESN'T SMOKE ANY-MORE, BUT THAT'S PRETTY MUCH THE ONLY CHANGE.
Gimme some booze, will ya?
She's grown up, kinda.

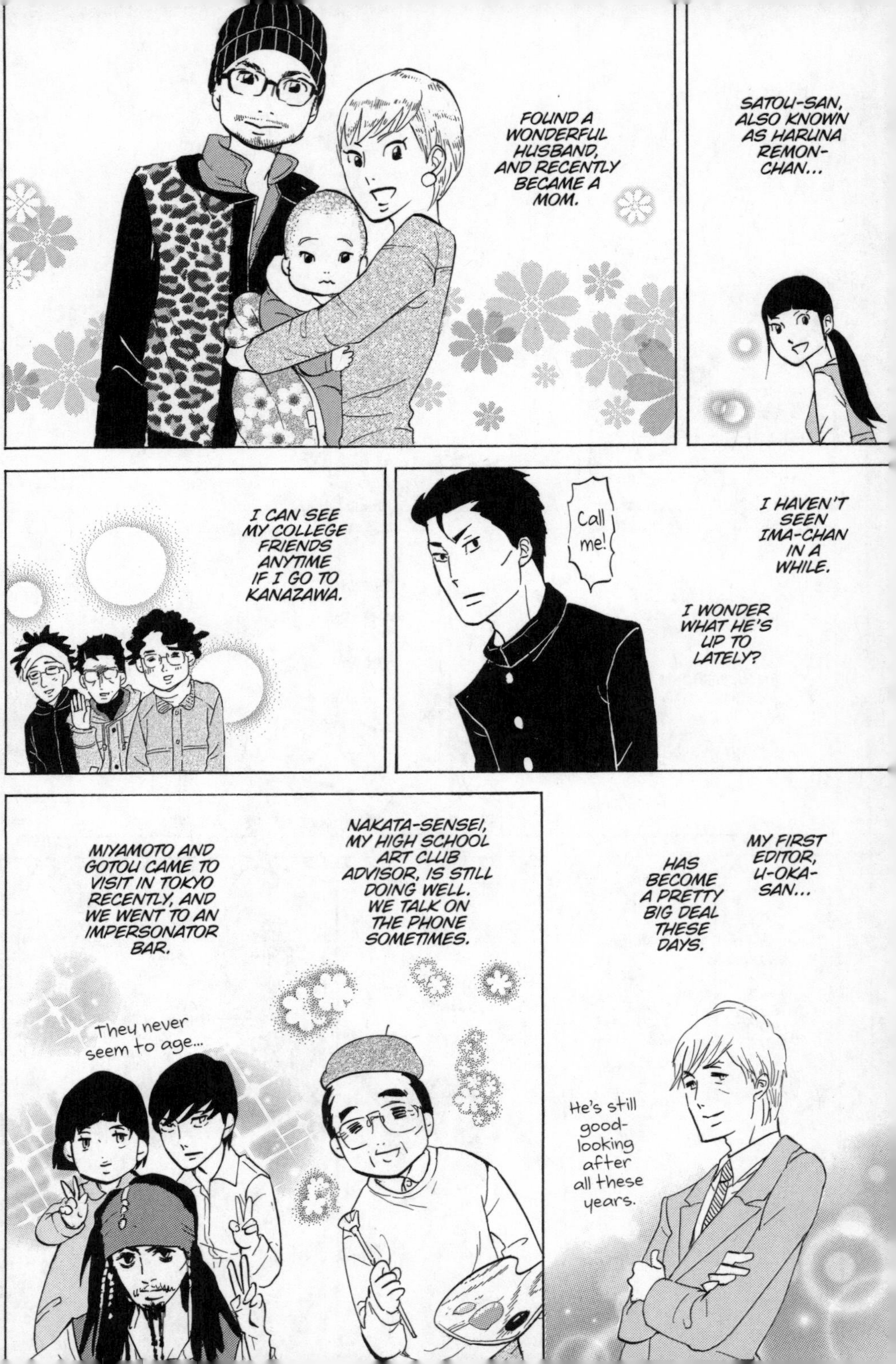
SATOU-SAN, ALSO KNOWN AS HARUNA REMON-CHAN...
FOUND A WONDERFUL HUSBAND, AND RECENTLY BECAME A MOM.
I HAVEN'T SEEN IMA-CHAN IN A WHILE.
Call me!
I WONDER WHAT HE'S UP TO LATELY?
I CAN SEE MY COLLEGE FRIENDS ANYTIME IF I GO TO KANAZAWA.
MY FIRST EDITOR, U-OKA-SAN...
HAS BECOME A PRETTY BIG DEAL THESE DAYS.
He's still good-looking after all these years.
NAKATA-SENSEI, MY HIGH SCHOOL ART CLUB ADVISOR, IS STILL DOING WELL. WE TALK ON THE PHONE SOMETIMES.
MIYAMOTO AND GOTOU CAME TO VISIT IN TOKYO RECENTLY, AND WE WENT TO AN IMPERSONATOR BAR.
They never seem to age...

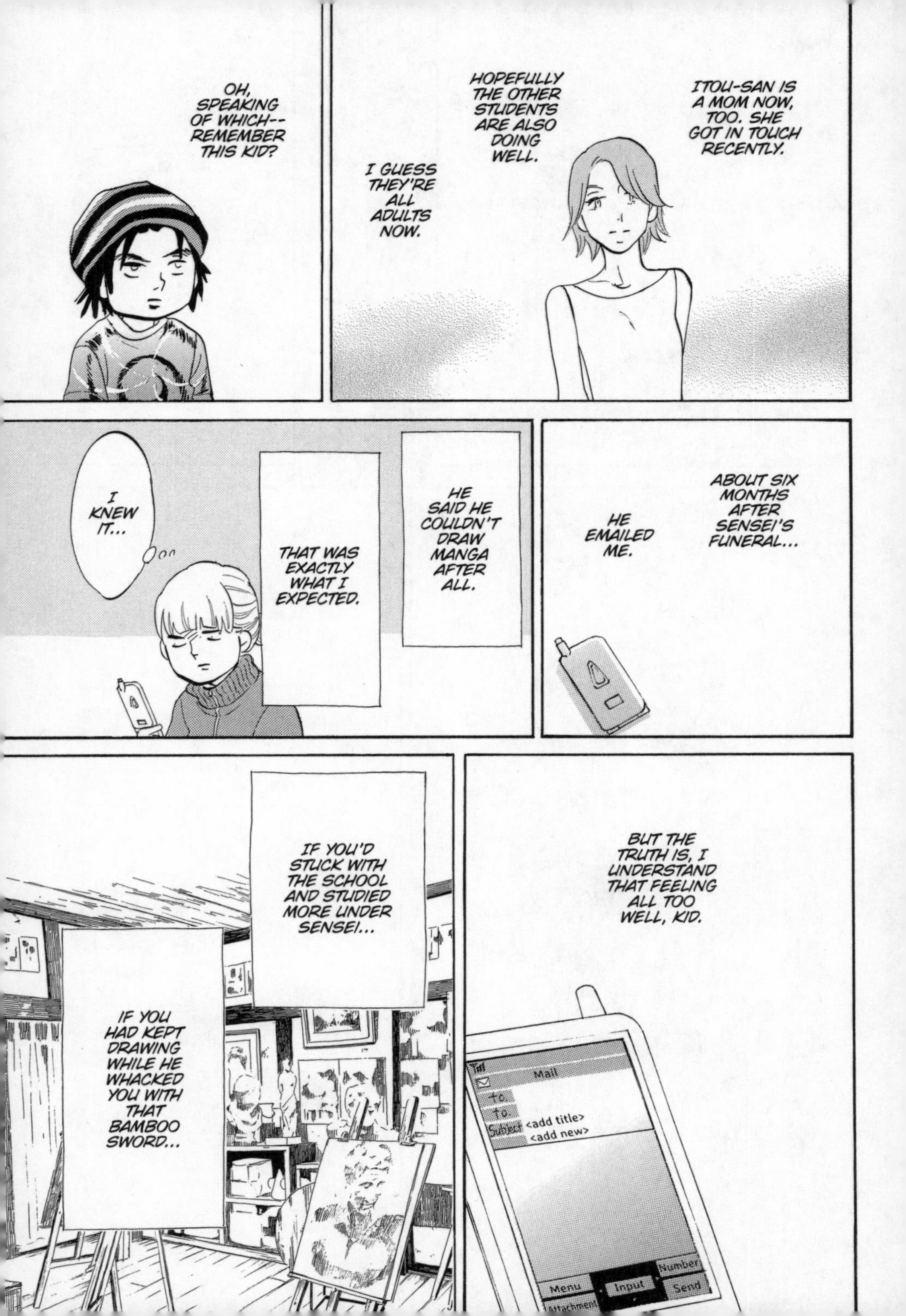
ITOU-SAN IS A MOM NOW, TOO. SHE GOT IN TOUCH RECENTLY.
HOPEFULLY THE OTHER STUDENTS ARE ALSO DOING WELL.
I GUESS THEY'RE ALL ADULTS NOW.
OH, SPEAKING OF WHICH-- REMEMBER THIS KID?
ABOUT SIX MONTHS AFTER SENSEI'S FUNERAL...
HE EMAILED ME.
HE SAID HE COULDN'T DRAW MANGA AFTER ALL.
THAT WAS EXACTLY WHAT I EXPECTED.
I KNEW IT...
BUT THE TRUTH IS, I UNDERSTAND THAT FEELING ALL TOO WELL, KID.
Mail
Subject <add title>
<add new>
Menu
Input
Send
IF YOU'D STUCK WITH THE SCHOOL AND STUDIED MORE UNDER SENSEI...
IF YOU HAD KEPT DRAWING WHILE HE WHACKED YOU WITH THAT BAMBOO SWORD...

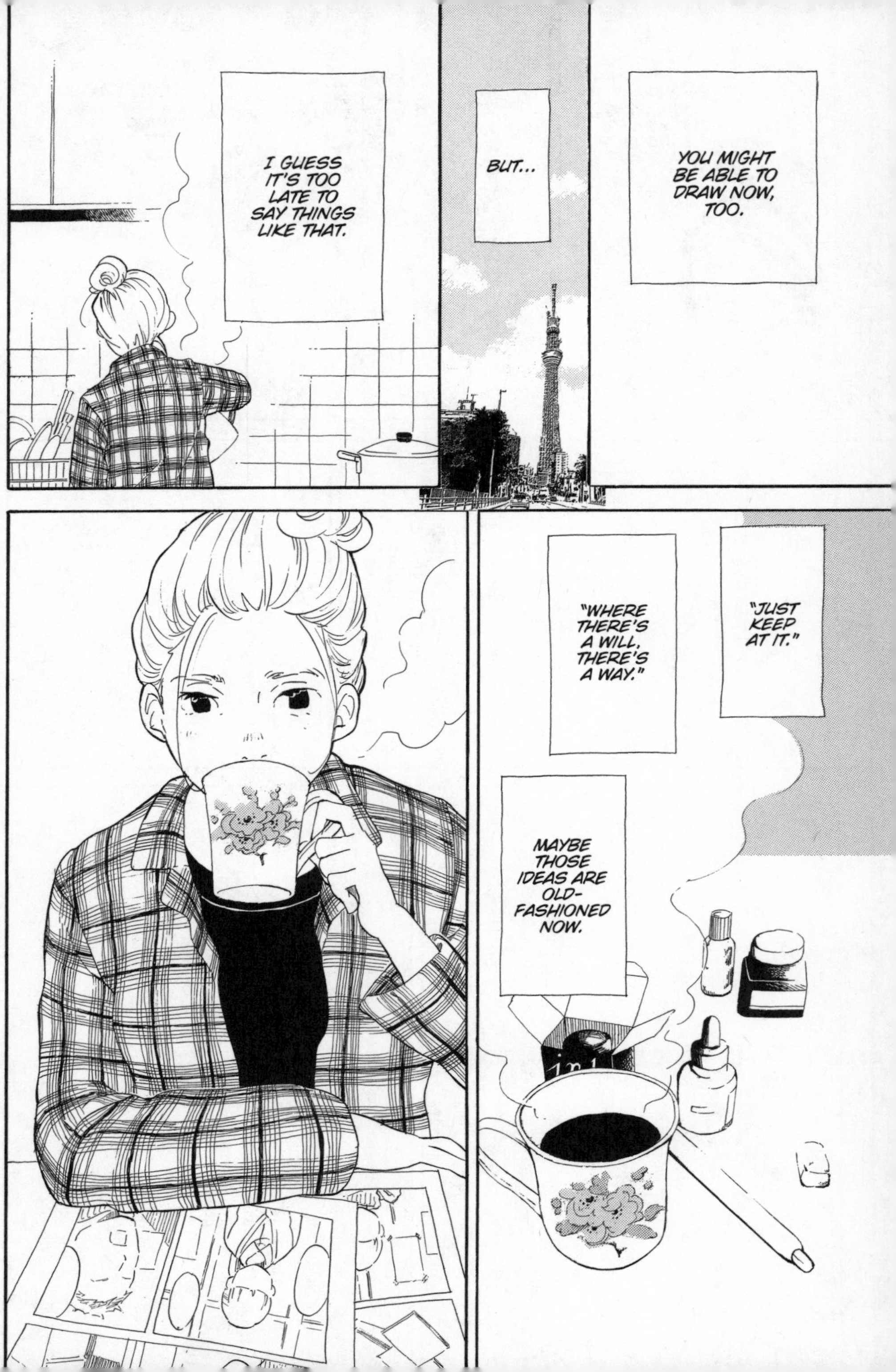
YOU MIGHT BE ABLE TO DRAW NOW, TOO.
BUT...
I GUESS IT'S TOO LATE TO SAY THINGS LIKE THAT.
"JUST KEEP AT IT."
"WHERE THERE'S A WILL, THERE'S A WAY."
MAYBE THOSE IDEAS ARE OLD-FASHIONED NOW.

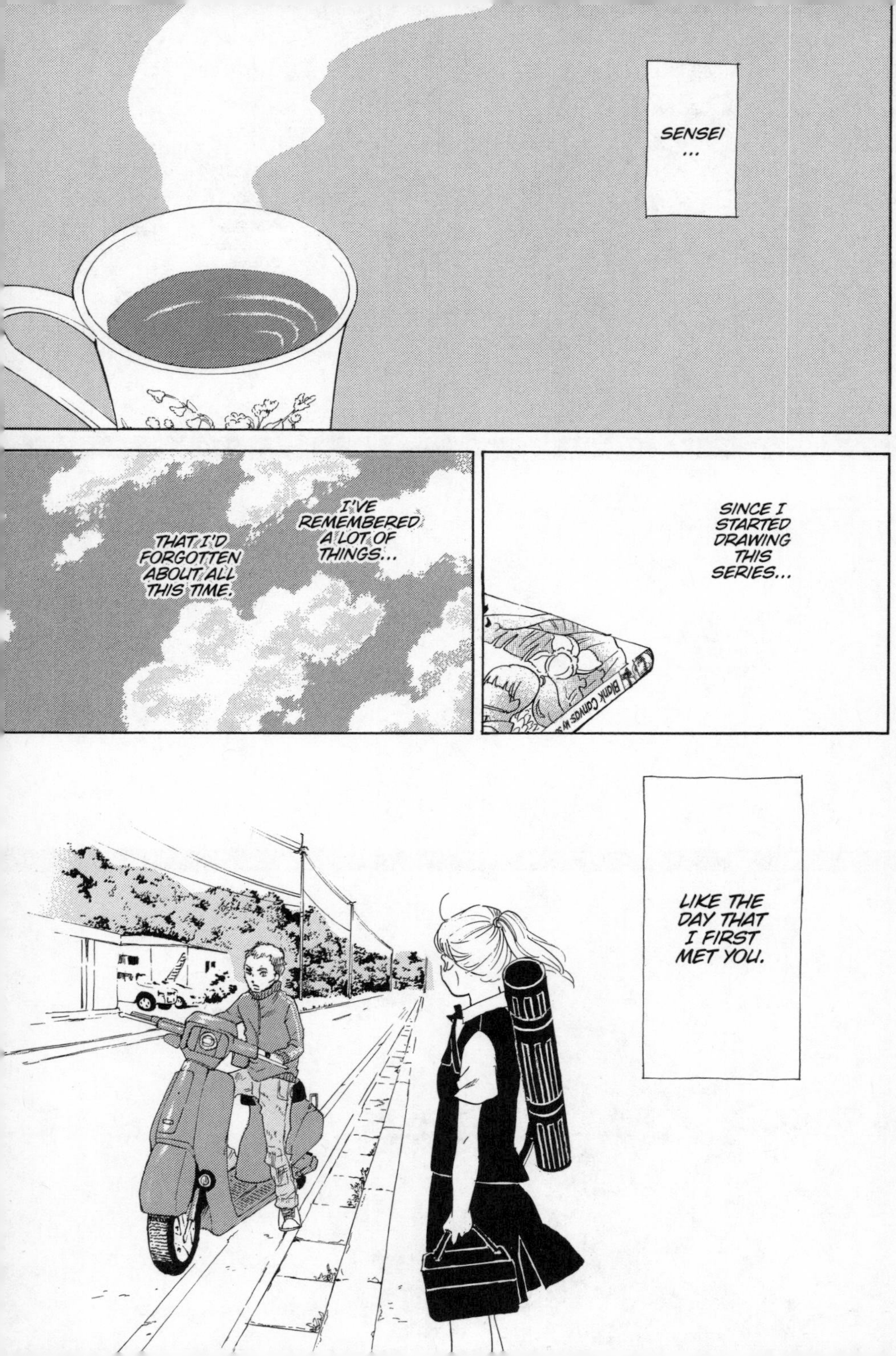
SENSEI ...
SINCE I STARTED DRAWING THIS SERIES...
I'VE REMEMBERED A LOT OF THINGS...
THAT I'D FORGOTTEN ABOUT ALL THIS TIME.
LIKE THE DAY THAT I FIRST MET YOU.

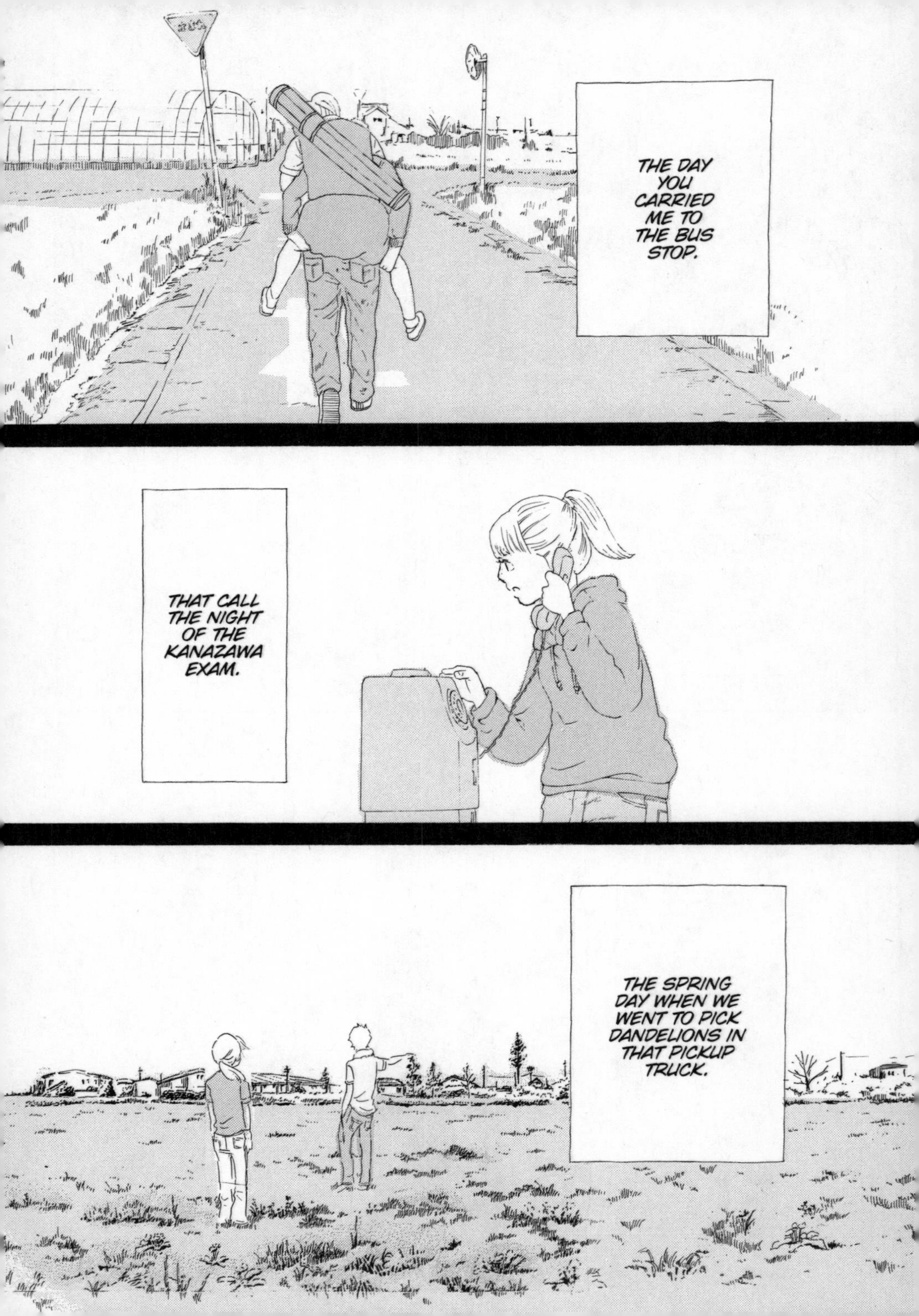
THE DAY YOU CARRIED ME TO THE BUS STOP.
THAT CALL THE NIGHT OF THE KANAZAWA EXAM.
THE SPRING DAY WHEN WE WENT TO PICK DANDELIONS IN THAT PICKUP TRUCK.

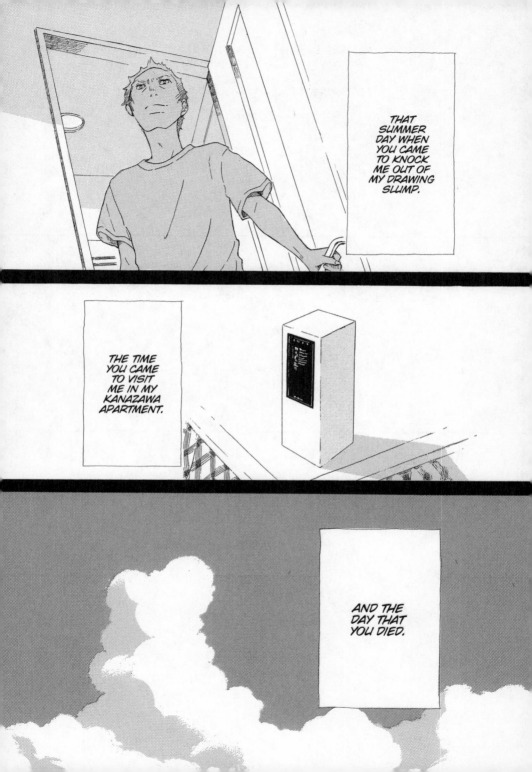

THAT SUMMER DAY WHEN YOU CAME TO KNOCK ME OUT OF MY DRAWING SLUMP.

THE TIME YOU CAME TO VISIT ME IN MY KANAZAWA APARTMENT.

AND THE DAY THAT YOU DIED.

SELFISH.

EGOTISTICAL.

COCKY.

CONCEITED.

BACK THEN,
I WAS SO
STUPID.

DISHONEST.

SNEAKY.

HEARTLESS.

GREEDY.

ALL OF
THAT WAS
WHY I
LOVED YOU,
SENSEI.

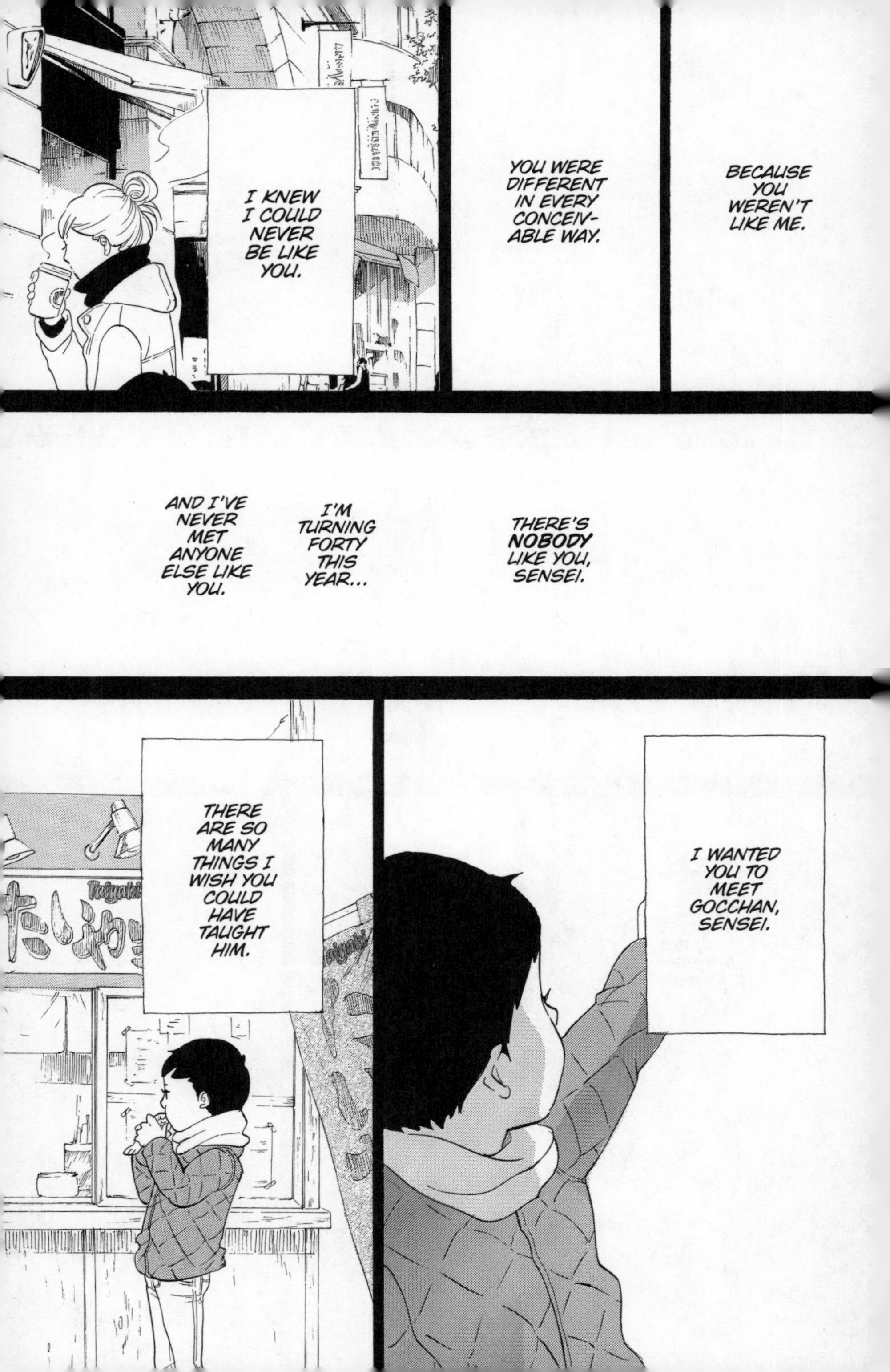
BECAUSE YOU WEREN'T LIKE ME.
YOU WERE DIFFERENT IN EVERY CONCEIV-ABLE WAY.
I KNEW I COULD NEVER BE LIKE YOU.
THERE'S NOBODY LIKE YOU, SENSEI.
I'M TURNING FORTY THIS YEAR...
AND I'VE NEVER MET ANYONE ELSE LIKE YOU.
I WANTED YOU TO MEET GOCCHAN, SENSEI.
THERE ARE SO MANY THINGS I WISH YOU COULD HAVE TAUGHT HIM.

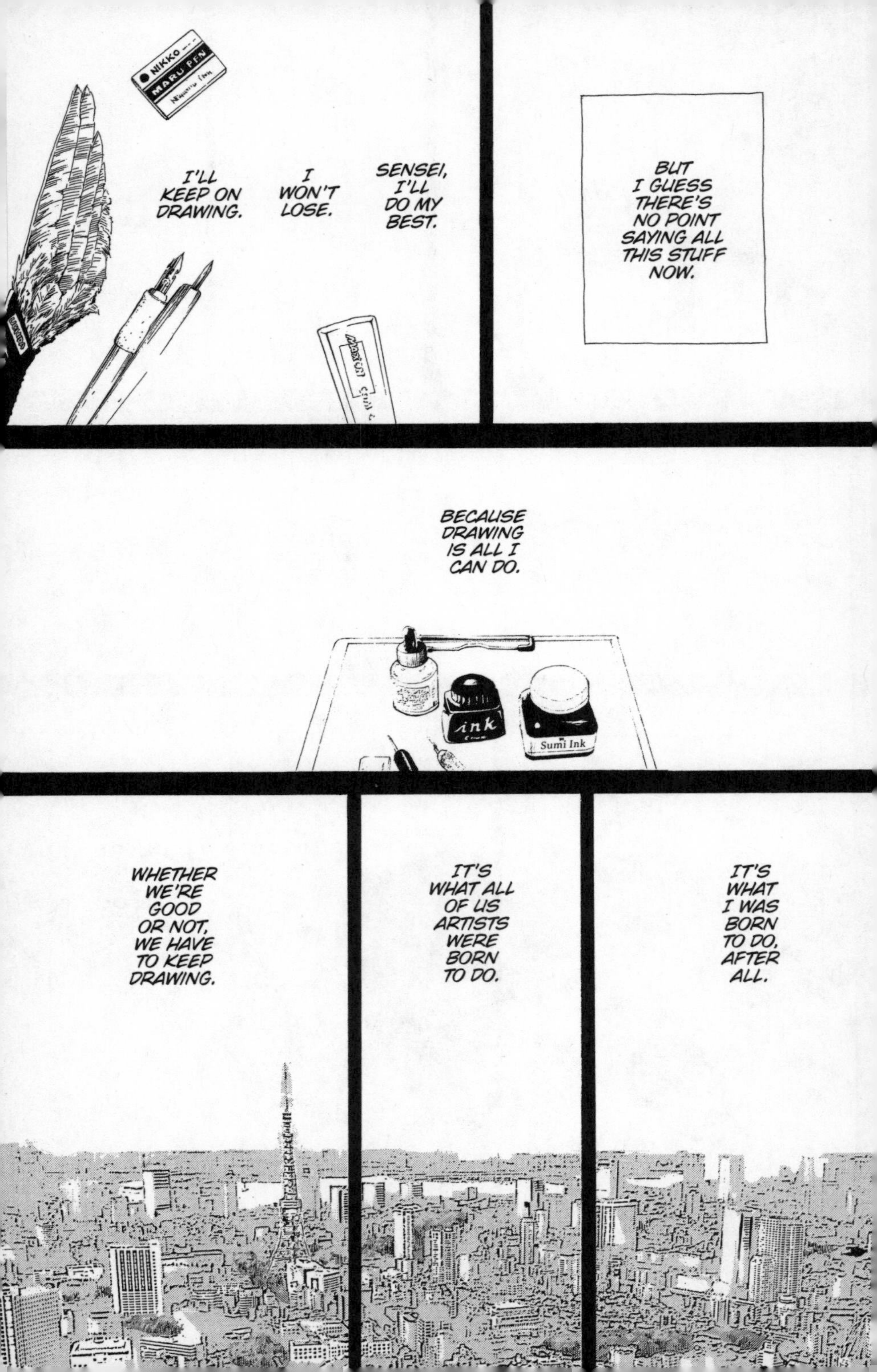
BUT I GUESS THERE'S NO POINT SAYING ALL THIS STUFF NOW.
NIKKO
MARU PEN
SENSEI, I'LL DO MY BEST.
I WON'T LOSE.
I'LL KEEP ON DRAWING.
BECAUSE DRAWING IS ALL I CAN DO.
Sumi Ink
ink
IT'S WHAT I WAS BORN TO DO, AFTER ALL.
IT'S WHAT ALL OF US ARTISTS WERE BORN TO DO.
WHETHER WE'RE GOOD OR NOT, WE HAVE TO KEEP DRAWING.

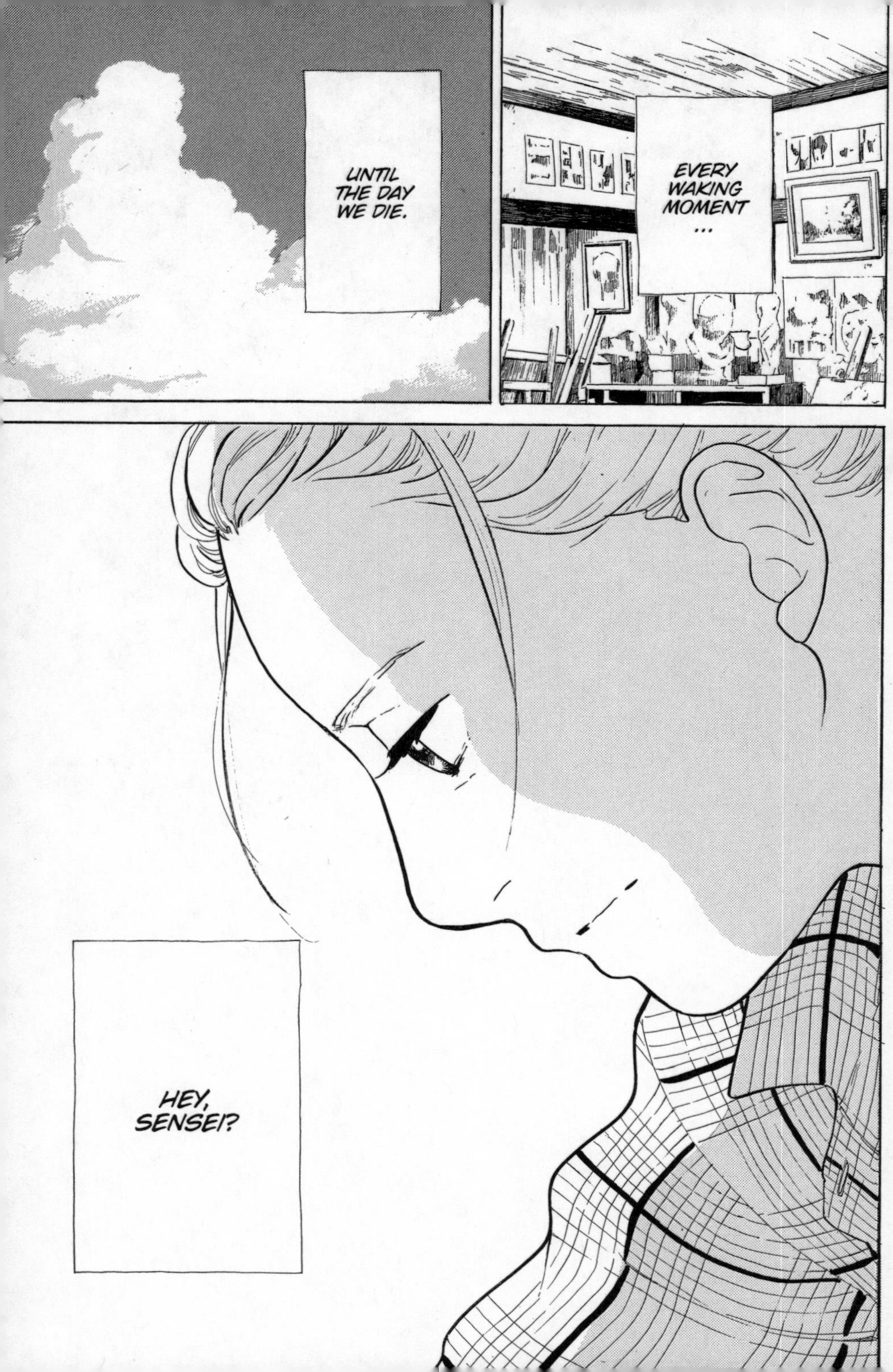
EVERY WAKING MOMENT ...
UNTIL THE DAY WE DIE.
HEY, SENSEI?

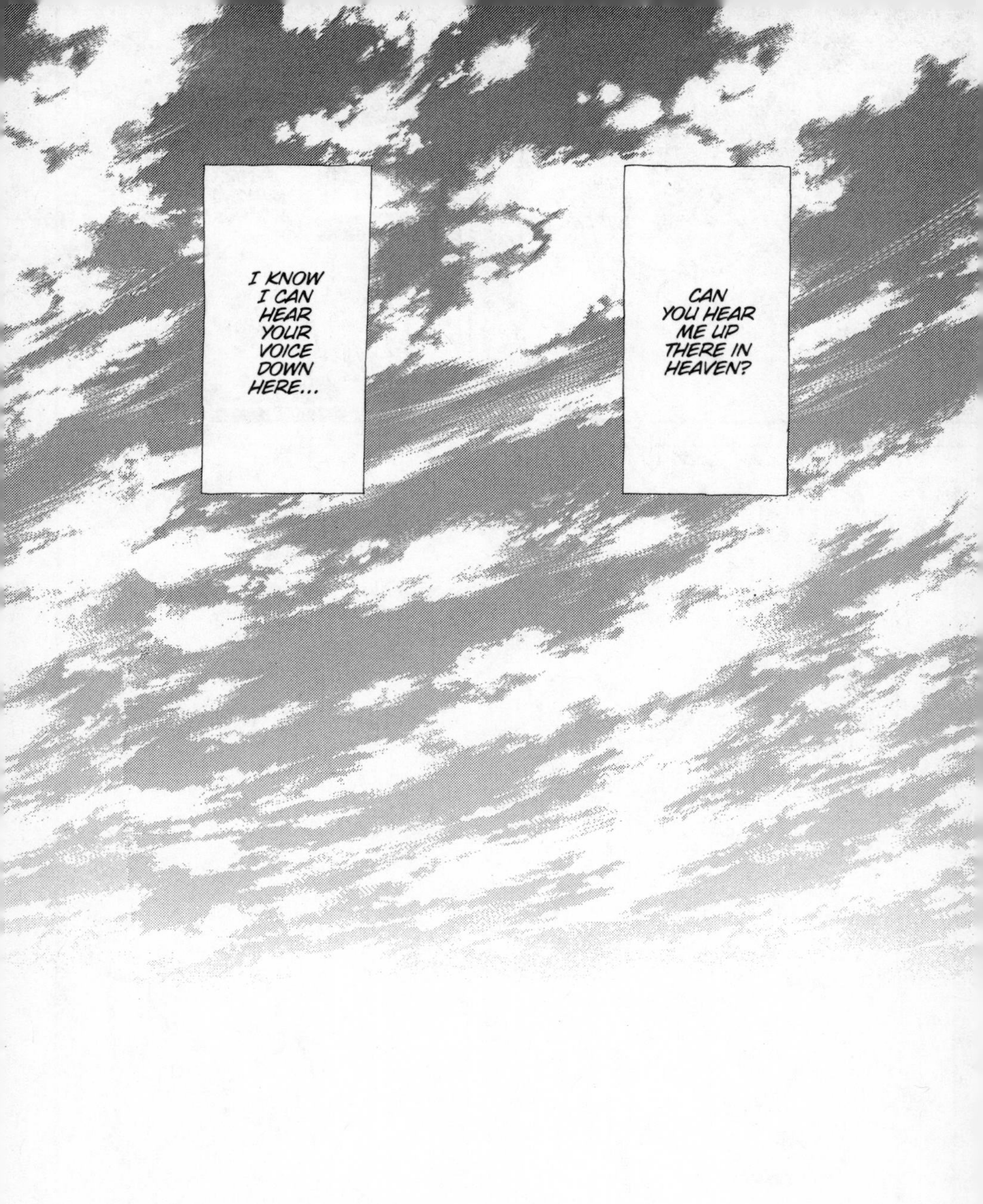
CAN YOU HEAR ME UP THERE IN HEAVEN?
I KNOW I CAN HEAR YOUR VOICE DOWN HERE...

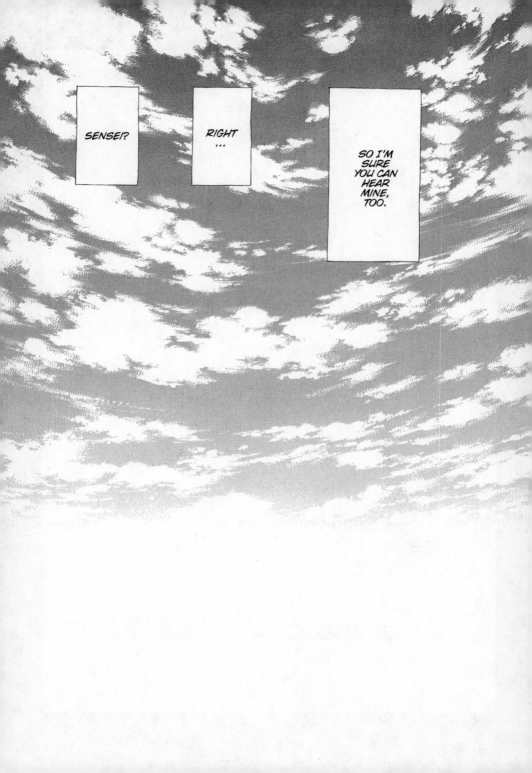

SENSEI?

RIGHT
...

SO I'M
SURE
YOU CAN
HEAR
MINE,
TOO.

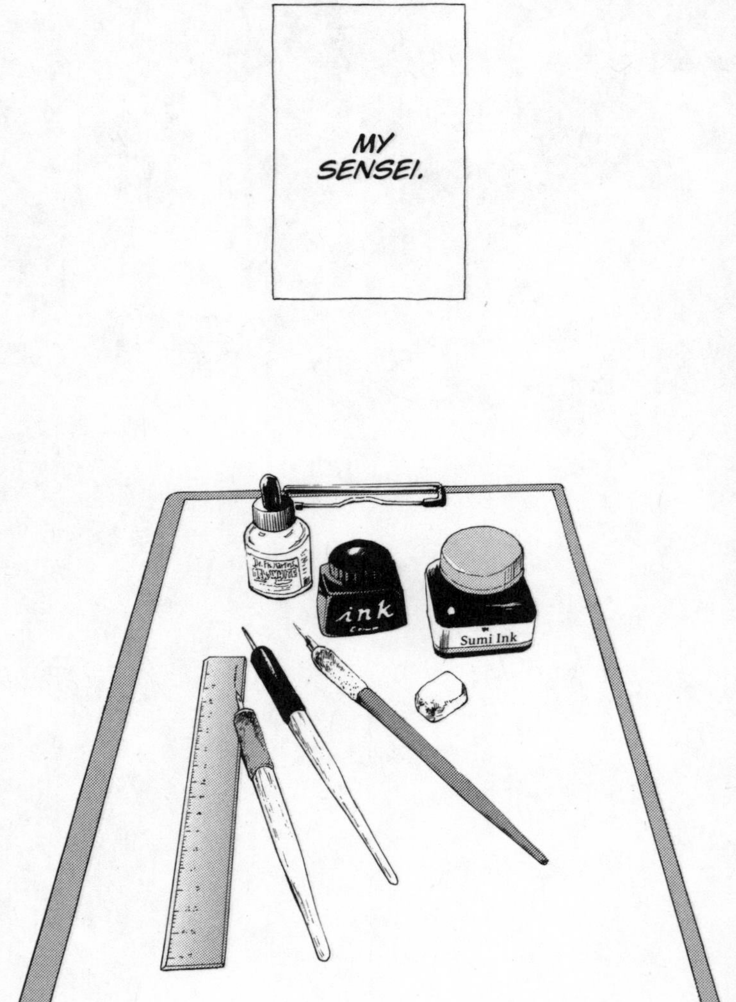
MY SENSEI.
ink
Sumi Ink

Blank Canvas: My So-Called Artist's Journey —END—

Blank Canvas

My So-Called Artist's Journey

Blank Canvas My So-Called Artist's Journey sketch book

New Year's, 2015.
Right before I drew the last chapter of this story, I went home to Miyazaki.

I dragged the box of college photos out of my closet and sorted through them.

I didn't take any pictures in high school, but I realized that I took a lot in college because I had a photography class. I think they made us buy an expensive single-lens reflex camera.

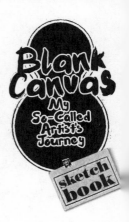

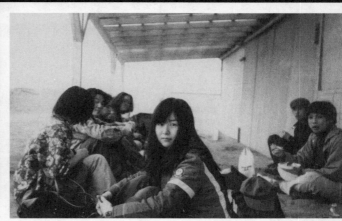

The oils majors.

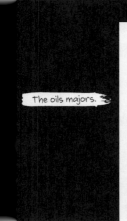

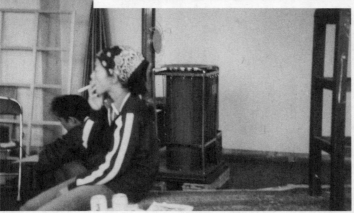

Our studio.

turally, there weren't that many photos of
g or painting. LOL!

did any of that, so it makes sense.

just tons of pictures of me messing aroun

I found this photo where I'm actually workin

s really is the only one there was.

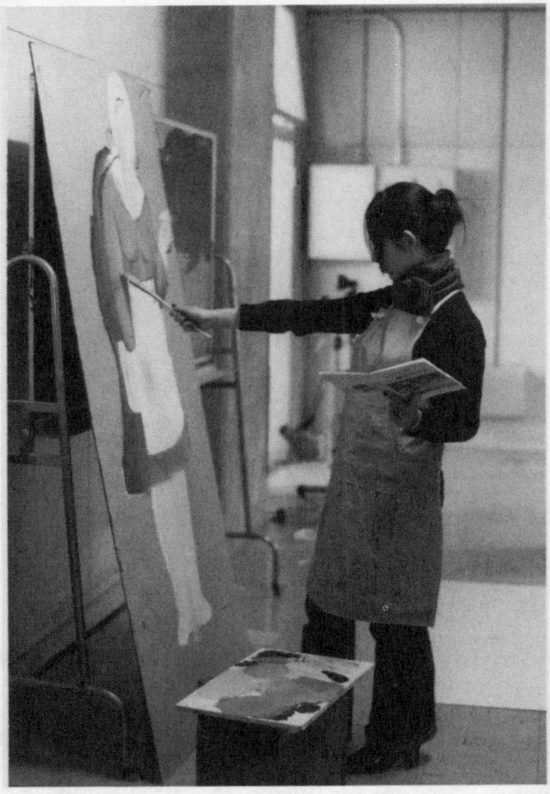

There were some photos of events I depicted in *Blank Canvas*, too.

Plus lots of pictures of my college friends...

and lots and ***lots*** of the scenery in Kanagawa.

Last but not least...

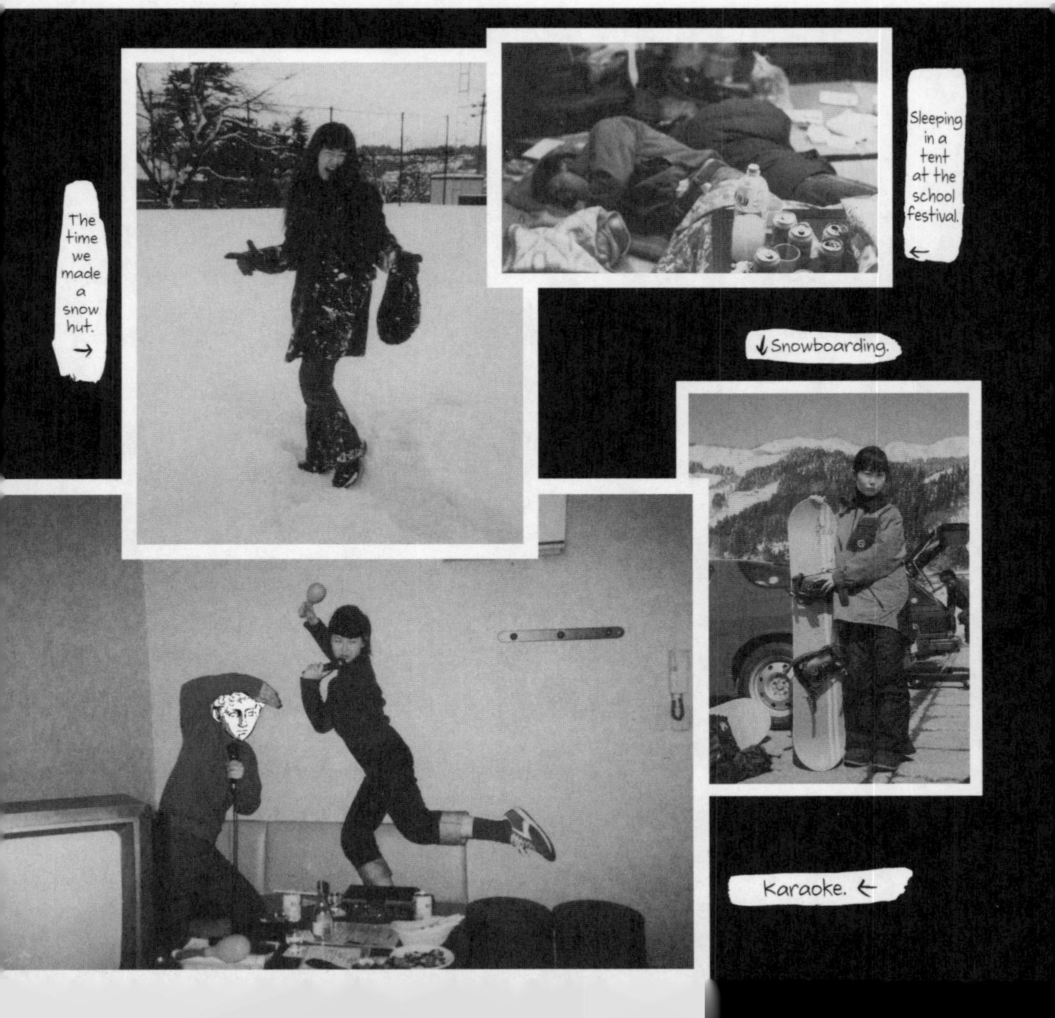

Sleeping in a tent at the school festival. ←
The time we made a snow hut. →
↓Snowboarding.
Karaoke. ←

Miraculously, I managed to find just one photo of Sensei.

I believe it was taken when I was back in Miyazaki for summer break during college.

For some reason, Sensei is wearing my hat and smiling a little in the photo.

Once I got back to Tokyo and finished drawing the last chapter, I put this photo under the transparent mat on my work desk, next to a portrait of me that Gocchan drew.

Then I got to work on my next story.

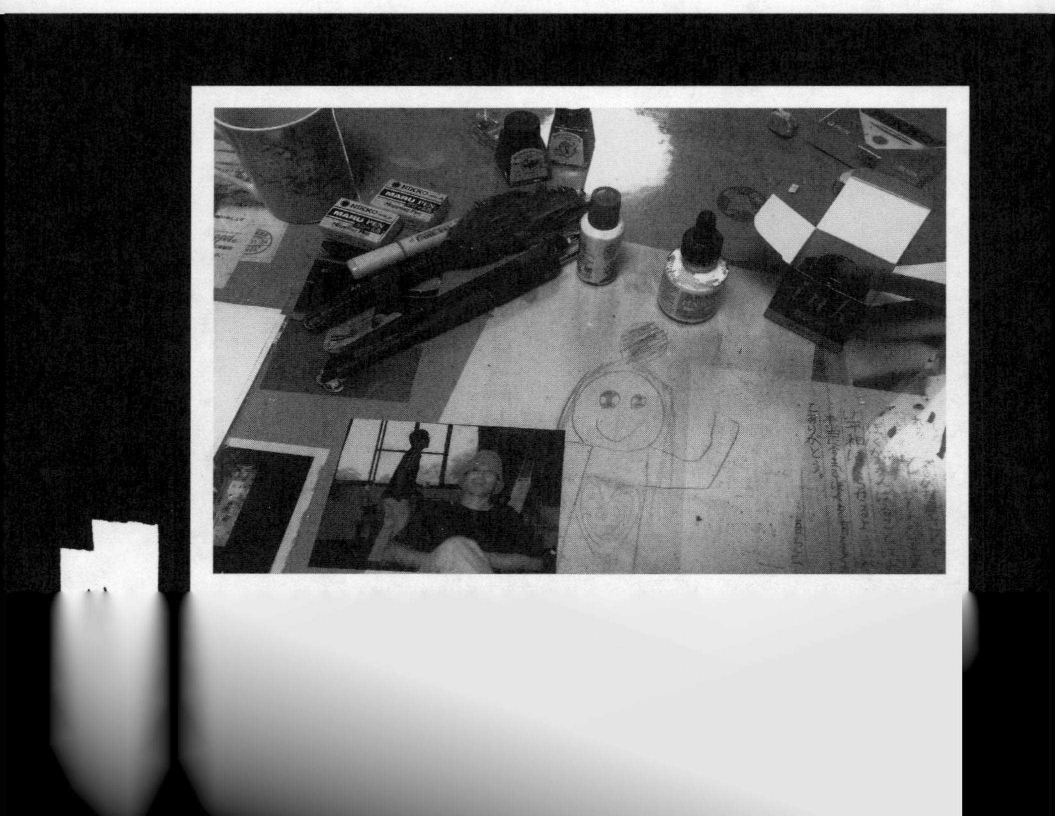
NIKKO
MARU PEN
NIKKO
MARU PEN

SEVEN SEAS ENTERTAINMENT PRESENTS

Blank Canvas
My So-Called Artist's Journey

story and art by AKIKO HIGASHIMURA   VOLUME 5

TRANSLATION
Jenny McKeon

ADAPTATION
Ysabet MacFarlane

LETTERING AND LAYOUT
Lys Blakeslee

COVER DESIGN
KC Fabellon

PROOFREADER
Kurestin Armada

EDITOR
Jenn Grunigen

PREPRESS TECHNICIAN
Rhiannon Rasmussen-Silverstein

PRODUCTION MANAGER
Lissa Pattillo

MANAGING EDITOR
Julie Davis

ASSOCIATE PUBLISHER
Adam Arnold

PUBLISHER
Jason DeAngelis

KAKUKAKU SHIKAJIKA © 2011 by Akiko Higashimura
All rights reserved.
First published in Japan in 2011 by SHUEISHA Inc., Tokyo.
English translation rights arranged by SHUEISHA Inc.
through TOHAN CORPORATION, Tokyo.

Seven Seas press and purchase enquiries can be sent to Marketing Manager
Lianne Sentar at press@gomanga.com. Information regarding the distribution
and purchase of digital editions is available from Digital Manager CK Russell
at digital@gomanga.com.

Seven Seas and the Seven Seas logo are trademarks of
Seven Seas Entertainment. All rights reserved.

ISBN: 978-1-64275-073-7

Printed in Canada

First Printing: June 2020

10 9 8 7 6 5 4 3 2 1

FOLLOW US ONLINE: www.sevenseasentertainment.com

READING DIRECTIONS

This book reads from **right to left**, Japanese style.
If this is your first time reading manga, you start
reading from the top right panel on each page and
take it from there. If you get lost, just follow the
numbered diagram here. It may seem backwards at
first, but you'll get the hang of it! Have fun!!

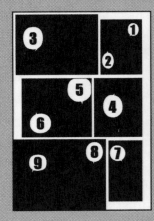